SECRET SHARERS

Secret Sharers

**THE INTIMATE RIVALRIES OF MODERNISM
AND PSYCHOANALYSIS**

Jennifer Spitzer

FORDHAM UNIVERSITY PRESS   NEW YORK   2023

Copyright © 2023 Fordham University Press

All rights reserved. No part of this publication may be reproduced, stored in a retrieval system, or transmitted in any form or by any means—electronic, mechanical, photocopy, recording, or any other—except for brief quotations in printed reviews, without the prior permission of the publisher.

Fordham University Press has no responsibility for the persistence or accuracy of URLs for external or third-party Internet websites referred to in this publication and does not guarantee that any content on such websites is, or will remain, accurate or appropriate.

Fordham University Press also publishes its books in a variety of electronic formats. Some content that appears in print may not be available in electronic books.

Visit us online at www.fordhampress.com.

Library of Congress Cataloging-in-Publication Data available online at https://catalog.loc.gov.

25 24 23   5 4 3 2 1

First edition

To Abby, Michael, Jacob, and Auden

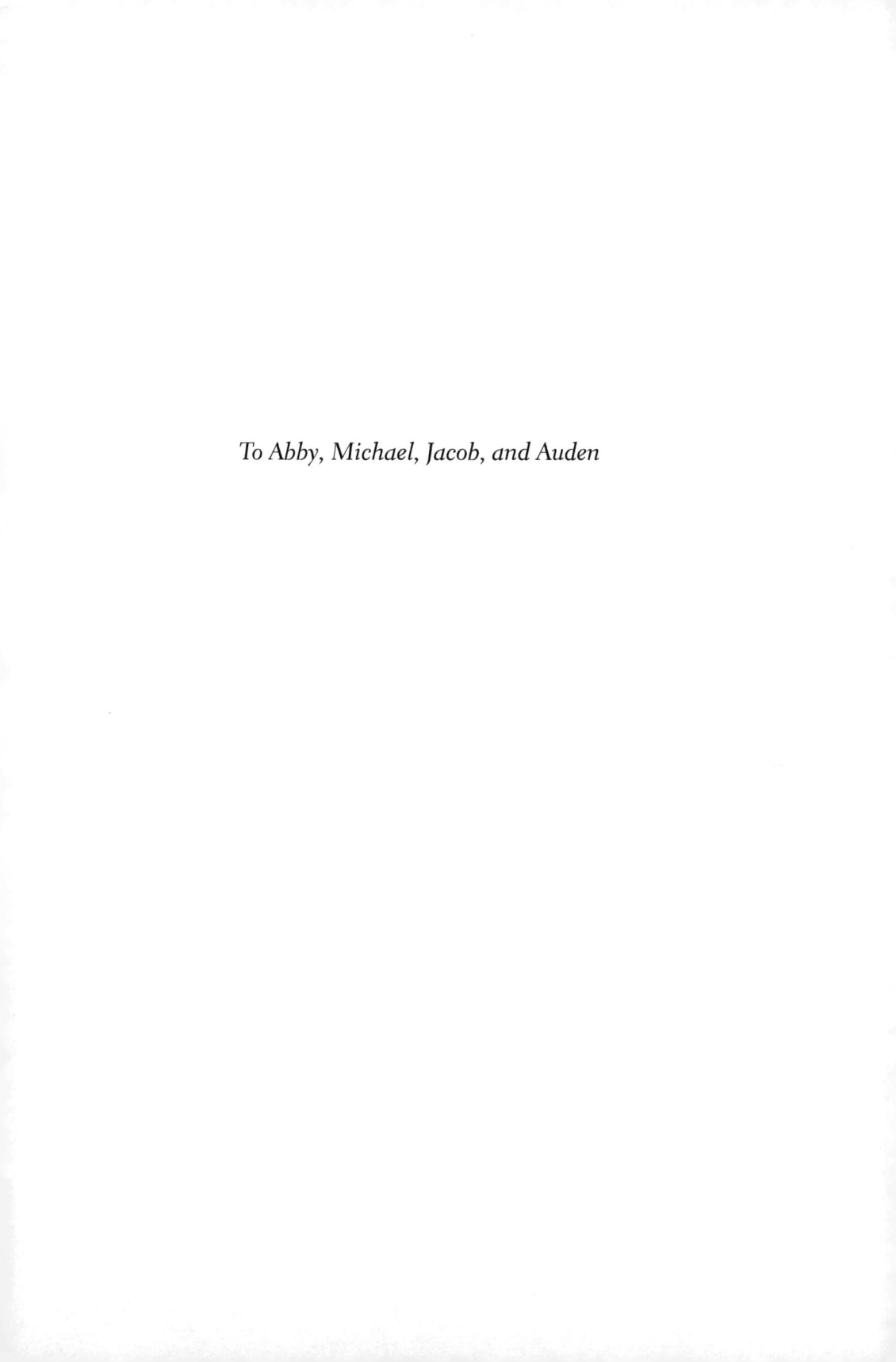

Contents

Introduction: Intimate Others   1

1 On Not Reading Freud: Amateurism, Expertise, and the "Pristine Unconscious" in D. H. Lawrence   31

2 The Soul under Psychoanalysis: Virginia Woolf and the Ethics of Intimacy   59

3 The Heterodox Psychology and Queer Poetics of Auden in the 1930s   88

4 Nabokov and the Lure of Freudian Forms   115

Conclusion: Modernist Afterlives and the Legacies of Suspicion   143

ACKNOWLEDGMENTS   155

NOTES   159

INDEX   191

SECRET SHARERS

Introduction
Intimate Others

> He was not a bit like me, really; yet, as we stood leaning over my bedplace, whispering side by side, with our dark heads together and our backs to the door, anybody bold enough to open it stealthily would have been treated to the uncanny sight of a double captain busy talking whispers with his other self.
>
> —JOSEPH CONRAD, "THE SECRET SHARER"

In this memorable passage from Joseph Conrad's "The Secret Sharer" (1910), the narrator, an unnamed ship's captain, imagines what it would look like for one of his crew members to catch him side by side with Leggatt, the fugitive sailor he has rescued and concealed below deck. He worries that the observer would confront not two separate men, but uncanny doubles engrossed in intimate conversation. At first, the captain denies the resemblance between himself and Leggatt ("He was not a bit like me"), but he quickly qualifies and admits the possibility of another view: "yet . . . anybody bold enough to open it stealthily would have been treated to the uncanny sight of a double captain busy talking whispers with his other self."[1]

This image of "secret sharers" captures the relationship between modernism and psychoanalysis that this book explores. Denying resemblances, trying to distance themselves from each other, modernist literature and psychoanalysis are also at times uncanny doubles of one another. Both address the difficulties of self-knowledge and the vexed challenges of moving across the boundaries between self and other. Secret sharing not only describes the relation between them, but also the concerns at the heart of both the literary and psychoanalytic projects.

With its unreliable first-person narrator and its layered accounts of the past, Conrad's story emerges as a prototypically modernist work of literature. It also reveals a psychoanalytic fascination with the self's division and its capacity to obstruct self-knowledge. Indeed, "The Secret Sharer" could be viewed as a dramatization of the analytic scenario insofar as the "sharing" it depicts between two characters, who are "busy talking whispers," evokes the discursive nature of analysis and its business of sharing intimate secrets. The tale not only dramatizes the perils of self-discovery that psychoanalysis theorizes, it also evokes the asymmetrical, intimate, transferential dynamics of the psychoanalytic encounter.[2]

At the beginning of Conrad's tale, the narrator informs us that he has been appointed captain only two weeks in advance of a journey from the Gulf of Siam to England, and that the trip marks "the first preparatory stage of our homeward journey," evoking the uncanny routes through which one returns homeward and "inward towards the self."[3] While taking the anchor watch alone, the captain spots a naked man clinging to a rope on the ship's side who identifies himself as Leggatt. With remarkable recklessness, the captain invites Leggatt aboard, and the two establish an immediate rapport. Leggatt puts on the captain's clothes, which fit perfectly, and a quick inspection of Leggatt's face reveals his resemblance to the captain himself: "It was, in the night, as though I had been faced by my own reflection in the depths of a somber and immense mirror."[4] Observing their many similarities (age, physical appearance, and shared military training), the narrator identifies Leggatt as his "double," a trope the story deploys insistently. As Leggatt shares his story of how he murdered a man and became a fugitive from the law, it becomes evident that everything in the story is doubled: there are two protagonists, two ships, two tales, and a double narrative structure—a tale within a tale—that dramatizes the act of sharing itself.

Yet the double can hardly be the secret to which the title refers, as Marjorie Garber and Barbara Johnson point out, since the narrator offers this interpretation explicitly on every page, describing Leggatt alternately as "my double," "my other self," "my secret self," "my second self," "my secret double," "the secret sharer of my life," and finally "my very own self." The doubling generates ambiguity about Leggatt's relationship to the captain: Is Leggatt same or other, real or imagined? Is he the "ideal conception of one's own personality every man sets up for himself secretly," the decisive leader the captain hopes himself to be? The story seems to offer every interpretive possibility.[5] The tale is readily available to a psychoanalytic reading of its first-person narrator who suffers from the narcissistic projection of a second self, whom he views as simultaneously like and unlike himself. In fact, Johnson and Garber suggest that the story "seems an ideal—indeed, almost too ideal—text on which to base an introduction to the varieties of psychoanalytic criticism."[6]

But my interest in "The Secret Sharer" turns on the story's preoccupations with self-narration and self-division—with the parts of us we conceal below deck and the parts we project as socially acceptable—which reveal the shared nature of the modernist and psychoanalytic projects. Like the captain and Leggatt, modernism and psychoanalysis were not so much contiguous, parallel figures as *secret sharers*—united as much by the fact that they do not coincide as by the fact that they do. The emergence of these fields in the early part of the twentieth century and their shared fascination with consciousness and the unconscious, perception, and memory elicited both productive engagements and intense competitive rivalries that helped shape the contours of modernism. Yet, despite these shared preoccupations, literary modernists often resisted psychoanalysis and sought to distinguish themselves from it in a variety of complex ways. Some modernists engaged directly and intensely with Freud and Freudian psychoanalysis, with unmistakable rivalry and critique (D. H. Lawrence, Vladimir Nabokov), while others wrestled in more complex ways with Freud's legacy and appeared willing to embrace certain concepts while distancing themselves from others.

I argue, however, that the intensity with which some writers distanced themselves from psychoanalysis registers the power it exerted over them. The key protagonists of my study—D. H. Lawrence, Virginia Woolf, W. H. Auden, and Vladimir Nabokov—are noteworthy for the way they engaged with, popularized, and revised the terms of Freudian psychoanalysis, while also struggling with it as an encroaching discourse. I am interested in how modernists read psychoanalysis, misread psychoanalysis, or refused to read it altogether, and am equally interested in the anxiety modernists expressed about being *read by* psychoanalysis, subjecting themselves or their art to psychoanalytic readings. Lawrence and Nabokov went so far as to declare their works invulnerable to the hermeneutic of the Freudians, while they engaged in obsessive conversation with psychoanalysis in their writing.

Literature and psychoanalysis were closest bedfellows during the first half of the twentieth century; yet modernism's frequent resistance to this contiguous form of knowledge was intensified by a climate of specialization and professionalization in which authorial identities and levels of expertise were at stake, a climate that gives birth to the "paranoid modernism" David Trotter identifies as a distinctive feature of late nineteenth- and early twentieth-century writing.[7] Modernists explicitly addressed psychoanalysts as they made the case for the distinctiveness and self-sufficiency of literature and the symbolic capital of authorship, and as they managed the reception and interpretation of their works against the pressure of critic outsiders. Several psychoanalysts sought insight and confirmation from literature, and envisioned their work as necessarily cross-disciplinary; but certain authors responded defensively to such literary adoptions. When the British analyst Alfred Kuttner hailed D. H. Lawrence's novel *Sons and Lovers* (1913) as the fictional case study *par excellence* of Oedipal theory, Lawrence responded with outrage: "My poor book: it was, as art, a fairly complete truth: so they carve a half-lie out of it, and say 'Voila.' Swine! Your little brochure—how soul-wearied you are by society and social experiments."[8] Lawrence advocates for the self-sufficiency of his novel as a "fairly complete truth," asking to be valued on its own terms and requiring no hermeneutic to make its truths apparent. In this defense of aesthetic autonomy, Lawrence elevates the novel—with its expressiveness and truth content—over the low form of the "brochure," with its reductive theorizing. Such a recognizably modernist response to psychoanalysis might be read as reactionary or elitist in that it seems to confirm a modernist defense of the purity of the artwork, one which, in the words of Renato Poggioli "aspires to abolish the discursive and syntactic element, to liberate art from any connection with psychological and empirical reality, to reduce every work to the intimate laws of its own essence or the given absolutes of its own of its own genre or means."[9] And yet, as Lawrence Rainey and other scholars have pointed out, aesthetic autonomy was also an essential marketing strategy for modernists as they negotiated the imperatives of the marketplace.[10] Aesthetic autonomy was also a strategy invoked against psychoanalytic incursions into the domain of literary criticism.

Psychoanalysis seemed threatening in part because it was viewed as seeking to demystify the process and product of aesthetic creation, in favor of a disenchanted and reductively biographical reading of art and literature. As Freud, Ernest Jones, Alfred Kuttner, Hanns Sachs, Marie Bonaparte, and other analysts turned to literary works as case studies, modernists invoked arguments on behalf of aesthetic autonomy to challenge what they viewed as the generalizing, demystifying, and reductive literary readings of psychoanalysis. In examining how Anglo-American modernists responded to the advent of psychoanalysis, I show how modernists often repudiated a rival hermeneutic that claimed the upper hand in generating insight about literary texts. Freud acknowledged such ambitions directly, declaring that psychoanalysis is "in a position to speak the decisive word in all questions that touch upon the imaginative life of man."[11] Modernists not only worried about the reduction of their works to psychoanalytic metanarratives, they also objected to the reduction of themselves to symptomatic beings who could be analyzed through their works. While Freud and his followers emphasized the unconscious as the origin of the artistic impulse, some modernists were eager to demonstrate their conscious artistry or the impersonality of authorship, like T. S. Eliot, who urged the distinction between "the man who suffers and the mind that creates."[12] As I argue throughout, many of the key concerns of modernism—aesthetic autonomy, formal self-consciousness, authorial expressivity, and artistic impersonality—were inflected by modernism's ongoing exchanges with psychoanalysis.

Discursive Debates

Modernism and psychoanalysis emerged simultaneously in the late nineteenth and early twentieth centuries. Both movements were revolutionary within the realms of art, politics, and culture. Both proclaimed their radical principles through innovative formal experiments and bravura rhetorical performances, including the manifesto and the stream-of-consciousness narrative, and, on the psychoanalytic side, the case study. Driven by similar investments in a fragmented human subject with precarious knowledge of self and world—a self that was no longer, to use Freud's famous phrase, "master in its own house"—both fields embarked upon quintessentially modern aesthetic and intellectual projects. The literary adaptation of stream of consciousness as a narrative device influenced by psychological theories of consciousness and perception led to productive experiments in the representation of time, memory, and subjectivity that became signature features of modernism. As Malcolm Bradbury and James McFarlane have argued, "if anything distinguishes [the interwar] decades and gives them their intellectual and historical character it is a fascination with evolving consciousness: consciousness aesthetic, psychological, and historical."[13] Modernism and psychoanalysis not only reflected changing ideas of consciousness, they also shaped consciousness by envisioning a human subject with uncharted depths and potentialities, a subject whose powers of perception were both enhanced and compromised by consciousness itself. Rather than merely reflect a psychological modernity, modernism and psychoanalysis were co-architects in the construction of the modern category of the psychological.[14]

Nonetheless, the very proximity of psychoanalysis rendered it a disorienting force for modernism.[15] As Michael Levenson observes, "The agon of modernism was not a collision between novelty and tradition but *a contest of novelties*, a struggle to define the trajectory of the new."[16] The intimate involvement of members of the Bloomsbury Group in translating, editing, publishing, popularizing, and practicing psychoanalysis virtually ensured that British writers and intellectuals were exposed to its ideas. Few modernists have been more closely linked to psychoanalysis than Virginia Woolf, but her response to Freud was famously fraught. While she and her husband, Leonard, were the first publishers of Freud's collected works in English, Woolf lampooned Freud in *Mrs. Dalloway* (1925) and in her essay "Freudian Fiction" (1920), in which she characterized fiction inspired by psychoanalysis as the "bastard child" of Freud, a degenerate offspring of this new discursive acquaintance. Woolf strategically opposed "Freudian fiction" to the experimentalism of modern fiction, pitting what she saw as the simplistic, reductive narratives of the former against the irreducible complexity of the latter. Woolf's contemporary, Katherine Mansfield, decried the "sudden 'mushroom growth' of cheap psycho-analysis in fiction," arguing that fiction inspired by psychoanalysis presented formulaic plots and characters.[17] The Bloomsbury art critics Roger Fry and Clive Bell ridiculed psychoanalytically inspired art as part of a feminized mass culture keyed to the endless gratification of wishes. D. H. Lawrence categorically refused to read Freud's writing and declared psychoanalysis a "public danger"—as if it were a signal threat to the prevailing social order. And T. S. Eliot proclaimed in 1927 that the "contemporary novel" is "either directly affected by a study of psycho-analysis, or affected by the atmosphere created by psycho-analysis, or inspired by a desire to escape from psycho-analysis."[18] Turning modernists into outraged defenders of the aesthetic, psychoanalysis claimed the distinction of seeming intimate yet other, alluring yet threatening, an extra-literary force corrupting the literary from within.

There have been a small handful of full-length studies of the relation between modernism and psychoanalysis: Maud Ellmann's influential collection, *The Nets of Modernism*,[19] examines the complex networks of circulation, exchange, and indebtedness across the works of Freud, Woolf, Joyce, and James. Lyndsey Stonebridge's *The Destructive Element*[20] traces the destructive fantasies and impulses that dominate modernist writing, and connects this modernist death drive to theories of British psychoanalysis, especially those of Melanie Klein. Laura Marcus's *Dreams of Modernity*[21] analyzes the fascinating interconnections between railway, cinema, and psychoanalysis as technologies of modernity, and the ways these technologies shaped and were shaped by the aesthetic experiments of H.D., Virginia Woolf, and Dorothy Richardson. Over the last two decades, scholarship on modernism and theories of mind has also focused on non-psychoanalytic and pre-Freudian forms of dynamic psychology, including empiricist psychology (Judith Ryan); vitalist philosophy (Omri Moses); spiritualism, mysticism, and psychical research (Pamela Thurschwell, Helen Sword, Roger Luckhurst, Leigh Wilson); behaviorism and reflex (Timothy Wientzen); modernism and self-help (Beth Blum); and contemporary fields of neuroscience and cognition. By insisting, in contrast, upon the centrally formative impact of psychoanalysis, my book shares thematic continuity with earlier literary-historical accounts of the relationship between literature and psychoanalysis offered by Frederick J. Hoffman, Stephen Marcus, Maud Ellmann, Perry Meisel, Jean-Michel Rabaté, Elizabeth Abel, and Susan Stanford Friedman. My book builds on these essential works, but has a different inflection. It aims to reanimate the lively and sometimes contentious debates and disagreements between modernists and psychoanalysts, with an eye to how Freudian psychoanalysis was crucial to modernism as a cultural and intellectual field, and to an emergent literary criticism that grew out of the modernist moment. Engaging the work of key modernist writers and critics, as well as greater and lesser-known psychoanalysts, it aims to reconstruct a cross-disciplinary matrix of modernist creation while tracking current debates in literary studies back to the early and mid-twentieth century. Ultimately, my project seeks to understand how particular modernist authors engaged Freudian psychoanalysis, sometimes contentiously, in ways that shaped their works.

Or to put it another way: the explicit repudiations of psychoanalysis by Anglo-American modernists should not obscure the complexity and intricacy of the interactions between these two fields, nor should it offer yet another instance of a "great divide" between modernism and a repressed cultural other. If anything, psychoanalysis and modernist literature were both so dialectical, so riven by similar tensions and contradictions, that they could never be understood as properly "other" to each other. This book recovers the complex play of rivalry and complicity between modernist writers and the psychoanalysts they claimed as aesthetic and intellectual antagonists, revealing the intuitive affinities, concrete interactions, and competitive rivalries that helped shape the aesthetic and intellectual contours of Anglo-American modernism. Indeed, it is impossible to disentangle some of modernism's key aesthetic innovations from the influence of psychoanalysis: Woolf's free indirect style, Lawrence's aesthetics of unconsciousness and embodied response, Auden's queer poetic criticism, and Nabokov's late modernist parody were all, as we will see, linked to psychoanalysis. I analyze how these aesthetic and intellectual transformations emerge in dialectical relation to the theories of psychic life and aesthetic production offered by psychoanalysis. Focusing more on intertextuality than on influence, I explain how psychoanalytic ideas and methodologies helped shape modernist culture, examining modernists' idiosyncratic reworkings and creative misreadings of Freudian psychoanalysis rather than in positioning Freud as a straw man, even as Anglo-American modernists did precisely this.

Writers such as Ezra Pound, Wyndham Lewis, Roger Fry, Clive Bell, and T. S. Eliot emerge as supporting characters in this narrative, although they mostly dismissed psychoanalysis wholesale. Their reactions reflect the more extreme and phobic responses to psychoanalysis, which includes Ezra Pound's antisemitic tirades against Freud and his endorsement of fascism as the only force that could triumph over the "quagmire" of the unconscious. (It should be emphasized that while many modernist writers viewed psychoanalysis as a repressive force, they experimented with repressive mechanisms themselves, including abstraction, authoritarianism, diagnosis, and critique.) Then there were figures like Samuel Beckett, who read extensively within psychoanalytic theory in the 1930s and was analyzed by Wilfred Bion at the Tavistock Clinic for two years before breaking off treatment; but Bion persuaded him to attend Jung's 1935 Tavistock lectures on the dissociative states produced by neurosis and psychosis.[22] Scholars have also detailed his romantic involvement with Lucia Joyce, James Joyce's daughter, who suffered from schizophrenia and sought treatment from Carl Jung, and his close proximity to, and translation of, the work of French surrealists, who were adapting psychoanalytic ideas about the unconscious and experimenting with irrationality and automatic writing. Beckett thus presents an example of a modernist who engaged with psychoanalysis during the interwar years and drew on the resources of psychoanalysis to explore extreme states of consciousness in his work, but who still held reservations about psychoanalysis as a single source of truth about the self.

Like Beckett, Auden and H.D. had productive yet ambivalent exchanges with psychoanalysis, as both poets drew on Freud's findings to catalyze their poetic projects. Auden was an early reader of Freud and Jung and modeled some of his early poetic experiments on psychoanalytic forms; but he became convinced in the 1930s that orthodox psychoanalysis was insufficiently radical as a social theory, and turned to more heterodox lay analysts to frame his emerging queer poetic practice. Extending psychoanalytic insights beyond their Freudian limitations, Auden embraced a more idiosyncratic version of psychoanalysis that could diagnose the ills of the social body and address its oppressive conformity and heteronormativity. H.D., along with her partner Bryher, was at the center of the ferment around psychoanalysis in Vienna in the 1930s and was analyzed by the Austrian psychoanalyst Hanns Sachs and later by Sigmund Freud, whose treatments became the subject matter of her memoir *Tribute to Freud*.

Attraction, envy, resistance, ambivalence, and disavowal were among the complex rhetorical and affective positions that writers adopted toward psychoanalysis; nor did any of these positions remain static over time. I track the ways in which psychoanalysis as a proximate discipline, helped give form to the aesthetic and discursive concerns of literary modernism. Woolf and Lawrence's claims not to have read Freud while helping to disseminate Freud's ideas to a broader British public, and Auden's turn away from an earlier allegiance to Freud's theories to a more idiosyncratic set of psychologies, bring into view the atmosphere of mutual critique and competition which—surprisingly—reveals how dependent modernism was on psychoanalysis. To think in terms of sharing and resistance, identification and disavowal, is also to bring the affective language of psychoanalysis to bear on a discussion of disciplinarity—discussions that have become reanimated in literary studies today.

Modernists offered a varied set of responses to the skeptical mood that psychoanalysis helped evolve—a "suspicious" reading style that looked to texts for their veiled events and repressed secrets. Freud often analogized his practice of interpreting signs to the work of the detective, who decodes resistant material and investigates errant or overlooked details. In his essay "The Moses of Michelangelo" (1914), he compared the work of the analyst to that of Giovanni Morelli, an art connoisseur who detected artistic fakes by "laying stress on the significance of minor details, of things like the drawing of a fingernail . . . which the copyist neglects to imitate and yet which every artist executes in his own characteristic way." Freud goes on to emphasize how Morelli's method is "closely related to the technique of psychoanalysis. It too, is accustomed to divine secret and concealed things from despised or unnoticed features, from the rubbish-heap, as it were, of our observations."[23]

One of the secondary aims of this study is to emphasize how recent debates within literary studies about the value of suspicious and symptomatic reading can be traced back to early twentieth-century debates about the value of psychoanalytic literary criticism. Modernism was not only a field of cultural production, but an intellectual field with a special relationship to the emergence of literary criticism as a discipline. David Trotter's book *Paranoid Modernism* argues that the works of early-twentieth-century modernists—in particular those of Ford, Lewis, Lawrence, and Conrad—reflect new fears about expertise and its consequences in an era marked by the rise of the professional classes. Trotter associates this particular strand of modernism with an obsessive search for professional status and symbolic capital (beyond mere commercial success), and with a paranoid madness that expressed itself in hyper-masculine, elitist, and anti-democratic ways.[24] Trotter's book, although differently focused, helps me address modernism's intense professional rivalries and robust defense of literary autonomy in the face of an emergent psychoanalytic criticism. Furthermore, in reassessing the historical and intellectual legacies of modernism, I argue that modernist responses to psychoanalytic criticism as it was applied to literature anticipate discussions that have taken place since the 1990s about "paranoid" reading and the "hermeneutics of suspicion" offered by Eve Kosofsky Sedgwick, Rita Felski, Sharon Marcus and Stephen Best, and others. In so doing, I suggest new ways we might treat disciplines and cultural fields as themselves in possession of instincts, desires, anxieties, and aversions that help shape their identities.

Secret Sharers asks a series of core questions: What formal and rhetorical strategies did modernists offer in response to a modernity that was becoming increasingly shaped by psychoanalysis? To what extent did modernists assimilate psychoanalytic theories and methods of reading into their practice, and to what extent did they offer inventive misreadings and aesthetic alternatives (alternatives that were sometimes shaped by the very paradigms they were eager to replace)? What aesthetic strategies, interpretive practices, and forms of knowledge were produced in the encounter between fields? As analysts turned to literature and art to illustrate psychoanalytic theories, modernists sought to counter the reductive and totalizing narratives of psychoanalysis by envisioning competing formulations of the relationship between literature and psychic life. This book reveals how modernists transformed the hermeneutic and diagnostic priorities of psychoanalysis into novel aesthetic strategies and distinctive modes of epistemological and critical engagement.

Modernists were skeptical of a psychoanalytic hermeneutic that aimed to resolve the ambiguity and penetrate the opacity so crucial to modernist aesthetics; yet they were also inspired by ideas of the unconscious and techniques like "free association," which endeavored to suspend the conscious control of thought to make way for involuntary ideas. Freud's understanding of the unconscious as resistant to chronological sequence and temporal structure, and his utilization of the techniques of dream analysis and "free association," may have helped inspire the disjointed, non-linear, and dreamlike experiments of modernism.[25] Moreover, Freud's understanding of dream formation—with its literary mechanisms of displacement, condensation, and secondary elaboration—bore affinities to the condensed, abstract, and cryptic poetics of modernism. As Lionel Trilling expressed in his essay "Freud and Literature" (1940), "of all mental systems, the Freudian psychology is the one which makes poetry indigenous to the very constitution of the mind."[26] But Trilling challenges Freud's notion of the unconscious origins of art when he stresses that the final product of literary creation requires the "formal control of the conscious mind." Literary critics and analysts alike were fascinated by the application of psychoanalysis to literature. Hanns Sachs, the Austrian psychoanalyst and member of Freud's inner circle, was another example of a figure who worked across fields, translating Kipling's poems into German and co-founding the journal *Imago*, inspired by Carl Spitteler's 1906 novel of the same title. Developing the idea of "collective day-dreaming,"[27] Sachs saw literary production not as the product of individual talent but as a social performance, in which the raw materials of a collective unconscious were processed in language.[28]

Both modernism and psychoanalysis described the project of culture in remarkably similar terms—as a will to mastery over the unruly forces of the unconscious and the forceful drives of the body ("where id was, there ego shall be," in Freud's famous formulation). We might say that if psychoanalysis endeavored to discover the sources of the irrational, modernism helped render the unconscious legible by generating formal and thematic analogues to its operations.[29]

Post-War Freudianity

By the early 1920s, psychoanalysis had become the dominant mode of psychological thought in Britain and the United States. As it gained visibility in the interwar years, it generated both anxiety and ambivalent appeal for modernists. Bloomsbury's hospitality to psychoanalysis in the 1910s and 1920s propelled both enthusiasm and skepticism among Anglo-American writers and critics about the ascendance of psychoanalysis as a discourse.[30] English journalists portrayed psychoanalysis (perhaps not unfairly) as a dangerous theoretical import from the continent with a prurient interest in sexuality and an unscientific methodology—but it was precisely these qualities that made it appealing to members of Bloomsbury.[31] Lytton Strachey attended psychoanalytic lectures at the British Psychological Society and reported his scandalous new insights to Virginia Woolf, who responded at first with curiosity and eventually with derision. Leonard Woolf provided the first nontechnical English review of A. A. Brill's 1914 English translation of *The Psychopathology of Everyday Life* and marketed it to his readers as a major literary event: "[Freud] writes with the subtlety of mind, a broad and sweeping imagination more characteristic of the poet than the scientist or the medical practitioner."[32] A decade later, in 1924, James Strachey convinced the Woolfs to form a publishing alliance between the International Psycho-analytical Library and the Hogarth Press, an alliance that would result in Hogarth's publication of all of Freud's works, both past and future.[33] And in 1925 Melanie Klein delivered her first English lecture in the home of Adrian and Karin Stephen, Woolf's brother and his wife—an event that would mark the beginnings of England's first home-grown brand of psychoanalysis: object-relations theory.[34]

Bloomsbury not only served as an intellectual enclave for psychoanalysis, it gave psychoanalysis a literary complexion: several members of Bloomsbury dabbled in psychoanalysis as an enrichment to their aesthetic and intellectual projects. Virginia Woolf's brother became an analyst, as did his wife; both were initiated into the field after being analyzed by Freud. Other figures in the Bloomsbury circle became analysts and disciples of Freud, including James and Alix Strachey, who moved back and forth between the aesthetic bohemia of Bloomsbury and the professional world of analysis, importing the intellectual transformations of the Continent to a variously receptive English intelligentsia. The convergence of psychoanalytic and modernist discourses led to cross-disciplinary projects such as Freud and Ernest Jones' psychoanalytic readings of *Oedipus* and *Hamlet* and the Hogarth Press's publication of the *Standard Edition of Freud*, with James Strachey's translations offering a uniquely British and aestheticized interpretation of Freud's work.[35] Hogarth's publication of Woolf's *Mrs. Dalloway* and the first volume of Freud's *Collected Papers* on the same day in 1925 was more than mere coincidence: It signified the mutually reinforcing ascendance of literary modernism and psychoanalysis in England. The International Psycho-analytical Library would ultimately become the greatest source of revenue for the Hogarth Press, helping to subsidize its experimental projects and thus joining modernist aesthetics to new theories of mind.

Psychoanalysis gained visibility in the interwar years, in part through its entanglement with Bloomsbury. In Graham Richards' terms, an inescapable atmosphere of "Freudishness" pervaded interwar England, especially within literary circles. Dorothy Richardson, who helped popularize modern psychological ideas by introducing stream-of-consciousness techniques into fiction, described the era as one of "post-War Freudianity."[36] The English writer and editor, Bryher, proclaimed: "You could not have escaped Freud in the literary world of the early twenties. Freud! All literary London discovered Freud about 1920 . . . the theories were the great subject of conversation wherever one went at that date. To me Freud is literary London . . . after the first war. People did not always agree but he was always taken with the utmost seriousness."[37]

In England, psychoanalysis circulated primarily among intellectual and literary elites. In the United States it was viewed as a liberatory discourse that challenged American sexual puritanism, as well as a popular amusement along the lines of jazz and cabaret.[38] After World War I, Freud and other analysts took on British and U.S. patients and students, because they had the financial capital to help sustain the enterprise and because they would help disseminate psychoanalysis abroad.[39] Freud and Jung delivered a series of lectures at Clark University in 1909, which helped set the stage for what cultural historians have described as the "psychologization" of American culture that was unrivaled in other places.[40] But its absorption into more mainstream channels in the United States alarmed Freud, who took aim at America as philistine for its failure to cultivate the instinctual renunciation that was the highest achievement of culture.[41] As Henry Abelove reminds us, Freud found Americans moralistic and materialistic, having sublimated their repressed sexual impulses into acquisition and accumulation, rather than into art, literature, science, and law.[42]

England on the other hand seemed to Freud to possess the sensibility and refinement, and the literary and cultural capital, that made it the next great center for psychoanalytic thought, on a par with Vienna and Berlin. It is perhaps ironic then that American, British, and Irish modernists—including Virginia Woolf, D. H. Lawrence, Roger Fry, Clive Bell, Wyndham Lewis, T. S. Eliot, Ezra Pound, Aldous Huxley, Gertrude Stein, and James Joyce—were notoriously critical of Freud's ideas.

Joyce worked to distance himself from Freud after the publication of *Ulysses*, announcing, "I have recorded, simultaneously, what a man says, sees, thinks, and what such seeing, thinking, saying does, to what you Freudians call the subconscious—but as for psychoanalysis it is neither more nor less than blackmail."[43] Joyce's final production, *Finnegans Wake* (1939), a novel indebted to the discourse of dreams and the unconscious, turns to parody to ward off its psychoanalytic rivals. In its satire of the incest fantasy, old men who are described as "farther potential" fantasize about taking advantage of girls who are "yung and easily Freudened." The verbal trickery here reflects the wordplay and double entendre that so appealed to Joyce, as it burlesques the reduction of social relations to sexual symbolism.

D. H. Lawrence mounted perhaps the most sustained critique of Freudian psychoanalysis, casting it as a foil to his own developing psychologies. In his two anti-psychoanalytic polemics from the 1920s, *Psychoanalysis and the Unconscious* (1921) and *Fantasia of the Unconscious* (1922), Lawrence defines the "pristine unconscious" as an embodied source of dynamic creativity temporally prior to intellection, which he contrasts to the cauldron of repressed impulses he associates with the Freudian unconscious. In the opening passages of *Psychoanalysis and the Unconscious*, he caricatures psychoanalysis's reception and popularization in Britain:

> The ears of the ethnologists began to tingle, the philosopher felt his gorge rise, and at last the moralist knew he must rush in. By this time psychoanalysis had become a public danger. The mob was on the alert. The Oedipus complex was a household word, the incest motive a commonplace of tea-table chat. Amateur analyses became the vogue. "Wait till you've been analyzed," said one man to another, with varying intonation. A sinister look came into the eyes of the initiates—the famous, or infamous, Freud look. You could recognize it everywhere, wherever you went.
>
> Psychoanalysts know what the end will be. They have crept in among us as healers and physicians; growing bolder, they have asserted their authority as scientists; two more minutes they will appear as apostles.[44]

Anyone familiar with Lawrence's writing will recognize the hyperbolic prose and destabilizing mixture of prophecy and satire. Yet the caricature captures something of the subversive and seductive qualities of psychoanalysis in the image of a clan of initiates whose eyes widen with prurient interest when analysis is invoked. Whether the object of ridicule is the psychoanalytic "initiates" or the alarmed "moralists" who fear the power of the new discourse, Lawrence conveys the sense of threat to official morality that psychoanalysis represented, developing into a "public danger" so thorough that it menaces mainstream culture.

Lawrence's caricature is not far from the depictions of psychoanalysis in the British and American general press, which decried its illegitimacy as a science, its faddish complexion and cultlike appeal, and its exaggerated attention to the "sex instinct." In English newspapers of the 1920s, reviewers consistently referred to the sex obsession of the Freudians and to their mystical, unscientific conjectures. But like many of these reviewers, Lawrence captures the vogue for psychoanalytic jargon and its absorption into "tea-table chat." By the early 1920s, technical terms like the Oedipus complex, inferiority complex, libido, and instinct had migrated into a popular idiom, so that individuals could invoke such concepts without direct knowledge of the literature. In his discussion of the American reception of psychoanalysis, Joel Pfister argues that the performance of psychoanalytic knowledge conferred intellectual prestige and urbanity to the speaker and granted individuals permission to be safely transgressive.[45] Lawrence plays up its faddish qualities and its potential abuse by charlatans.

Equally threatening to Lawrence was psychoanalysts' claims to expertise: Psychoanalysts not only pose as doctors and scientists, they assume the mantle of religious authorities: "This new doctrine—it will be called no less—has been subtly and insidiously suggested to us, gradually inoculated into us. It is true that doctors are the priests, nay worse, the medicine-men of our decadent society."[46] Lawrence mixes metaphors to register the subtlety with which psychoanalysis has penetrated popular thought: "Doctrine" compares psychoanalysis to religion; "suggests" equates psychoanalysis with the powers of hypnosis; while "inoculates" implies the mysteriously invasive powers of medicine. Lawrence's critique is aimed at psychoanalysis's pretensions to authority, to its exalted sense of its own powers. Like Freud, Lawrence was acutely aware of the waning power of religious faith in his own era: in *Women in Love* (1916), for example, the nihilistic Birkin proclaims God's death: "The old ideals are dead as nails—nothing there . . . there's no God."[47] But by the time of *Psychoanalysis and the Unconscious* (1921), Lawrence seems convinced that psychoanalysis is poised to eclipse the authority of religion by acting as a "new morality." If he was originally attracted to psychoanalysis for its occult formulations of the unconscious and its promises of psychosexual liberation, he soon rejected its elevation to the status of a science or religion, its aspirations to a totalizing theory of the subject.

Lawrence equates psychoanalysis with a vague yet alarming sense of the "new," as if it embodied both the radical uncertainty of modernity and the collective hunger for new articles of faith. Foucault has similarly emphasized how in the modern era the psychologist came to absorb the authority that had been divested from religious figures and institutions, suggesting in *Madness and Civilization* (1964) that Freud elevated the status of the medical personage to quasi-divine omnipotence. In the schism between science and faith that occupied late nineteenth- and early twentieth-century moralists and critics, psychoanalysis becomes equated with the ascendance of materialism and science, and with their degrading effects; it also comes to stand as a sign of the erosion of faith and spirituality characteristic of the modern era. Although Freud, the committed atheist, augured the eclipse of religion by science, in the minds of his followers he was also a kind of ecclesiastical authority of a newly secular age.

To be sure, the assimilation of psychoanalytic ideas into England and the United States, particularly in the aftermath of the Great War, intensified the sense of rupture from the past that gave modernism its revolutionary force. Psychoanalysis became for many a new dogma in a world shaken by war, class struggle, and political and sexual revolution; and yet psychoanalysis simultaneously intensified this sense of rupture by subverting Enlightenment concepts of progress, reason, and civilization, while offering to explain the collapse of these values. As Graham Richards argues, the British were "desperately seeking a modern psychological vocabulary" appropriate to their situation, one in which "the now glaring limitations and failures of 'reason' could first be understood . . . and then rectified," and in which "the underlying mechanisms of human sociality and harmony could be identified and harnessed in the face of radical social breakdown."[48]

Psychoanalysis encountered intense hostility from the scientific and medical establishment when it was first introduced into England in the 1910s. Ernest Jones, Edward Glover, and other members of the British Psychoanalytical Society, engaged in fierce battles with the medical establishment over the legitimacy and effectiveness of psychoanalysis.[49] But it was really the First World War and its aftermath that helped shift the perception of psychoanalysis as a useful tool in the treatment of shell shock and traumatic neurosis.[50] The British anthropologist and psychologist W. H. R. Rivers defended the role of psychoanalysis in comprehending the social impact of war and the reality of "shell shock" as a post-traumatic disorder. Rivers helped move psychology away from the materialism of English psychiatry, which had focused on brain anatomy as the origin of pathology, and toward the experimental psychotherapeutic methods of Freud. Unlike Freud, however, he focused on the instinct of "self-preservation" rather than the sexual instinct as the force behind neurosis, arguing that neurosis resulted from a repressed impulse to flee the battlefield.[51] Siegfried Sassoon's semi-autobiographical accounts of his transformative work with Rivers at Craiglockhart during the war, and Pat Barker's novelistic reconstruction of this relationship in *Regeneration* (1991) have turned Rivers into a literary icon of sorts; but for the purposes of this study, he is significant for popularizing theories of psychoanalysis to the British and for helping establish a thriving psychotherapeutic practice for the treatment of shell shock.

Graham Richards suggests that "the sudden inward turn of the traditionally non-introspective British" had much to do with the trauma of the war and the social crisis it catalyzed.[52] Part of the appeal of psychoanalysis was the scale upon which it operated: psychoanalysis interpreted large-scale conflicts through the prisms of the intra-personal and inter-personal, contracting what seemed like the anarchic social forces of history into a repertoire of narratives about the self and its intimate relations with others.[53] In a post-war society that was experiencing both belated and anticipatory forms of trauma, psychoanalysis was adept at narrativizing sources of aggression and explaining the unique temporalities of traumatic experience.[54] In Rebecca West's 1918 novella, *The Return of the Soldier*, for example, the psychoanalyst figure, Dr. Anderson, explains to Kitty, the wife of the amnesiac soldier recently returned from the front, the connection between psychic trauma, wish fulfillment, and amnesia: "His unconscious self is refusing to let him resume his relations with his normal life, and so we get this loss of memory."[55] Narrated by Jenny, the female cousin of the traumatized soldier, Chris Baldry, the tightly drawn novel understands the war as partly a problem of scale: how to make sense of a global conflagration via the social and psychic mechanisms of British upper-middle-class domesticity, which turns on its own forms of evasion and exclusion. As West's *The Return of the Soldier* and Woolf's *Mrs. Dalloway* make clear, modernism was highly invested in this question of scale, and how to make the war representable through the aesthetic affordances of the novel.

Freud's own work underwent revision toward the end of World War I, casting beyond the exclusivity of the sexual instincts to a consideration of the psyche's management of pleasure and pain. *Beyond the Pleasure Principle* (1920) concerns itself with how the psychic mechanism, ostensibly under the sway of the pleasure principle, repeats and recollects sources of "unpleasure." Written in the immediate aftermath of the war, and translated into English in 1928,

Freud's monograph attributes traumatic neurosis both to a lack of preparation and to an absence of physical wounds, the presence of which would, according to Freud, help to stave off neurosis by offering a physiological site of cathexis.[56] Invoking an anecdote about his eighteen-month-old grandson who stages a seemingly pleasurable game of *fort/da*, during which he casts off a wooden cotton reel and then pulls it back in, Freud concludes that this is a game designed to manage the distressing disappearance of his parents, to exert mastery in an otherwise powerless situation. The child re-creates the primal separation from the mother by creating a symbolic substitute to manage the psychic stress of the event. Such scenes offer powerful interpretive gestures and animating fictions about the subject's efforts to cope with overwhelming social forces. Just as significantly, as Anne-Claire Mulder points out, the story of Freud's grandson is a paradigmatic scene of representation, for the subject moves from his immediate reality to symbolic mediation.[57] As such, it articulates some of the forceful connections between psychoanalysis and literature, for the subject uses linguistic signs and images to mediate their experiential reality. Or, put another way, psychoanalysis didn't simply make use of mimesis, but imagined the unconscious as itself a kind of artist, in a way that undercut the Romantic ideal of the genius who is exclusively able to turn the world of things into a world of representations.

Freud's own sources were largely literary, and his works continually make reference to Shakespeare, Goethe, and Heine. Forging connections between trauma and representation, Freud compares the activities of the unconscious to those of the artist, suggesting that the mental apparatus produces the kinds of condensations and displacements achieved in literary texts. Even though Freud bore little curiosity about his modernist contemporaries, he praised creative writers as the precursor poets of psychoanalytic knowledge, and even remarked that literature was one of the fields psychoanalysts should master in their training.[58]

Many critics have addressed the literary qualities of Freud's writing, or seen Freud as a modernist in his own right. In *The Literary Freud* (2007), Perry Meisel underscores Freud's focus on language and representation, his theoretical grounding in literary and mythological sources, and his rhetorical performances "by which its fictions are presented as revealed truths."[59] Meisel also highlights psychoanalysis's attachment to literary tropes and its comparisons of the mechanisms of the psyche to those of language.[60] Stephen Marcus famously reads Freud's case studies as psychoanalytic novels; Freud's "Dora," with its unreliable first-person perspective, its non-linear narration, and its self-conscious formal innovation, "bears certain suggestive resemblances to a modern experimental novel."[61] Marcus reminds us that in Freud's hands the case study becomes something it never was before: self-consciously incomplete in its presentation as textual fragment. Freud features less as a confident scientist methodically using evidence to confirm a hypothesis than as a modernist author aware of the "problematic status of his undertaking and the dubious quality of his achievement."[62] We see him descending into the world of narrative after traditional empirical methods fail to secure the desired results. And although Freud wanted psychoanalysis to bear the authority of a science, his own admission at the beginning of *Studies on Hysteria* that "the case histories I write should read like short stories" and that "they lack the serious stamp of science" registers the generic instability and literary self-consciousness of his studies. I must console myself," Freud goes on to say, "with the reflection that the nature of the subject is evidently responsible for this, rather than any preference of my own."[63] Literariness was arguably there at the start, as psychoanalysis emerged not as a study of biology, but as a study of patients' narratives about themselves. Freud's reliance on tropes borrowed from literature and myth, his focus on narrative as a means of diagnosis and cure, and his development of an elaborate system for analyzing linguistic utterance all point to the profoundly literary nature of his project. Freud insisted that psychoanalysis was a positivist science of the mind, but the question of whether it was closer to an expressive art form or a science bedeviled the field from its inception.

"Footling Interiors": Modernism, Psychoanalysis, and the Inward Turn

Modernist writers were not only conflicted about Freud, they were conflicted about their relation to psychology itself. Astradur Eysteinsson has argued that we might identify two influential strains within modernism, one that more eagerly embraced psychology and another that we might call anti-subjectivist or impersonal (although many modernists would be difficult to categorize as either).[64] This psychological modernism, on the one hand, attends to the deep structures of the psyche and to non-rational levels of human experience and cognition, and admits the compatibility of modernist practice with psychological theories of mind. It turns to expressionist and surrealist poetics, stream of consciousness prose, and the use of multiple "centers of consciousness." At its most extreme, psychological modernism evokes the image of the isolated mind absorbed in contemplation of its own mental processes. And yet, as Eysteinsson reminds us, the magnification of subjectivity sometimes coincides with an erasure of subjectivity, as the modernist subject comes to lose their tenuous hold on social reality.[65] This is not far from the critique of modernism offered by Lukács, who sees in modernism's inward turn and focus on the viewer's crisis of perception a negation and degradation of a reality beyond the subject.[66]

On the other hand, we can view a powerful anti-subjectivist and impersonal strain of Anglo-American modernism in the work of T. E. Hulme, Ezra Pound, T. S. Eliot, and Wyndham Lewis.[67] Concerned with exorcising "the specter of psychologism,"[68] this anti-subjectivist strain includes the hard, crystalline poetics and geometrical abstraction of Hulme's anti-humanism, Pound and Lewis's objectivism, and Eliot's impersonality. Pound ridiculed the inward tendencies of modernism and psychoanalysis as so much "introspective idiocy,"[69] while Eliot demanded an "escape from emotion" and a "continual extinction of personality."[70] For these writers, psychological inwardness is an affectively messy and irrational formlessness. Even Virginia Woolf and Wallace Stevens can often be understood as turning away from the human toward solid objects, returning the viewer to the concreteness of the material world. Referencing Woolf's depictions of a world without humans, Lewis's tributes to physical objects, and Stevens' poetry of discrete things, Douglas Mao suggests that modernist writers sought refuge from a modernity construed "as an affair of consciousness gone awry, a phenomenon of subjectivity grown rapacious and fantastically powerful. . . ."[71] Lewis's literary surrogate Tarr declares that "good art must have no inside."[72] For these modernists, objectivity and impersonality indexed a weariness with consciousness itself, and with the deformations of experience that an abstracting consciousness was seen as producing.[73]

Anti-psychological modernists associated psychoanalysis with the excessive solipsism of Romantic poetry and the sentimentality of Victorian literature.[74] Pound's Imagism emphasized precision, concreteness, and visual distinctness as a call to abolish the abstraction, emotional excess, and ornamentation in poetry. In Pound's polemical essay "Prolegomena" (1912), he calls for a poetry that is like "granite": "austere, direct, free from emotional slither."[75] This emotional "slither" would become increasingly associated with the solipsism and emotional excess that he felt psychoanalysis promoted. In a 1935 article in *The New English Weekly*, Pound described Freudianism as a wallowing in self-absorption and suffering: "People treated by Freudians, etc. get steadily more and more interested in their own footling interiors, and . . . less interesting to anyone else. . . . They are at the nadir from Spinoza's sane and hearty: the more perfect a thing is the more it acts and the less it suffers."[76] He maintained that psychoanalysis precipitated a turning away from the external world in favor of an obsessive attention to interiority, an attention which was the very source of pathology. Well into the 1950s, Pound inveighed against the Freudians, which became a source of contention with H.D., whose decision to be analyzed by Freud in 1933 likely catalyzed their split.[77] H.D. had been for

Pound the poet whose work encapsulated the hard, crystalline precision of Imagism; so her turn to psychoanalysis was something of a betrayal.

What scholars have observed as the reactionary character of Anglo-American modernism—its misogyny, its xenophobia, its "genteel" or overt antisemitism, and its flirtation with fascism—clearly underwrote some of modernism's fantasies about the dangers of psychoanalysis.[78] For example, Lawrence's screeds against Freud often trade in antisemitic stereotypes; in *Psychoanalysis and the Unconscious*, he refers repeatedly to Freud's inventory of "merchandise," as though Freud were a Jewish merchant or pawnbroker trafficking his wares. Pound's distaste for modern psychology was intimately entangled with his antisemitism, as is evident in his description of psychoanalysis as "the Viennese poison . . . whole pewk of kiketry, aimed at destroying the will/introspective idiocy/non objective."[79] This may seem like inarticulate sputtering, but the vile amalgam of slurs and stereotypes bring into view how Pound's antisemitism was connected to his longstanding horror of formlessness and emotional "slither."

As recent criticism on Pound has shown, it is impossible to disentangle Pound's aesthetic and political views, even his early aesthetic avant-gardism, from his endorsement of fascism.[80] Parsing the complexities and contradictions of Pound's fascist imaginary, Robert Casillo connects Pound's agrarian, mythological, and patriarchal values to his antisemitism and fascism. Pound associated Jews with a range of evils—including usury, foreignness, effeminacy, emotional excess, and the blurring of cultural origins. His anti-Jewish sentiments developed, by the early 1940s, into explicit theories of international Jewish conspiracy, or what Pound called the "crawling slime of a secret [Jewish] rule."[81] In *The Cantos* and other writings from these decades, Pound traded in stereotypes of Jews as linked to emotional excess, sentimentality, and neurosis, denouncing the "formless, abstract 'squish' of Jewish thought."[82] He associated Jews with the "unnatural" fluidity of the inner life, with the mysterious forces of the unconscious, and with an excess of introspection.[83] Pound's emphasis on "order, shape, and definition," on clear outlines and hard exteriors, became both an aesthetic position and a political ideology aimed at containing the amorphous disorder he associated with Jewishness.[84]

Pound's anti-psychologism is thus clearly related to his antisemitism, but it was also linked to a misogyny that expressed anxieties about male autonomy.[85] In this regard, Pound is similar to figures like Lewis, whose assertions of aesthetic autonomy rested on both a disavowal of psychologism and an assertion of sexual difference. Wyndham Lewis was explicit in linking the success of psychoanalysis to a newly liberated female subject, both of which he saw as threats to the autonomy of the male artist.[86] Although Lewis and his stated rival, D. H. Lawrence, considered the politically, intellectually, and sexually liberated woman to be a threat to male individuation, Lewis's anxieties about psychoanalysis and the feminine converged in his distinctly misogynist caricatures of Lawrence. Whereas Lawrence saw himself as refuting psychoanalysis, Lewis conflated the two in an effort to discredit them both.[87] In *Paleface*, Lewis accuses Lawrence of a "glorification of the Feminine principle" and of exploiting "the fashionable Oedipal Complex": "the cry of Mr. Lawrence (great little Freudian that he has always been) is 'back to the womb.'"[88] If for Lawrence "blood-consciousness," the non-rational knowledge rooted in the body, represented a longed-for absence of the agonized self-consciousness that afflicted modern humanity, for Lewis, mindlessness—the loss of reason and intellect—represented the most threatening element of modern culture, and precisely that which linked the ideas of Freud with the irrationality of the masses.[89] Associating femininity and psychoanalysis with self-absorption and introspection, Lewis looked to objective, impersonal art forms to rupture the Romantic attachment to solipsism. Lewis's drama of male individuation, depicted most clearly in *Tarr* (1918), illustrates a central tension for these male modernists: how to assert a robust individualism without succumbing to the lure of psychologism.

The male modernist defense of an authentic aesthetic culture that depended on the repudiation of a feminized mass cultural aesthetic constituted, at the very least, an ideology of art as a refuge from the vicissitudes of modernity, and at the most extreme, a form of fascism. Women were, as Andreas Huyssen reminds us, the masses knocking at the gate of male power and privilege. At the same time, they were the receptacle for various fantasies, projections and displaced fears brought upon by modernization, the expansion of industrial capitalism, and the convulsions in the social and political order.[90] No doubt, the centrality of women's subjectivity to Freudian psychoanalysis (especially in its focus on hysteria) reinforced the connection between psychoanalysis and women's empowerment. And yet, this strain of anti-psychological modernism converges with Freudian psychoanalysis in their equation of the feminine with an unruly irrationality that had to be mastered through the distancing power of male intellect.

The American expatriate poet H.D. is a notable exception to this anxious retreat from psychologism in modernist poetry. She viewed psychoanalysis as an analogue to her aesthetic practices, although she did engage in an ongoing debate with Freud's ideas, as Susan Stanford Friedman and Laura Marcus have compellingly shown.[91] In *Tribute to Freud* (1956), a text that recounts her treatment by Freud in 1933–34 in Vienna, H.D. acknowledges psychoanalysis's revitalizing potential at a time in which repeated traumas on the personal and world stage had short-circuited her creativity.[92] She had survived the blitz, the death of her brother in war, the death of her father thereafter, a miscarriage, and the loss of her marriage. Like Freud, she was interested in the "hieroglyph of the dream," and its link to "supernormal" or "abnormal" states of mind. Drawing on the more mystical language of psychical research and popular spiritualism, H.D. inventively misreads Freud by returning to psychoanalysis some of the spiritual residuum it had purged, a residuum that she associates with repressed female artistry. Inverting the usual gendered tropes, H.D. invokes Freud as a "Midwife of the soul" or spiritual medium, offering access to occult knowledge and hidden depths of experience.

H.D. argues that poetic composition and psychoanalysis are both practices that rely on the recollection of fragments and the association of seemingly unrelated ideas. In describing her analysis with Freud, she says: "Thoughts were things, to be collected, collated, analyzed, shelved or resolved. Fragmentary ideas, apparently unrelated, were often found to be part of a special layer or stratum of thought and memory, therefore to belong together."[93] This process of recollection and recovery seemed particularly significant for H.D. in a postwar context in which bodies, psyches, communities, and traditions were in fragments. H.D. embodies a more nuanced relation to psychoanalysis, as she contests the absolute authority of Freud and challenges his views on women, while leveraging the psychoanalytic process to help her translate personal experience and idiosyncratic visions into poetic practice.[94]

Freud's death in 1939 did nothing to weaken the impact of psychoanalysis on literature; if anything, it only intensified its authority. Auden's well-known elegy, "In Memory of Sigmund Freud," (1939) honors Freud as "no more a person / now but a whole climate of opinion / under whom we conduct our different lives."[95] The initial shock associated with Freud's ideas in the 1910s and 1920s gives way to a "climate" of Freud, an atmosphere so pervasive that it "quietly surrounds all our habits of growth." The poem hinges on a complex presentation of Freud as both a common person, mortal and flawed, and a defining cultural force whose worldview people have come to accept as their own, even if they are unconscious of it. While Auden had largely rejected Freud's theories in the early 1930s in his turn to a more radical set of psychologies, his rapprochement with Freud in 1939 speaks to a more thorough assimilation of psychoanalytic ideas within British and American culture, and to an acknowledgment of Freud's ongoing relevance in a world disfigured by war, fascism, and mass death. Freud died the year Germany invaded Poland, and his death features in Auden's elegy not merely on its own but in relation to the mounting death of the "European crisis." Auden's humanizing elegy concedes the flaws in Freud's thinking, "often he was wrong and, at times, absurd," while paying tribute to a figure committed to leading us out of ignorance and self-deception. A different orientation to Freud emerges here—one that is respectful, even reverential, toward a figure who generated a storm of intensity among modernists in the early decades of the century. "In Memory of Sigmund Freud" unfolds Auden's deep understanding of Freud's ideas, revealing the poet's sympathy for a man who functioned alternatively as an intellectual precursor, a muse, and an opponent.[96]

"The Artist Is Being X-Rayed"

One of the principal objections of modernists to psychoanalysis was its conflation of artwork with artist. In psychoanalytic readings of art and literature, the artwork could have no separate ontology from that of the artist; the artist's projective and identificatory impulses could only produce disguised versions of the self, a kind of never-ending mimesis. Anticipating what would become New Critical arguments about "biographical" and "intentional" fallacy, many writers insisted on a separation between artist and artistic creation on the grounds that psycho-biographical readings misinterpreted the artistic process and overlooked the formal and rhetorical complexity of the literary work itself.

In 1925 the German novelist Thomas Mann remarked that "as an artist . . . I am not at all satisfied with Freudian ideas; rather, I feel disquieted and reduced by them. The artist is being X-rayed by Freud's ideas to the point where it violates the secret of his creative art."[97] Mann's "confession" draws together the synecdochal violations that inhere between artwork and artist when the former is viewed as symptomatic of the artist's psychic conflicts. The X-ray serves as metaphor for Freud's methods, but it also serves as a synecdoche for a larger constellation of new technologies of perception and scientific practices deemed threatening to the sphere of art. Developed within a year of each other, X-ray technology and psychoanalytic techniques become identified with a similar aim—penetrating the outer layers of human form and behavior in order to gain knowledge of the interior.[98] Jean-Michel Rabaté has described how this modern scientific consciousness entailed a "vivisective spirit" for modern art, which applied "a mental scalpel to the lyrical self."[99] Indeed, the modernist imaginary is filled with the tableau of the artist's subjection to science and psychiatry: consider Prufrock etherized upon a table or the unnamed protagonist of *Invisible Man* hooked up to the mother-machine, mentally reprogrammed by electroshock therapy. The modern subject is anatomized, laid bare by the processes of scientific and psychological modernity. Mann's remarks about psychoanalysis betray a related anxiety, that if artists submit to analytic treatment, they will forfeit the mysterious capacity to create. That neurosis and art are mutually reinforcing is a narrative subtended by Romantic associations of madness and genius.[100] Mann's reference to art's "secret" invokes a larger constellation of related theories about the aesthetic, including a perception of the artwork as self-enclosed and as qualitatively different from other modes of labor and production.

While Mann falls outside the bounds of this study, he evinces a set of anxieties shared by many modernists about the demystification and disenchantment of art by psychoanalysis. Nabokov's opinions of Freud were characteristically acid, but some of his statements about the demystification of art echo Mann's anxieties: "I think that the creative artist is an exile in [Freud's] study, in his bedroom, in the circle of his lamplight. He's quite alone there; he's the lone wolf. As soon as he's together with somebody else he shares his secret, he shares his mystery, he shares his God with somebody else."[101] Although Nabokov's response is elliptical, it seems to equate psychoanalysis with the effort to purge artistic creation of its mysteries and pleasures. In her essay "Freudian Fiction," Virginia Woolf satirized psychoanalysis as the "key that opens every door," reducing literary character to the unimaginative case study.[102] Such images of invasion and violation speak to a perceived threat psychoanalysis posed to literature as it extended its rational procedures to literary artifacts.[103] To the extent that psychoanalysis offered itself as a hermeneutical key to literature and culture it threatened to dissolve the expressive singularity and authenticity of the artwork. Indeed it vowed to transform the meaning of authorship itself, by insisting that the meanings art disclosed were unconscious.[104] An anonymous 1913 review of *The Interpretation of Dreams* in *The New Statesman*, a British left-leaning newspaper, expressed such a view of psychoanalysis's demystifying and reductive tendencies: "Not only has [Professor Freud] invented an entirely new theory of the dream, but he uses it with a fanatic's splendid recklessness as a master key to unlock the secrets both of dreams and literature."[105]

Such ideas carry over into a critical debate between Freud's ambassador to Britain, Ernest Jones, and the Bloomsbury art critic Roger Fry over the meaning and function of art, which was more specifically a debate about the role of psychology and emotion in the interpretation of art. In a speech Jones gave in 1927, published as an essay the following year entitled "Psycho-analysis and the Artist" (1928), Jones reinforces the privileged role of the psychoanalytic interpreter who can bridge the gap between aesthetic technique and human emotion.[106] Jones offers three reasons why the psychoanalyst is uniquely qualified to engage with literature and art: First, with their knowledge of the unconscious, the psychoanalyst can analyze the sources of inspiration that propel the artistic process. Poetic inspiration, once a vague and mystical concept, can be systematically investigated through its link to unconscious processes. Second, since the psychoanalyst is accustomed to navigating the patient's resistances, they are prepared to uncover motivations of which the artist is unaware. "Aesthetic feelings," Jones argues, are symptoms concealing "repressed and buried tendencies which it was the main aim of the analyst to uncover."[107] That is, the formal and aesthetic features of the artwork act as a resistant surface disclosing deeper and truer meanings to the analyst. Finally, the psychoanalyst recognizes the resemblance between "the working of the artist's creative impulse" and "other mental processes."[108] Jones contends that "what the artist is really trying to do, quite unconsciously, is to convert as completely as possible into aesthetic terms whatever emotions or wishes may be deeply stirring him."[109] Jones's defense of psychoanalytic criticism here notably jettisons considerations of form, undermining an earlier promise in the essay to take aesthetic "technique" seriously. Freud and Jones describe the aesthetic process as the "bait" that lures both artist and spectator toward the expression of unconscious impulses. In the end, Jones's essay fails to reassure artists or critics who are skeptical of the reductions of art to psychoanalytic formulas; instead it appears to confirm Thomas Mann's suspicion that the aim of psychoanalysis is to discover art's secret.

Modernists' reservations about psychoanalysis were not only a response to psychoanalytic readings of their works, but a response to psychoanalytic theories of art as such. This book tracks both the common concerns that underpin psychoanalysis and artistic modernism and the fundamental disagreements between psychoanalysts and modernist authors about the relationship between art and psychic life. Freud's view that art offered symbolic fictions that could compensate the artist for the psychic costs of civilization was a major affront to a modernist sensibility, even as modernists turned to art as a vital, if self-reflexively inadequate, response to what Ezra Pound termed a "botched civilization" in the wake of two world wars.[110] For Freud, art is instrumental, therapeutic, even narcotic in helping to reconcile individuals to the sacrifices they must make for culture. As he says in *Civilization and Its Discontents* (1930): "Life, as we find it, is too hard for us; it brings us too many pains, disappointments and impossible tasks. In order to bear it we cannot dispense with palliative measures."[111] If the increase of pleasure and the avoidance of unpleasure are our single-minded aims (Freud groups them under the sway of the pleasure principle), then art charts a middle path between total deflection of unwanted misery and an intoxicated insensitivity to it. Art is a palliative measure intended to diminish our pains, closely related to those "intoxicating substances" that can make us insensitive to those pains.[112] Art is both the highest achievement of civilization and a necessary vehicle to fending off our misery.

Art is also, for Freud, a surrogate for unsatisfied wishes. Since our internal world of instinctual needs is fundamentally at odds with the external world with its uncompromising insistence that we sacrifice our instincts or reroute them, art becomes a vehicle for shifting the direction of the instincts toward more socially acceptable aims. In Freud's earliest statement on art and the creative process, "Creative Writers and Day-dreaming" (1908), he compares the poet to the neurotic who has learned to project such fantasy onto reality without its being subject to reality testing.[113] In his *Introductory Lectures* (1922) Freud declares, "There is in fact a path from phantasy and back again to reality, and that is—art."[114] This is the same passage in which Freud refers to the "introverted" and "neurotic" disposition of the artist, the artist who can nonetheless transform his desire for "honour, power, riches, fame, and the love of women" into artistic achievement.[115] The "true artist," Freud declares, has a "powerful capacity for sublimation," and can channel his unfulfilled desires into art that can be consumed by spectators eager for the consolations that art offers:

> [The artist] possesses the mysterious ability to mould his particular material until it expresses the idea of his phantasy faithfully; and then he knows how to attach to this reflection of his phantasy-life so strong a stream of pleasure that, for a time at least, the repressions are out-balanced and dispelled by it. When he can do all this, he opens out to others the way back to the comfort and consolation of their own unconscious sources of pleasure.[116]

Turning to art to sublimate unconscious wishes, the artist can simultaneously satisfy their own desires and those of their audience, while reaping the audience's "gratitude and admiration."[117] Nor should those desires be read as exclusively erotic, for Freud suggests that art and literature can act as compensation for all manner of deficiencies, becoming an artistic supplement to an impoverished reality.

In viewing art as both a projection of inner conflict and as a psychic surrogate for unsatisfied wishes, Freud deemphasizes the heightened formal awareness that was crucial to modernism. If art is the communication of fantasies, disguised through aesthetic and formal presentation, literary form is reduced to a shimmering and seductive lure to wish-fulfillment, which it is also form's obligation to mask. Freud refers to the lure of form as "fore-pleasure," which disguises the pleasure achieved through deeper psychical sources. Even Lionel Trilling, who helped pave the way for the assimilation of psychoanalysis into academic literary discourse, agreed that psychoanalytic interpretations neglected the form of art in favor of a biographical determinism that pinned literary meaning to the sublimation of authorial neurosis. Freud, writes Trilling, "has less to say about beauty than about most other things," beholden as he is to the interpretation of content at the expense of formal elements like tone, feeling, and style.[118]

Theodor Adorno will go further than Trilling, arguing in his robust defense of modernist art in *Aesthetic Theory* (1970) that the biographical determinism of psychoanalysis wholly negates the mediation of form, most crucially the formal strategies by which art can challenge the status quo. In Adorno's critique, psychoanalysis reduces the artist to a "performance of gaining mastery over instinctual renunciation," and thus to the "achievement of conformity."[119] If psychoanalysis treats art's negativity as concentrated on instinctual conflicts, whose successful sublimation is the condition of the artwork's production, then it disavows not only art's autonomy, its "inner truth," but also its potential for social critique. In *Aesthetic Theory*, Adorno understands psychoanalysis to be an ideological tool for reconciling us to existing social structures. But there is an important counter-argument to be made: that psychoanalytic discourse did little to render its followers, or the culture at large, complacent. As a thorn in the side of established doctrine, psychoanalysis preserved an intensely adversarial function, made manifest in the resistance people held out against it.[120]

The modernist responses I track here and in the chapters that follow unfold a typology of anxieties about psychoanalysis and its approach to art: 1) that it would demystify the process and product of aesthetic creation, 2) that it would neglect the self-determining nature of the artwork in favor of a disenchanted and reductively biographical view of art, in which art is mere reflection of the artist's psyche, 3) that it would disregard the heighted formal awareness that was crucial to modernism, and 4) that it would neutralize art's potential for critique by reducing all art to the process of sublimation. Psychoanalysis posed some serious challenges for modernism, as it stressed content over form, context over text, and desire over disinterest. Adorno's characterization of psychoanalysis captures the modernist complaint most succinctly: "psychoanalysis treats artworks as nothing but facts, yet it neglects their own objectivity, their inner consistency, their level of form, their critical impulse, their relation to nonpsychical reality, and, finally, their idea of truth."[121] Moreover, psychoanalysis, by definition, sees itself as a practice that moves across disciplinary boundaries and discourses. At stake for modernist authors, then, as we will see, is the influence and authority of their own literary practice in relation to psychoanalysis, a field that was not only arrogating to itself the authority to interpret psychological selfhood, but also, and more provocatively, enlisting literary artifacts to support its theories.

Itinerary

Literary modernism's struggle with psychoanalysis did not end at midcentury. I argue here that attention to the vexed and ambivalent relationship between literary autonomy and psychoanalytic methods provides a crucial context for the current "method wars" in literary studies, debates about methods of reading and styles of textual engagement. In the words of Rita Felski, literary criticism's "distinctive sensibility" is "knowing, distrustful, self-conscious, hard-headed, tirelessly vigilant."[122] Psychoanalysis is still playing a starring role in the effort to outline the work of literary studies. I show in this book how the epistemological, ethical, and aesthetic consequences of psychoanalysis still haunt the language of disciplinary boundaries and aesthetic self-determination. Following this line of inquiry from the early twentieth century to the present, this book addresses the "hermeneutics of suspicion" that psychoanalysis helped codify and that still forms a site of contest in the field. I demonstrate how current critical methods, from "reparative" reading and "surface" reading to other postcritical methods are descendants—and more recent rivals—of literary modernism's conflicted responses to the protocols of suspicion.

The chapters that follow trace the ambivalent reception of Freudian psychoanalysis by modernists who were intimately affiliated with the new discourse. Several key events organize this account: Leonard Woolf's first non-technical reviews of Freud's essays in 1914, Hogarth Press's translation and publication of Freud's *Standard Edition* and the International Psycho-analytical Library in 1924, Auden's engagement with a group of eccentric psychologists in Weimar Berlin in 1929–30, and Nabokov's publication of *Lolita*, a parodic psychological case study, at the apex of the popularity of psychoanalysis in the United States.

In Chapter One, I read D. H. Lawrence's two extended essays *Psychoanalysis and the Unconscious* (1921) and *Fantasia of the Unconscious* (1922) as explicit counter-statements to psychoanalysis. I argue that in these idiosyncratic texts, as in the novel *Women in Love* (1920), Lawrence participates in the production of new psychological genres and becomes, ironically, one of the key disseminators of popular Freudianism, while simultaneously indicting psychoanalysis for its privileging of mental life at the expense of the body. Challenging the emphasis of psychoanalysis on expertise and critical distance, Lawrence champions amateurism and promotes intuition as a more direct vehicle to knowledge of the self. Lawrence and Freud can be deemed *sharers* in their effort to transform human consciousness through language and in their self-presentation as radical truth-tellers working amid resistance. But it is equally significant that Lawrence envisioned Freud as fundamentally antagonistic to his utopian ideas of social transformation, which aimed to reawaken modern subjects to the embodied consciousness that modern habits of "idealism" had jeopardized. As this chapter illustrates, the textual kinship that Lawrence shares with Freud is both the engine of Lawrence's developing philosophy of self, as well as a source of the agonizing self-contradictions in his work.

Chapter Two begins by tracing the entanglements between Bloomsbury and psychoanalysis as a backdrop to Woolf's ongoing discursive battles with Freud. While Bloomsbury by 1924 had largely embraced psychoanalysis as part of its aesthetic philosophies, Woolf was among a handful of Bloomsbury figures, including Roger Fry and Clive Bell, who rejected psychoanalytic advances into the sphere of art. The Woolfs were the first publishers of Freud's complete works in English, and while the profits of the Psycho-analytical Library helped subsidize the Hogarth Press, Woolf remained wary of psychoanalysis and refused to read Freud's work until the last years of her life. To understand this conflicted relationship, I turn first to "Modern Fiction" (1919), in which Woolf identifies a shared preoccupation with psychoanalysis in the "dark places of psychology." Woolf entreats the moderns to "Look within!"—to direct aesthetic attention to personal, subjective experience. But she also draws distinctions between the impressionist methods of modernism and the positivism of Freud. In her essay "Freudian Fiction" and in *Mrs. Dalloway*, Woolf hyperbolizes the dangers of psychoanalysis and psychiatry as scientific dissections of the soul. Chapter Two contends that despite Woolf's resistance to psychoanalysis, her narrative style sometimes echoes the intimate, asymmetrical dynamics of the analytic encounter.

In Chapter Three, I track Auden's productive ambivalence about psychoanalysis and his embrace of a radical set of psychologies that proposed the liberation of desire from all forms of repression. Auden identified psychoanalysis early on as a model for his poetics of difficulty and as an epistemology of same-sex desire, only to turn to more heterodox psychologies that recast psychoanalysis as a mode of repression and ideological consensus. Within the experimental laboratory of late Weimar Berlin, Auden began to challenge psychoanalytic views of same-sex desire as failed maturation and psychic regression, although he never fully abandons these ideas. Reading Auden's poetry and critical prose of the early and mid-1930s, I explore his idiosyncratic readings of psychoanalysis and his adoption of a group of marginal psychologists who helped him challenge the epistemological and diagnostic activities of psychoanalysis and to develop a queer poetics. Auden's 1930s modernist style emerges here as a turn away from the heuristic model of Freudian encryption and its relation to a poetics of difficulty, and toward a strategically amateurish poetics that preempts the need for expert critical interpretation. Challenging the "certain diagnosis" and "expertise" he saw emerging from within the modern disciplines, Auden in the 1930s seems to have anticipated the prevalence of a symptomatic style in criticism long before this style was recognized.

The main focus of Chapter Four is Vladimir Nabokov, not only because he presents the most well-known and explicit rejection of Freud by a twentieth-century author, but also because he dedicates his pivotal work, *Lolita*, to an extended satire of Freudian forms. *Lolita* is structured as a parodic case study, and is reliant on Freud's theories of child sexual development, traumatic repetition, and father-child incest, while proliferating Freudian puns and wordplay. I am interested in how *Lolita* burlesques psychoanalytic interpretation, including its "symbol hunting" and paranoid style, while also relying on a hermeneutics of suspicion. As I go on to suggest, the only ethical orientation to *Lolita* is in fact precisely a hermeneutics of suspicion, one that reads Humbert's discourse against the grain and looks for flashes of Lolita and her experience through the confusing mesh of Humbert's perspective.

My book concludes by suggesting that contemporary literary studies has, unwittingly, inherited a long-standing conflict about the relationship between psychoanalysis and literature. Current debates about the value of "suspicious" and "paranoid" reading practices date back to the formative years of Anglo-American modernism and its entanglement with psychoanalysis. This inheritance is especially evident in current methodological debates over "postcritical" reading, with its ambivalence about critique and its suspicious style of interpretation. Drawing on a critical tradition that includes Susan Sontag, Eve K. Sedgwick, Rita Felski, and others, I show how modernist writers and midcentury critical defenders of modernism were direct about the perils of a psychoanalytic and suspicious approach. Sontag argued that modernist artifacts, from Pound's poetry to abstract expressionist art, displayed a built-in resistance to the critical demystification that Marxist and psychoanalytic interpretations demanded.[123] Adorno argued in *Aesthetic Theory* (1970) that psychoanalysis violates the inner truth and aesthetic self-determination of the art work, and that it wrests authority from the work itself. Both thinkers were responding to a midcentury ethos that had thoroughly assimilated psychoanalytic theory into its literary criticism. Echoing modernist arguments about of aesthetic autonomy, Sontag and Adorno anticipate postcritical appeals to engage with artworks in ways that are less abstract and dogmatic and more affective and embodied. I conclude by showing how modernist and late modernist debates with psychoanalysis have occasioned a set of post-Freudian modes and practices that propose alternatives to reading "deeply" and "suspiciously."

1
On Not Reading Freud
Amateurism, Expertise, and the "Pristine Unconscious" in D. H. Lawrence

> There is something irreversible about what Freud has done to twentieth-century culture.
> —JOHN FORRESTER, DISPATCHES FROM THE FREUD WARS (1997)

In the opening section of his 1921 essay "Psychoanalysis and the Unconscious," D. H. Lawrence stages a highly theatrical parody of Freud's narrative of the unconscious:

> With dilated hearts we watched Freud disappearing into the cavern of darkness, which is sleep and unconsciousness to us, darkness which issues in the foam of all consciousness. He was making for the origins. We watched his ideal candle flutter and go small. . . .
> But sweet heaven, what merchandise! What dreams, dear heart! What was there in the cave? Alas that we ever looked! Nothing but a huge slimy serpent of sex, and heaps of excrement, and a myriad repulsive little horrors spawned between sex and excrement.
> Is it true? Does the great unknown of sleep contain nothing else? . . . Imagine the unspeakable horror of the repressions Freud brought home to us. Gagged, bound, maniacal repressions, sexual complexes, fecal inhibitions, dream monsters. We tried to repudiate them. But no, they were there, demonstrable. These were the horrid things that ate our souls and caused our helpless neurosis.[1]

It is impossible to minimize, first and foremost, the extremity of this caricature, particularly in its rapid transition from the melodramatic to the grotesque. Lawrence revels in his satirical description of this primal scene, as he accumulates a series of explicit images to shock his reader. With rhetorical flourish, Lawrence adopts the melodramatic exclamations of a squeamish and feminized observer—"Sweet heaven," "dear heart!" "Alas that we ever looked!"— to underscore the shocking and offensive nature of Freud's discoveries— the "heaps of excrement," "slimy serpent of sex," and "myriad repulsive little horrors"—figures rendered even more lascivious by their sibilance. However exaggerated, the caricature provides a window into Lawrence's view of the Freudian unconscious, full of dream monsters and maniacal repressions; it is a hellish underworld of "repulsive horrors" so extreme they are "unspeakable." While satirizing these horrors, Lawrence suggests that "they were there, demonstrable," as if Freud's narrative were not only irresistible, but potentially *true*. And here we note a peculiar irony: Lawrence satirizes psychoanalysis and points up its horrors, while simultaneously acknowledging, even performing, its seductive qualities for the reader. It is as if Lawrence is not only participant in, but also producer of, the manifold pleasures of Freudian forms of knowledge.

Of course, Lawrence does not affirm Freud's interpretation of the unconscious; he goes on to suggest that we moderns have planted our monsters ourselves: that "the mind acts as incubus and procreator of its own horrors."[2] Lawrence argues that rather than discover the contents of the unconscious, psychoanalysis has found what it was trained to suspect lurked in the dark places of the soul—the complexes, conflicts, and repressed sexual secrets of which it was most afraid. Lawrence draws on Plato's allegory of the cave and offers the image of Freud's "ideal candle" to suggest a type of knowledge that is not generated from subjective experience, but is imposed deductively from without: that is, "idealism" becomes his rhetorical shorthand for the epistemological methods that he sees and opposes in Freud—the imposition of external ideas onto lived categories of experience.[3] While attempting to shatter the epistemological sleight of hand that he equates with psychoanalysis, Lawrence articulates his own model of knowledge-seeking, one that is intuitive, subjective, and based in states of bodily experience. He develops a revisionary account of Freud's unconscious to articulate a counter-discourse that provides an extended metaphor for such forms of knowledge. Lawrence's efforts to repudiate Freud, and to offer an alternative psychological system to oppose what he saw as the reductive hermeneutical practices of psychoanalysis, ironically enhanced the status of an emergent discourse that Lawrence, at least ostensibly, was trying to discredit.

To locate the discursive rivalries between Lawrence and Freud, I refer to Lawrence's essays deemed eccentric if not downright embarrassing by critics both then and now: *Psychoanalysis and the Unconscious* (1921) and *Fantasia of the Unconscious* (1922), his two published polemics on psychoanalysis. At stake for Lawrence, I suggest, is the influence and authority of his own literary practice in relation to psychoanalysis, a field that was not only arrogating to itself the authority to interpret psychological selfhood, but also, and more provocatively still, to appropriate literary texts (including Lawrence's own) to vindicate its theories. In these essays, Lawrence defends the literary from psychoanalytic reductions and indicts psychoanalysis for its symptomatic reading, with its assumption that literature is incomplete without the interventions of an expert interpreter. Highlighting the different use he will make of knowledge and evidence, Lawrence champions amateurism over psychoanalytic expertise and promotes intuition as a more direct vehicle to knowledge of the self. Such assaults on Freud's methodology occur most frequently on the terrain of the unconscious, which Lawrence interprets as a "pristine" state of pure embodiment temporally prior to intellect, rather than a reservoir of repressed sexual impulses surging below consciousness—or, in Lawrence's more dramatic phrasing, "a cellar in which the mind keeps its own bastard spawn."[4]

It is my contention that while Lawrence's quarrel with Freud reflects his differing conception of what constitutes knowledge and evidence, Lawrence evinces a willful blindness to the discourses that underwrite his critique—most notably the theoretical abstractions that are central to his thinking. Abstraction is in a sense a hysterical symptom of Lawrence's writing, a symptom that expresses the conflicts within his own ideas: Lawrence's ideas depend on a rationalist detachment as much as they implicitly valorize the powers of the mind. Moreover, the intensity with which Lawrence distances himself from Freud seems more than anything to underscore the power psychoanalysis exerts over him. As this chapter will illustrate, the textual kinship that Lawrence shares with Freud is both the engine of Lawrence's developing philosophy of self, as well as a source of the agonizing self-contradictions in his work.

An Amateur of Amateurs

In 1913 Lawrence wrote: "I never read Freud, but I have learned about him since I was in Germany."[5] Lawrence resisted reading Freud, a fact that may account for his tendency to replicate the vulgar Freudianism of his culture. Lawrence was never in analysis himself, and he consistently maintained a hostile attitude to those he called "the Freudians."[6] "I hate therapy altogether," he remarked on one occasion; neurotics assume "perfect conscious and automatic control when they're cured. . . . I would prefer that the neurotics died."[7] Lawrence protested elsewhere that psychoanalysis never "let one's feelings alone . . . they can never let you *have* any real feelings."[8] As these remarks suggest, Lawrence attributed to psychoanalysis the power of de-authenticating human feeling and of depriving human experience of the qualities of spontaneity and intuition that he prized so highly.[9] Fiona Beckett points out that Lawrence the linguist could have read Freud in the original German, especially during his first trip to Germany in 1912, and that he could have read any one of the English translations of Freud available to the British public in the 1910s.[10] He certainly could have read *The Psychopathology of Everyday Life* or *The Interpretation of Dreams* when they first appeared in English translation in 1914. Leonard Woolf wrote one of the first English reviews of *The Interpretation of Dreams*, praising its artfulness and lyricism, a review that no doubt broadened the reception of Freud to include intellectuals outside of the fields of medicine or psychology. But there is no evidence that Lawrence read any of these texts, either in English or in German.

And yet, despite his resistance to reading Freud's work, and despite his disdain for psychoanalytic treatment, Lawrence managed to produce a body of critical material devoted to the interrogation of this new and controversial science: indeed, his confidence in speaking about a discourse of which he had little direct knowledge seems truly amazing. But, as Lawrence consistently reminded his reader, the true psychologist is intuitive, using subjective experience to apprehend the world. In *Fantasia of the Unconscious*, Lawrence proudly parades his lack of credentials: "I am not a scientist. I am an amateur of amateurs . . . I am not a scholar of any sort . . . I proceed by intuition."[11] This faith in intuition and corresponding suspicion of theory and expertise served Lawrence in distancing his methods from those of the analysts he derided. In the words of Frederick Hoffman, "Lawrence had from the beginning insisted upon a dynamically personal and subjective tribunal at which ideas—any ideas—were to be tried."[12]

Lawrence accused psychoanalysis of relying on deductive modes of investigation, of fitting emotional experience into *a priori* categories, a process he called "idealism." Psychoanalysis imposes an "ideal nature upon the unconscious. . . . What we are suffering from is the restriction of the unconscious within certain ideal limits."[13] In contrast, Lawrence insisted that his insights about human psychology were cultivated inductively, from his own experience, rather than through the second-hand deductions of the psychoanalyst. "How do we know the unconscious?" he asks in *Psychoanalysis and the Unconscious*. "We know it by direct experience." We know it as "we know the sun."[14] Earlier in the essay, Lawrence declares, in his emphatically idiosyncratic vocabulary and strident style, "The motivizing of the passional sphere from the ideal is the final peril of human consciousness. It is the death of all spontaneous, creative life."[15] Lawrence's qualms about method here are not merely conflicts about a theory of the subject; they reflect deeply held beliefs about what constitutes knowledge and its apprehension. Real truths are not arrived at through philosophical deductions or through the labors of qualified analysts: true knowledge is that which is immediately available to the senses.

Lawrence's pronouncements against psychoanalytic "idealism" must be tempered by an awareness of the extent to which Freud's discoveries were also subjective in nature, derived from the analysis of his own dreams and childhood experience. In Freud's own words, "no psychoanalyst goes further than his own complexes and internal resistances permit; and we consequently require that he shall begin his activity with self-analysis and continually carry it deeper while he is making his observations on his patients."[16] Freud nonetheless acknowledged the difficulty of self-analysis as a purely intuitive process: Self-analysis, he remarked in a letter to Wilhelm Fliess, is impossible without "knowledge obtained objectively."[17] After World War I, Freud's perspective would become considerably bleaker, and he would appear to change his mind about the potential of self-analysis, insisting that if it were genuinely possible there would be no neurotic illness, hence the need for objective interpreters. If Freud was increasingly convinced of the importance of expertise in psychological treatment, of the need for trained interpreters who could decode resistant human phenomena in search of underlying meaning—something the subject could not do for himself—Lawrence seemed to express a more populist view that self-knowledge was a matter of personal prerogative and that it required no more than the sensuous encounter with the world.

The Novel as Case Study

Initially attracted to Freudian psychoanalysis for its potentially liberatory investigations of instinct and the unconscious, Lawrence would soon come to loathe it, especially after psychoanalytic theory chose Sons and Lovers as its case study par excellence.[18] The British analysts who discovered the novel shortly after its publication in 1913 lauded Sons and Lovers as the most penetrating exploration of the Oedipal scenario ever described in literature, so perfectly did the arc of protagonist Paul Morel align with the developmental narrative articulated by Freud. Paul's rivalry with his father, his intense allegiance to his mother, and his inability to substitute his affections for his mother with those for other women, bore resemblance to the neurotic features described by Freud, so much so that British analysts began to wonder at the interchangeability of novel and case study, as if Sons and Lovers might in fact be a more compelling guide to psychological experience than the Freudian monograph.

Three years before the publication of Sons and Lovers in 1913, the term "Oedipus complex" made its first appearance, although the concept was alive in Freud's writing at least a decade before. In an 1897 letter to Wilhelm Fliess, Freud ties this self-discovery to the story of *Oedipus Rex*, and goes on to declare it a universal phenomenon of early childhood development: "I have found, in my own case too, [the phenomenon of] being in love with my mother and jealous of my father, and I now consider it a universal event in early childhood. . . ."[19] Little Hans became a defining illustration of this theory, as Freud interpreted Hans's phobia of horses as an unconscious fear of the father, who would punish and renounce Hans for desiring his mother. Freud called the Oedipus complex "the nucleus of the neuroses" and emphasized its universal complexion, though critics have criticized its highly gendered articulation through the experience of boyhood. For Freud, proper psychosexual development is tied to the renunciation of the incestuous love object, generally the mother, and to the transfer of the boy's identification to his father, a process that unfolds because of the child's repressed fear of being castrated by the father. But as critics have pointed out, this model reinforces heterosexist and patriarchal associations of women with lack: the lack of visible genitals of the male tied to sensations of inferiority. In her feminist reply to Freud, Karen Horney redescribes penis envy as a women's symbolic longing for the social prestige and position that men achieve—a socio-cultural argument about gender hierarchies, rather than a biologically essentialist one. Women do not suffer inferiority because they lack the anatomical penis, but because their gender confers a subordinate social position.[20]

Critics have suggested that the psychoanalytic complexion of *Sons and Lovers* was likely attributed to the influence of Frieda Weekley on the book's final draft. Frieda, Lawrence's mistress whom he eventually married, had become aware of psychoanalysis through her family, her frequent trips to Germany, and through her affair in Munich in 1907–8 with Otto Gross, a young psychiatrist on the fringes of Freud's circle, whom Ernest Jones would come to criticize for his esoteric ideas about free love. Lawrence's early statements to his editor about the novel in 1912 appear to strengthen the Oedipal reading of the novel, although such a reading would come to offend him:

> . . . a woman of character and refinement goes into the lower class, and has no satisfaction in her own life. She has had a passion for her husband, so her children are born of passion, and have heaps of vitality. But as her sons grow up she selects them as lovers—first the eldest, then the second. These sons are *urged* into life by their reciprocal love of their mother. . . . But when they come to manhood, they can't love, because their mother is the strongest power in their lives, and holds them. As soon as the young men come into contact with women, there's a split.[21]

Lawrence's description emphasizes the mother's role in igniting her sons' passions and then obstructing their romantic attachments to other women. Indeed, within the book there are multiple episodes of overt romantic behavior between mother and son. Lawrence's description to his editor is undoubtedly more interesting than a mere Oedipal triangle, engaging dimensions of class, education, and gender roles, and introducing us to the vitalistic language Lawrence applies to the charged interpersonal dynamics in his fictions.[22] But it does complicate Lawrence's subsequent disavowals of a psychoanalytic approach and lends ironic support to the psychoanalytic concept of denial as a mode of affirmation. The novel ultimately emphasizes the family as a crucible for determining the individual's future relationships, and concerns itself with Paul's struggle—and eventual failure—to become a self-determining subject with his own romantic script.

The narration ultimately projects Paul's predicament as a generalized condition of "virginity" for men of his generation: "the tragedy of thousands of young men in England":

> A good many of the nicest men he knew were like himself, bound in by their own virginity, which they could not break out of. . . . Being the sons of mothers whose husbands had blundered rather brutally through their feminine sanctities, they were themselves too diffident and shy. They could easier deny themselves than incur any reproach from a woman; for a woman was like their mother, and they were full of the sense of their mother. They preferred themselves to suffer the misery of celibacy, rather than risk the other person.[23]

Stuck between blundering fathers and overbearing mothers who no longer find their husbands to be fitting romantic partners, these "diffident and shy" young men find individuation and romantic fulfillment impossible, and end in a prison of "virginity." In other writings, Lawrence associates virginity with an intellectually distanced relationship to sex that doesn't yield a fully embodied experience of it. Indeed, his parents' tumultuous relationship—with his father's drunken abuse and his mother's possessiveness and interference—offers no romantic model for Paul and is, in the symbolic idiom of the novel, a form of castration.

The analyst and critic Alfred Kuttner, in his 1916 article "Sons and Lovers: A Freudian Appreciation" in the *Psychoanalytic Review*, traces the persistence of Oedipal themes across Lawrence's oeuvre: sons insistently struggle against oppressive mothers and find romantic relationships outside the family circle impossible; women are chronically dissatisfied with marriage and transfer their affections to sons; fathers and sons vie for the mother's affections; and (male) individuals fail to realize complete selfhood because of the arresting effects of the family dynamic.[24] Kuttner praised *Sons and Lovers*' "freshness" and "amazing style" but insisted that it would be unremarkable were it not for "added significance" acquired "by virtue of the support it gives to the scientific study of human motives."[25] As an advertisement for Kuttner's practice, the review emphasizes the novel's value as psychoanalytic evidence: *Sons and Lovers* is able to "attest the truth of what is the most far-reaching psychological theory ever propounded . . . Professor Sigmund Freud's theory of psychological evolution of the emotion of love as finally expressed by a man or a woman towards a member of the other sex."[26]

Lawrence's reaction to Kuttner's reading was characteristically intense. He was outraged by the reduction of his novel to psychoanalytic evidence. If Kuttner and his predecessors Freud and Ernest Jones are eager to reconcile literature with psychoanalysis as mutually reinforcing discourses, Lawrence is highly suspicious of the reduction of his novel to a psychoanalytic narrative: indeed, he thinks his novel is more "complete" than the psychoanalytic reading of it. In a letter to his friend Barbara Low, a British psychoanalyst trained by Ernest Jones and Hanns Sachs and a founding member of the British Psychoanalytical Society, Lawrence writes:

> I hated the Psychoanalysis Review of *Sons and Lovers*. You know I think "complexes" are vicious half-statements of the Freudians: sort of can't see the wood for the trees. When you've said Mutter-complex, you've said nothing—no more than if you called hysteria a nervous disease. Hysteria isn't nerves, a complex is not simply a sex relation: far from it.—My poor book: it was, as art, a fairly complete truth: so they carve a half-lie out of it, and say "Voila." Swine! Your little brochure—how soul-wearied you are by society and social experiments.[27]

Eager to defend the autonomous sphere of art, Lawrence insists on the self-sufficiency of his novel: as art it is a "fairly complete truth," asking to be valued on its own terms and requiring no hermeneutic to make its truths apparent. Lawrence insists on the epistemic degradation enacted upon his novel when read according to a psychoanalytic meta-narrative. Such meta-narratives prioritized an external theoretical framework—what Lawrence calls in his poem "Thought," "the juggling and twisting of already existent ideas"—over an affective, experiential encounter with the text—"a man in his wholeness wholly attending." He accuses such reading of being ineffectual and superficial, and of deploying empty categories and labels that fail to highlight the work's meaning. A psychoanalytic reading of the text prioritizes the act of interpretation as a critical unmasking of repressed content, a search for the latent beneath the manifest. But Lawrence made it clear in his writings that he prioritized the work's capacity to confer its own truths.

Perhaps more to the point is Lawrence's opposition to what might be called "symptomatic" reading, a style of interpretation imputed to Freud, and later to those critics within literary studies who annexed Freud's method of "restor[ing] to the surface the deep history that the text represses."[28] The most notable of such critics, Fredric Jameson, saw symptomatic reading as an interpretive search for "a latent meaning behind a manifest one;" it being the interpreter's role to "rewrite the surface categories of a text in the stronger language of a more fundamental interpretive code."[29] Lawrence's resistance to Kuttner's symptomatic reading is evident not only in his defense of the literary work as "a whole truth," a repository of meaning that is already available to the reader without the assistance of an interpreter, but in his accusation that analysts "can't see the wood for the trees." Lawrence was concerned with how the analysis of the literary object diminished aesthetic experience, hence his investment in a method of intuition as a subjective mode of insight into "an essential reality" beyond the material world.[30] Intuition offers a subjective counterpoint to what Lawrence sees as the distortions of the intellect, with the intellect's deductive mode of sense making.

Lawrence's remarks here resemble his declaration in *Studies in Classic American Literature* (1923) that "Art-speech is the only truth,"[31] by which he meant that art could offer truth-claims that discursive statements could not. Given Lawrence's future as a literary critic, his hostility to the critical impulse is somewhat surprising: much like the psychoanalytic critics he derided, Lawrence practiced a style of literary criticism that would "save the tale from the artist who created it," or, in David J. Gordon's helpful gloss, "reveal deeper and truer implications of a work than the artist himself may be conscious of."[32] In *Studies in Classic American Literature*, Lawrence practices a kind of psychoanalytically informed symptomatic reading that identifies textual signs of psychic pathology of the author and the wider culture in which the work was produced. By the late teens and early twenties, Lawrence seems to have adopted a style of reading remarkably similar to the symptomatic reading to which his novels were subjected, a sign that he had appropriated the very methodologies he was in the process of challenging. Like Freud and Kuttner, Lawrence attributed a powerful role to the interpreter/critic who could detect and disclose meanings that were otherwise hidden beneath the manifest content of the work, provided of course that the critic was a producer of art himself. Lawrence's ambivalence about the role of criticism speaks powerfully to his opposition to the interpretive purchase of other disciplines on literary texts. The Lawrence-Kuttner agon engages larger questions about the definition of literary criticism, questions raised pointedly by Françoise Meltzer: Where does literature end and criticism begin? What topics are permitted for the literary critic to discuss, and what are off-limits? What is "inside" and what is "outside" literature?[33] Lawrence is most concerned with how authority is conferred on the literary critic. The posture of amateurism that he adopts suggests an effort to demarcate a literary field that could be impervious to the interventions of disciplinary outsiders; it also suggests the sense of threat that psychoanalysis posed to authors, as it used literary texts as allegories for its own speculations.

The reviews by Kuttner and other analysts helped make *Sons and Lovers* a financial success; however, this had no bearing upon Lawrence's hostility to the analysts who had encroached upon his art and repurposed it for their own use. In a psychoanalytic sense, Lawrence's vitriol could be read as a reaction formation: it must have been exceedingly difficult, even for Lawrence, to deny the parallels between *Sons and Lovers* and Oedipal theory, particularly as the latter continued to condition the reception of the former. The response to Kuttner, with its rejection of psychoanalytic definitions of terms like "complex" and "hysteria," highlights Lawrence's willingness to engage in dialogue with a set of theories about which he was only partially informed. The defensive posturing, parodic excess, and rhetorical outwitting Lawrence exhibits are precisely the strategic positions taken up in *Psychoanalysis of the Unconscious* and *Fantasia of the Unconscious*—his most fully realized rebuttals to Freudian psychoanalysis.

Sure Intuition

If Lawrence was offended by the infringement on literature by disciplinary outsiders, he had no qualms about writing in other disciplines. However appalled he was by Alfred Kuttner's psychoanalytic reading of *Sons and Lovers*, Lawrence himself freely trespassed on psychological topics and readily assimilated psychoanalytic language into his own writing in the years following Kuttner's review. Inverting interpretive hierarchies, Lawrence challenged the psychoanalytic responses to his novel by reading psychoanalysis literarily, thereby exposing the reversibility of this process. For Lawrence, writing discursively about psychoanalysis did not entail expertise in the subject matter. Rather, Lawrence endeavored to deconstruct the very concept of expertise by demonstrating that an amateur such as himself had as much intuitive access to psychological knowledge as any self-appointed expert. Alert to the hierarchies that inhere in the claim to expertise, Lawrence was notably suspicious of the gap of knowledge that removes the expert from being the designated object of scrutiny. Lawrence's anti-intellectual posture manifested itself in a glorification of subjective intuition as a vehicle to knowledge about self and world, and a corresponding denunciation of discursive or deductive methods. This reliance on intuition rather than expertise may partially explain Lawrence's refusal to read Freud directly, which may in turn explain his consistent misrepresentations of psychoanalysis. Not reading Freud, but discussing Freud at length, was for Lawrence the most rebellious act of amateur reading.

In spite of this resistance to reading Freud, it remains the case that after 1914, a British intellectual did not have to read Freud directly to achieve a level of cultural literacy in his theories. Psychoanalysis was in the ether, circulating among both high and popular culture as a kind of novelty. With its potentially freeing narratives of introspection, emotional candor, and frankness in matters of sexuality, it captivated the bohemian intellectual circles that Lawrence traversed. Frederick J. Hoffman, in his pioneering study of the relations between Anglo-American modernism and psychoanalysis, *Freudianism and the Literary Mind* (1956), offers an account of this form of cultural literacy during the first decades of the twentieth century:

> . . . it is hardly likely that any thinking person who in any way associated himself with the world of letters failed to encounter the new psychology. It is more than likely that he was unable to escape getting too much of it. If he had not read any books on the subject, he was bound to come across it in almost any discussion; if he did not go out, he was just as likely to discover it in newspaper or magazine.[34]

R. A. Gekoski affirms Hoffman's conclusions when he asserts that psychoanalysis had become a kind of intellectual slang that "entailed no necessary accompanying comprehension of Freudian theory."[35] For intellectuals and general audiences alike, much of the dissemination of psychoanalytic theory occurred through more popular channels, such as the lay press, advice columns, and self-help literature.[36] In Lawrence's own words, by the 1920s, the Oedipus complex had become "a household word, the incest motive a commonplace of tea-table chat."[37]

Psychoanalysis had colonized public attention so thoroughly through the power of its ideas that people claimed familiarity with its concepts without ever coming face to face with an authoritative text. Lawrence's two essays on psychoanalysis are a case in point, for they presume to speak authoritatively on a subject of which Lawrence had little direct knowledge. Yet even though Lawrence was no more than a dabbler in psychoanalytic theory, and even though the majority of critics failed to take Lawrence's statements on Freud seriously, there is every reason to believe that Lawrence intended the essays as serious contributions to the field.

Psychoanalysis and the Unconscious and *Fantasia of the Unconscious* were composed during Lawrence's most fertile artistic period, the years that saw the publication of *Women in Love* (1920); *The Lost Girl* (1920); *Mr. Noon* (written 1921–23); *Aaron's Rod* (1922); *Kangaroo* (1923); and *Studies in Classic American Literature* (1923). *Fantasia of the Unconscious* was crafted as a sequel to *Psychoanalysis and the Unconscious*: Lawrence spoke of it as an extension of the earlier essay and an opportunity to reinforce his message. If *Psychoanalysis* was seemingly crafted as a scientific treatise, an attempt to systematize a response to the psychoanalytic studies offered by Freud, Jung, and their acolytes, *Fantasia*, as its title suggests, is more fanciful and irregular in style, relying as it does on archetypical and mythological explanations of the unconscious. To say that Lawrence's first study is supposedly scientific may seem paradoxical, for in both essays his writing is associational and ambulatory, resistant to linear logic and systematic argumentation. Lawrence does, however, draw on scientific discourse and methodology, notably the method of empiricism as he saw it, to make a case for psychoanalysis's failure as a science—in particular, psychoanalysis's lack of attention to empirical and subjective experience and its overestimation of theory and deductive reasoning. As he says at the beginning of *Fantasia*, "to my mind there is a great field of science which is as yet quite closed to us. I refer to the science which proceeds in terms of life and is established on data of living experience and sure intuition."[38]

Lawrence's resistance to a systematic approach—to a structured argument or careful use of supporting evidence in either essay—seems consonant with his ideas about intuition and subjective response. As Aldous Huxley remarked, Lawrence's essays have a subjective immediacy that aims to render "the felt quality of experience."[39] Critics of Lawrence's freewheeling style of criticism with its logical inconsistencies and shifting terminology included T. S. Eliot, who charged Lawrence with having a lack of "intellectual and social training," and, more damningly, an "incapacity for what we ordinarily call thinking."[40] *Psychoanalysis and the Unconscious* and *Fantasia of the Unconscious* sprawl over seemingly random and disconnected topics: psychoanalysis, incest, "affective centers," illness, child education, and parenting. Chapter titles reveal this thematic instability: Chapter III of *Fantasia*, "Plexuses, Planes and So On," is followed by a chapter entitled "Trees and Babies and Papas and Mamas." In Chapter IV, a prolonged elaboration of the parent-child dynamic is prefaced by a highly digressive meditation on tree worship. The sheer strangeness of these texts would seem to explain their critical neglect. The bulk of critics who reviewed the essays when they were first published concluded that they were bizarre, illogical, or incomprehensible. A handful of reviewers questioned

Lawrence's sanity. One author suggested: "A system such as Mr. Lawrence wishes to establish would derationalize man. Eventually it might lead us all into the jungle."[41] One can't help but think of the unhinged Mr. Kurtz leading rational man into the heart of darkness. I would argue that the value of these texts lies precisely in their eccentricity, for they reveal the philosophical underpinnings of Lawrence's body of work and inform the kind of formal and stylistic choices that Lawrence makes elsewhere. Moreover, the essays highlight Lawrence's decentered position in relation to high modernism, which, as Eliot's critique reveals, was still concerned with traditional forms of education and training.

Sex in the Head

If modernism has often been associated with an inward turn, a fascination with and aestheticization of psychological processes, Lawrence presents a potential counterexample of a modernist who romanticized a state in which the individual would be released from their inwardness. Lawrence saw in psychoanalysis the apotheosis of modern civilization's obsession with introspection—a "scientific discipline of inwardness," as Philip Rieff put it.[42] In both *Psychoanalysis* and *Fantasia*, Lawrence elaborates a view that the Freudian mode of inquiry is an instigator of a distorted knowledge of the self—that psychoanalysis, to borrow the words of Foucault, constitutes a "perverse implantation" that incites and encourages the perverse forms of sexuality that it claims to have discovered.

As the opening passage of this chapter suggests, introspection for Lawrence conjures the very monsters, horrors, and repressions it purportedly examines. Psychoanalysis is not the cure, but rather the cause of pathology. By trusting in the power of rational investigation to achieve knowledge of the unconscious, psychoanalysis merely intensifies the repression of unconscious life that is already a pervasive feature of modern civilization.[43] If looking inward reveals nothing but excrement, if it fills the subject with horror at their own sexuality, then introspection and the kind of knowledge it produces may inspire the very neurosis that Freud undertakes to naturalize. Put another way, Lawrence rejects the type of interpretive reading of the self that psychoanalysis demands, insisting that such knowledge is merely the imposition of external ideas onto the unconscious, a process that distorts the inner dynamics of the self.

In the foreword to *Fantasia*, Lawrence pays tribute to psychoanalysis for "directing any light whatsoever on the taboo subjects" of sex and sexuality. Momentarily, Lawrence depicts Freud as liberating sex from its injunction to silence and invisibility." But Lawrence's praise is fleeting, for what ensues is a critique of the manner in which psychoanalysis "liberates" sex—by transforming it into discourse. Lawrence goes on to elaborate these ideas more fully:

> Sex, whatever else it is, is an utterly private affair, as private as personality, as secret as individuality. To go trashily bandying the word about is indecent. True every man is faced with the problem of himself, of his own individuality, and his own sex. But it is his own single, private, individual affair. He must fight it out with his own soul, alone, or with a book which is like his own self speaking, making him appeased in his aloneness. But he must not have sex oozing out of his mouth in words, and out of his eyes in glaucous looks, and out of his ears in greediness, and silkering like stagnant water in his mind.
> There should be an absolute taboo upon sex, to prevent all this mental indecency and dynamic impotency. For sex in the head means a mess everywhere else. And the more Freud you have, the more your head whirls with sex, and your effective centres atrophy.[44]

If earlier in the foreword to *Fantasia,* Lawrence credits psychoanalysis with lifting the taboo against sexual discourse, here he champions "an absolute taboo upon sex," a prohibition of the transformation of sex into discourse.

For Lawrence, the distortions perpetrated by psychoanalysis are the discursive constructions around sex and sexuality that psychoanalysis generates. Lawrence acknowledges the problematic nature of personal identity and sexuality (a concession to psychoanalytic theory, no doubt) but such conflict, he asserts, must go on within the subject; it must not be made the object of analysis. The image of sex "oozing" out of one's mouth, eyes, and ears is visceral, as if sex were a kind of bodily fluid threatening to flood the subject and dissolve its bodily boundaries. Lawrence insists on the containment of these bodily forces within the subject: sexuality is not something to unleash or explore, abstract or analyze, but rather something to secrete within the privacy of the "soul," a word he deploys repeatedly in clear opposition to a psychoanalytic vocabulary. Implicit in this passage is the sense that there is something violating about the psychoanalytic gaze, a "will to knowledge" that makes sex an object of analysis and intervention.[45] The language of "oozing" not only highlights the dissolution of boundaries of the putatively integral self, it speaks to an anxiety about psychoanalysis's power to violate personal privacy and sexual secrecy—a discursive oozing of sexuality that goes beyond/outside the self/individual.

What is most "indecent" to Lawrence here is what he calls "sex in the head"—a phrase that recurs throughout his body of work. "Sex in the head" has multiple resonances for Lawrence: a turning inward of man upon himself, an intensification of the mental at the expense of the physical, and any kind of intellectually distanced view of the sexual act. More obviously still, "sex in the head" stands in implicit opposition to "sex in the body" or the sex act, without which, Lawrence warns, the spontaneous "centers atrophy."[46] As Lawrence says in *Fantasia*: "I see sex as something more specific, not to be dissociated from actual sex functioning. . . . Sex without the consummating act of coition is never quite sex. . . ."[47] The "dynamic impotency" Lawrence imagines in the earlier passage seems to be the displacement of the embodied sex act into a discourse about sex. Nor is such "impotency" merely metaphorical: Lawrence firmly believes that the abstract and discursive approach to sex that psychoanalysis and modern culture have incited will lead to male impotence—hence Lawrence's oft-critiqued investment in "primitive" culture and working-class men as embodying a less "mentalized" and more embodied and sexually potent form of experience. Lawrence's shrill warnings about the relationship between mentalized sex and sexual impotence become embodied in his literary characters, including Paul in *Sons and Lovers* and Clifford in *Lady Chatterley's Lover*. Having been rendered impotent by the war and by the world of abstract ideas in which he is enclosed, Clifford Chatterley is unable to connect sexually to his wife. In contrast, the working-class Mellors, Chatterley's foil, embodies the non-intellectual earthiness and sexual potency that Lawrence equates with essential masculinity. If Freud expanded the definition of sex to encompass "everything, which, with a view to obtaining pleasure, is concerned with the body"—including homosexuality and masturbation, as well as the discursive formations surrounding sex[48]—Lawrence wants to contain "sex" within a more narrow prescription: heterosexual coitus between man and woman. As his chosen metaphor for psychoanalysis, "sex in the head" evokes the perils of an analytical engagement with sexuality, one that takes the subject away from the physical sex act (unequivocally heterosexual, undeniably normative), into a realm of abstraction.

In describing modern society's analytical attitude toward sex, Lawrence makes repeated reference to the Christian allegory of the fall. He asks, "Why did we fall into this gnawing disease of unappeasable dissatisfaction? . . . Not because we sinned, but because we got our sex into our head."[49] In this passage, Lawrence charges psychoanalytic discourse with creating the very "dissatisfaction" that Freud claims is engendered by repression. Anticipating Foucault's argument that discourses help produce the objects of which they speak, Lawrence suggests that it is not socially unacceptable sexual instincts that produce "unappeasable dissatisfaction," but rather psychoanalytic discourse that creates the very idea that sexual instincts require repression in the first place. Put in another way, psychoanalysis does not so much discover the repressed content of the unconscious as generate seductive narratives of repression that the modern individual accepts as truth. Lawrence's use of the serpent throughout *Psychoanalysis and the Unconscious*, with its evocation of the seduction before the fall, makes psychoanalysis an evil tempter (and arguably, a phallic symbol). Psychoanalysis becomes metaphorically linked to a fallen humanity, whereby an awareness of sexuality, which psychoanalysis initiates, constitutes a loss of innocence: "It is knowledge of sex that constitutes sin, and not sex itself . . . Adam and Eve fell, not because they had sex, or even because they committed the sexual act, but because they became aware of their sex and of the possibility of the act."[50]

In Lawrence's inventive use of religious allegory here, the "sin" that psychoanalysis commits is the transformation of physical sex into "a mental object": mankind has fallen because it has attributed omnipotence to thought. Lawrence's response to this cultural dominant as he sees it will be to romanticize a state prior to the intellectualization of sexuality that he equates with Freud, a state that offers the fully embodied experience of sex without the mental tortures—the guilt, complexes, and inhibitions that he claims psychoanalysis induces. He will invent an alternative version of the unconscious that is radically different from Freud's version and more in keeping with his own developing philosophies of consciousness. If Lawrence condemns the kind of mental knowledge produced by the Freudian method, he champions a form of knowledge yielded by an alternative version of the unconscious. The unconscious—an endlessly mutable category in its own right—becomes the locus of Lawrence's rival discourse with Freud.

The Pristine Unconscious

The gravitational center of Freud's narrative about the self was undeniably the unconscious, which, though it evolved over time, retained its basic definition as a reservoir of instincts, drives, and repressed content generally unavailable to consciousness.[51] In *Psychoanalysis and the Unconscious* Lawrence offers a reading of the Freudian unconscious as

> that which recoils from consciousness, that which reacts in the psyche away from mental consciousness. His unconscious is, we take it, that part of the human consciousness which, though mental, ideal in its nature, yet is unwilling to expose itself to full recognition, and so recoils back into the affective regions and acts there as a secret agent, unconfessed, unadmitted, potent, and usually destructive. The whole body of our repressions makes up our unconscious.[52]

By framing his interpretation of the Freudian unconscious around secrecy and destructiveness, as the metaphor of the secret agent and the language of "recoil" suggest, Lawrence repudiates a version of the unconscious charged with negative affects and impulses, a repository for everything "which is bad, anti-social, sick in individual experience."[53] The language of "recoil" *coils* back to the serpentine imagery at the beginning of the essay, to the "huge slimy serpent of sex" and the "serpent of sex coiled round the root of all our actions,"[54] to the phallic and religious images of seduction that Lawrence attaches to psychoanalysis. The chain of metonyms proliferates as the secret agent comes to substitute for the absent serpent. But is the secret agent a metaphor for the unconscious, as the grammar of the passage suggests, or is it a metaphor for the analyst, who roots out areas of repression and inhibition by seducing the analysand into a confession of dark secrets? Or is the secret agent Freud himself? As these readings indicate, Freud was to Lawrence a serpent in the grass, a charismatic, seductive, and deceptive, figure whom Lawrence could not evade, and whom he used productively to generate his own forms of knowledge.

Lawrence's own version of the unconscious began to emerge while he was making final revisions to *Sons and Lovers*, a time when he was first exposed to psychoanalysis through Frieda. In a letter to the artist Ernest Collins in January of 1913, Lawrence articulates what would become the most enduring metaphysic of his oeuvre: a basic distinction between "mental consciousness," or the conscious mind, and "blood consciousness," or the unconscious:

> My great religion is a belief in the blood, the flesh, as being wiser than the intellect. We can go wrong in our minds. But what our blood feels and believes and says, is always true. The intellect is only a bit and a bridle. . . . We know too much. No, we think we know such a lot. . . . And we have forgotten ourselves. . . . We cannot be.[55]

While Lawrence's vocabulary here is relatively new, the basic concepts are not. The novel Lawrence had just composed, *Sons and Lovers*, explores a similar dualism embodied in two rival characters: a sensuous, instinctive, and highly physical father and a cultured, intellectual, and often puritanical mother. Although the mother emerges as the more sympathetic character in the novel, the "great religion" Lawrence adopts in the letter favors the characteristics associated with the father. In the hierarchy Lawrence establishes, "blood consciousness" is granted ontological and temporal priority to mental knowledge, as a more direct vehicle to truth and to an authentic sense of self. Lawrence's deployment of the word "blood" (rather than "body," say), is intriguing, and merits some unpacking. Blood in Lawrence's vocabulary may be both the anatomical blood we assume and "a metaphor for sensory or non-rational life"[56]—that which will eventually evolve into Lawrence's version of the unconscious. "Blood-consciousness" as a theory becomes a way for Lawrence to close the gap between the mind and body, by imagining a form of consciousness that is biologically determined and rooted in the body, rather than the mind. Eager to challenge the Cartesian hierarchy of mind over body that orders his culture, Lawrence affirms another seat of consciousness independent of the mind, a "blood-consciousness" based in states of bodily experience. Given Lawrence's interest in the vitalist language of flows and currents, a language that becomes increasingly pronounced in Lawrence's writing in the 1920s, blood may have also been an appealing synecdoche for the body, as it connoted a dynamic life force that also brought individuals into physical communion. In *Women in Love*, we recall, Gerald and Birkin share blood as a sign of intimacy, a brotherhood that is also highly eroticized.

Nonetheless, we cannot discount the racialized and fascist connotations of "blood," especially as the Right used slogans of "blood" and "folk" to promote nationalist unity and "pure" blood lines. Philip Rieff has argued that Lawrence's use of blood as a metaphor did not have fascist connotations, but that it evolved from a literary language of blood as metaphoric of passionate states of experience. For Rieff, Lawrence's blood metaphors "remain traditional, expressing for him, as for Shakespeare and others between, the possibility of leading the impassioned and yet social life."[57] But Lawrence's interest in German folk culture and his ongoing investment in primitivism render this argument suspect. Although there is no evidence that he actively promoted fascist causes, as Pound did, Lawrence's belief that early civilizations and cultures have a more direct relationship to sensuality and embodiment certainly gives "blood" a primitivist and racist complexion.

The duality between blood-consciousness and mind-consciousness is articulated further in an essay on Hawthorne from *Studies in Classic American Literature* (1923). In the essay, Lawrence reads *The Scarlet Letter* as an allegory for the conflict between these two ways of being:

> We are divided against ourselves.
>
> For instance, the blood hates being KNOWN by the mind. It feels itself destroyed when it is KNOWN. Hence the profound instinct of privacy.
>
> And on the other hand, the mind and the spiritual consciousness of man simply hates the dark potency of blood-acts: hates the genuine dark sensual orgasms, which do, for the time being, actually obliterate the mind and the spiritual consciousness, plunge them in a suffocating flood of darkness. . . .

> We are all of us conscious in both ways. And the two wars are antagonistic in us
> They will always remain so.
> That is our cross.[58]

In these statements on blood- and mind-consciousness, Lawrence deploys an idiosyncratic Christian rhetoric to articulate a distinctly modern state of being. Christ's burden of man's mortal sin ("That is our cross") has been translated into a more modern, philosophical idiom of self-division. According to the passage, humans are divided because they are riven by competing forces of blood and mind, what might reasonably be compared to Freud's dualism of instincts and reality principle, or of *id* and *ego*. We see the familiar Lawrentian leitmotif of division and opposition, of dialectic without synthesis, but we also see a more affectively charged description of these forces here, which are personified as violent actors in perpetual struggle. The language of hate and destruction, of obliteration and suffocation, of flooding and plunging, suggest the vitality of these oppositions, which, for Lawrence, constituted the dynamic forces at work within the individual. In the same essay, Lawrence defines "blood-knowledge" as "instinct, intuition, all the vast vital flux of knowing that goes on in the dark, antecedent to the mind" and equates this knowledge with that which existed between Adam and Eve before the Fall.[59]

Lawrence's *Studies in American Literature* was published in 1923, the same year Freud published *Das Ich und Das Es* (The ego and the id). In Lawrence's essay on Benjamin Franklin in *Studies*, he writes that there is an "It" inside of us that is the real author "of our own deeds and works,"[60] and that we are never wholly in control of our actions: "But what we *think* we do is not very important. We never really know what we are doing. Either we are materialistic instruments, like Benjamin or we move in the gesture of creation, from our deepest self, usually unconscious. We are only the actors, we are never wholly the authors of our own deeds or works. IT is the author, the unknown inside us or outside us."[61]

Here Lawrence compares the conscious self to an "actor" (as opposed to an "author") working out scripts of which he is not fully conscious—an analogy that evokes Freud's well-known maxim: "The ego is not master in its own house." Lawrence's intriguing use of the term "IT" here, which he does not use much elsewhere, is the force of the unknown inside us, arguably akin to that instinctive libidinal part of the personality Freud describes. "IT" could in fact be a translation of Freud's "das Es," controversially translated by James Strachey as "id," although a literal translation into English would be "the It." Lawrence also implies that the work of art, like the deed, seems to have an agency of its own that the author is unaware of. Linking Lawrence's concept of the "IT" to an instinctive force of creation that remains elusive to our conscious selves, Lawrence is possibly rewriting the ideas of Freud in his own idiom—which suggests, once again, the uncomfortable adjacency of their ideas.[62]

In *Psychoanalysis and the Unconscious*, which is roughly contemporaneous with *Studies in American Literature*, Lawrence articulates the same basic tension between the mental and physical: The "emotional" or "passional sphere" is contrasted with the "logical," "abstract," or "ideal" spheres—those affiliated with reason and intellect. For Lawrence, reason is a defensive form of hyperintellectualism bearing little relationship to the experience of the body. Lawrence values the unconscious as he imagines it precisely because it promises access to the non-rational and intuitive parts of our being. He sees as destructive the supremacy granted to mental life by psychoanalysis and other "idealist" philosophies. Lawrence's primary objection to the Freudian unconscious, therefore, is its construction as a supposedly abstract, disembodied category. Although Freud's conception of the "instincts" was no doubt physiologically based, as was Freud's conception of hysteria, Lawrence reads, or rather misreads, Freud as representative of a pervasive cultural tendency towards intellectualism, especially as psychoanalysis insisted on making personal experience available for rational analysis. In 1924 Lawrence told his friend Mabel Luhan: "I know what lies back" of the fascination with psychoanalysis—the same indecent desire to have everything in the will and the head. Life itself comes from elsewhere."[63]

In his essay "Morality and the Novel" (1925), Lawrence offers a theory of reader response to the modern novel that bears the unmistakable traces of Freudian psychoanalysis. The novel may be judged authentically new, Lawrence claims, if it arouses pain or resistance, if it challenges the sensibilities of the reader, whom Lawrence assumes to be lulled by the consoling forms and fictions of the dominant culture: "To read a really new novel will *always* hurt, to some extent. There will always be resistance. The same with new pictures, new music. You may judge of their reality by the fact that they do arouse a certain resistance, and compel, at length, a certain acquiescence."[64]

Lawrence invests language with the power to radically transform consciousness. His articulation of a phenomenology of reading based on *resistance* reflects both the provocative character of his modernism and his faith in language as a medium of expressive transformation.[65] It also echoes Freudian understandings of resistance, conceived as a defense mechanism mounted by the analysand to anything that gives access to the unconscious.[66] For Freud, the critical objections mounted by the analysand within the analytic session validated the authenticity of those truths that were inadmissible to consciousness, and were therefore potential sources of psychopathology.[67] As he says in his *General Introduction to Psychoanalysis*: "Indeed, we at last understand that overcoming these resistances is the essential achievement of analysis and is that portion of the work which alone assures us that we have accomplished something with the patient."[68] Interpreting the resistance would eventually become the cornerstone of Freud's hermeneutics, affirming the value of the resistance even over and above the truths it presumably concealed.

Freud's "fundamental rule of psychoanalysis," delivered to his clients at the start of treatment, and exacted as a pledge, constituted an initial attempt to manage his patients' resistance, by making it imperative for the patient to relate everything that entered consciousness.[69] In *The Interpretation of Dreams*, Freud writes that the patient must be prepared for the techniques of free association and dream analysis: "We must aim at bringing about two changes in him: an increase in the attention he pays to his own psychical perceptions and the elimination of the criticism by which he normally sifts the thoughts that occur to him."[70] Nor was resistance confined to the relationship between analysand and analyst, for it came to encompass what Freud and his adherents interpreted as a widespread cultural intolerance to psychoanalytic ideas, "the general revolt against our science," which became paradoxical confirmation of the validity of psychoanalysis.[71] Similarly, for Lawrence, the resistance provoked in the reader of modern fiction indexed its authentic newness and truth-value. Both Lawrence and Freud interpreted the significance of their innovations to reside in the resistance that they provoked, and both saw this resistance as demanding a working through or, as Lawrence suggests, an "acquiescence." Both presupposed a skeptical reader and an adversarial dynamic between author and audience.[72] But of course this shared vocabulary of resistance contradicts Lawrence's stated resistance to Freud.

If Lawrence and Freud can be deemed *sharers* in their effort to transform human consciousness through the medium of language, in their epistemological pursuit of truth, and in their self-presentation as radical truth-tellers and conscious innovators working amid resistance, it is equally significant that Lawrence envisioned Freud as fundamentally antagonistic to his utopic program of social transformation, which aimed to reawaken modern subjects to the embodied consciousness that modern civilization had jeopardized. For Lawrence, Freud was not a fellow liberator, but a metonym for an abstract intellectualism, or "idealism," that enclosed modern subjects in a defensive shell, sundering mind from body, and subject from world. Lawrence refused to read Freud's writing while arguing at length about the deficiencies of Freudian psychoanalysis. The refusal to read Freud directly speaks to Lawrence's own resistive reading practices. The truth is, Lawrence was as captivated by its psychoanalysis's allurements as he was critical of its narratives and methods of interpretation.

"Beyond the Limits of Consciousness" and *Women in Love*

Lawrence does not confine his observations about the mind-body agon to his polemical essays. This same "metaphysic" is integrated into his fiction, inviting the criticism that his fictions seem more like polemics than stories and that his characters seem more like authorial mouthpieces than rounded or realistic characters. It might be more accurate to say that characters are staged so as to reflect the binaries that structure Lawrence's thinking. The conflict between blood-consciousness and mind-consciousness, for example, is dramatized in *Women in Love* by the interpersonal agon of Birkin and Hermione, whose romantic relationship is in the process of unraveling when the novel begins. When Birkin and Hermione charge into Ursula's classroom during a lesson on botany, their lovers' quarrel becomes a seemingly pedagogical moment for the reader. In a challenge to Birkin and her new rival, Hermione attempts to undercut Ursula's lesson by announcing that knowledge forecloses the possibility of spontaneous, non-deliberative action: "'Isn't the mind'—she said, with the convulsed movement of her body, 'isn't it our death? Doesn't it destroy all our spontaneity, all our instincts?'" Birkin, however, attempts to catch her in the lie and expose her hypocrisy with his response:

> "You are merely making words," he said; "knowledge means everything to you. Even your animalism, you want it in your head. You don't want to be an animal, you want to observe your own animal functions, to get a mental thrill out of them. It is all secondary—and more decadent than the most hidebound intellectualism...
>
> "Because you haven't got any real body, any dark sensual body of life. You have no sensuality. You have only your will and your conceit of consciousness, and your lust for power, to know."[73]

Hermione is one of several characters in the novel, including Birkin, who express a yearning for immediate, sensual experience; but, like many of the characters in Lawrence's fictions, she lacks access to the sensual body and is positioned as the epitome of self-consciousness. She says to Birkin early in the novel: "To me the pleasure of knowing is so great, so wonderful—nothing has meant so much to me in all life, as certain knowledge."[74] The narrator tells us that Birkin achieved "no real fulfillment in sensuality," with Hermione; instead, "he became disgusted and despised the whole process as if it were dirty." What is distinctly Lawrentian here is the association of independent women with mental life: while Hermione's self-reflexivity and intellectualism are associated with dirt and impurity, Birkin's expressions of physicality are portrayed as acts of purification and renewal.

Ironically, Hermione and Birkin never achieve erotic consummation until Hermione, in a spontaneous rage, attacks Birkin with a paperweight:

> A terrible voluptuous thrill ran down her arms—she was going to know her voluptuous consummation.... What delight, what delight in strength, what delirium of pleasure! She was going to have her consummation of voluptuous ecstasy at last.... Her hand closed on a blue, beautiful ball of lapis lazuli that stood on her desk for a paperweight.... Her heart was a pure flame in her breast, she was purely unconscious in ecstasy.... Then, swiftly, in a flame that drenched down her body like fluid lightning and gave her a perfect, unutterable consummation, unutterable satisfaction, she brought down the ball of jewel stone with all her force, crash on his head.[75]

This passage is climactic on multiple levels, for it is not only the moment when the pent-up sexual energy between Hermione and Birkin is discharged, when Hermione finally achieves her "consummation," but it is the first time Hermione becomes "unconscious in her ecstasy." Hermione's self-consciousness is dissolved in a frenzy of passionate, physical action that is no less erotic than it is violent. Meanwhile, Birkin loses consciousness after the blow to his head and is described as moving "in a sort of darkness." Baptizing himself in sensual communion with nature, Birkin achieves erotic consummation as "the coolness and subtlety of vegetation" travels into his blood: "It was such a fine, cool, subtle touch all over him, he seemed to saturate himself with [the primroses'] contact."[76] For Birkin, direct sexual contact with Hermione is displaced by a transcendent experience with the natural world. Ironically, Birkin, the most philosophical character in the novel, the character who is "abstract almost to be intangible,"[77] can express raw physicality and sensuality in this moment; but Hermione, despite her violent "consummation," remains linked symbolically to the paperweight, to the dead weight of culture and intellect. The paradox of *Women in Love* is that despite the anti-intellectual position it takes in deprioritizing mental-consciousness, it remains through and through a novel of ideas. The intellect for Lawrence is like Milton's Satan, a charismatic element that Lawrence cannot evade and that ultimately turns out to be the driving force of his aesthetic.

Epistemophilia, the "will to know" and to observe oneself in the process of knowing, is the charge leveled at psychoanalysis in both *Psychoanalysis* and *Fantasia*. For Lawrence and his literary counterpart Birkin, epistemophilia is the decadent by-product of a hyper-civilized, disenchanted, mechanical age; but it is clear that a return to the embodied sensuality of what Lawrence equates with "the primitive" is not possible. Still Lawrence and Freud both invest in the primitive as a space beyond culture, as a nostalgic counterpart to the modern world. In *Civilization and Its Discontents*, Freud offers the primitive as a counterpoint to modernity: "what we call our civilization is largely responsible for our misery, and that we should be much happier if we gave it up and returned to primitive conditions."[78] Indeed, Freud's developmental schemas, with their insistent analogies between "primitive" cultures and our infantile selves, are deeply rooted in Eurocentric racism and in colonialist evolutionary theories. Hardly a neutral scientific term, "primitive" for Freud indexed both the earliest stages of psychic development and the so-called primitive, societies which were viewed as less developed (temporally, culturally, technologically) than modern European society.[79] Modernist primitivism took its cues partly from Freudian psychology, as both extoled "primitive" peoples for enjoying a more direct relationship to the natural world and to their own embodied instincts than their hyper-civilized European counterparts. *Women in Love* enacts such a construction of the primitive, for it continuously evokes the primitive as an unalienated origin, making it a critical foil to contemporary life. For Lawrence, the misery of the modern world was a result of the overestimation of the mind at the expense of the body, a duality he reinforces as he searches out discursive paths back to physical, pre-mental consciousness.

Lawrence's idealization of the primitive, and its tropes of bodily knowledge, is most pronounced in *The Plumed Serpent* (1926), "The Woman Who Rode Away" (1928), and *Women in Love*. The bohemian set of men in *Women in Love* with whom Gerald and Birkin consort, collect primitive art and relentlessly discuss it. The conversation in Halliday's apartment about the West African sculpture of the woman in childbirth rehearses what can only be described as a set of modernist clichés about the primitive, conveying to the men "the suggestion of the extreme of physical sensation, beyond the limits of mental consciousness."[80] After Gerald questions its status as an art object, Birkin asserts that "it conveys a complete truth," the same argument that Lawrence invokes in his defense of *Sons and Lovers* from psychoanalytic readings. Both objects, the African statue and Lawrence's novel, are invoked as self-sufficient expressive objects that should be impenetrable to rational analysis; and yet Birkin purports to be the privileged interpreter of the statue. Birkin evokes a teleological narrative of development to explain the statue's primitiveness: It is "pure culture in sensation, culture in the physical consciousness really ultimate physical consciousness, mindless, utterly sensual. It is so sensual as to be final, supreme."[81] In its nudity and extravagant sexual features, its subject matter (fertility, child-birth), and its non-Western origin, the statue is viewed as a symbol of all of the qualities that Lawrence condenses in his primitivist idea of blood-consciousness: physicality, sensuality, mindlessness. Birkin does not perceive the African statue as an art object in its capacity as representation; rather, he views it as a site of pure sensual expressivity. But Birkin, in his idealization of the statue, fails to acknowledge its commodified status, as well as its role as a sign of all the qualities from which the upper-class men are distanced.

Marianna Torgovnick makes the convincing argument that Lawrence freely substituted the primitive for many of the other categories that obsessed him during his career, such as working-class men, vital masculinity, and phallic power.[82] To this list I would add the varied qualities affiliated with "blood-consciousness:" embodied sexuality, physicality, mindlessness. Lawrence's equation of non-white peoples with such qualities casts suspicion on Philip Rieff's assertion that blood-consciousness was innocent of racist and fascist connotations; indeed, there seems to be no way to separate Lawrence's allegory of blood consciousness from the fascist, white supremacist beliefs circulating in Europe and the United States at the time. Lawrence clearly inherited and embraced a racialized conception of human progress that contained within it the notion that non-white peoples were temporally retrograde, stalled at an earlier stage of human development. Lawrence fetishizes primitive life as a complement to the physical and sensual experience contained in his ideas of blood-consciousness. Perhaps similarly, Freud made a shrine of his office with antiquities and fetishes, a collection that visually reinforced his belief that unconscious processes replicated not only our earliest wishes, fantasies, and conflicts, but also those of a primitive past. Freud used archeology as a master metaphor for psychoanalysis and compared himself to an archaeologist methodically working his way into the past. Torgovnick suggests that Freud deployed the primitive as "the testing ground, the laboratory, the key" to universal truths about human nature.[83] Ultimately, both Freud and Lawrence look to the primitive as a founding myth for their different narratives of psychic life.

Lawrence's representation of the Freudian unconscious (as distinct from his conception of blood-consciousness) provides a platform for the presentation of rival theories: Lawrence is eager to wrest his version of the unconscious from any trace of the repressions that he associates with the Freudian model. Indeed, he attempts to conceive of the unconscious as it might exist without repression, for repression, he concludes, distorts and misrepresents the true unconscious. On this point, Lawrence and Freud's views appear to be harmonious: Both acknowledge the deleterious consequences of repression and purport to liberate their audiences from historically debilitating forms of repression. Indeed, the cornerstone of Freud's philosophy was the view that the etiology of the psychoneurosis could be traced to sexual repression. Lawrence, however, conceives himself to be offering something quite new by recognizing in psychoanalysis the very machinery of repression, rather than its putative cure. Lawrence does not so much reinterpret the Freudian unconscious as offer a different model, one more consistent with his own theory of mind/body dualism.

To the "sack of horrors" of the Freudian unconscious, dominated by conflicts and complexes, Lawrence opposes his model of the "pristine unconscious," in which "all of our genuine impulse arises."[84] In place of a hellish internal world plagued by repressions and inhibitions, Lawrence imagines an edenic state of innocence, a realm of pure instinct that is temporally and ontologically prior to cognition. The pristine unconscious exists "prior to any mentality"; it is "the bubbling life in us, which is innocent of any mental alteration":

> We have actually to go back to our own unconscious. But not to the unconscious which is the inverted reflection of our ideal consciousness. We must discover, if we can, the true unconscious, where our life bubbles up in us, prior to any mentality. The first bubbling of life in us, which is innocent of any mental alteration, this is the unconscious. It is pristine, not in any way ideal. It is the spontaneous origin from which it behooves us to live.[85]

Lawrence goes on to say that the "true unconscious" is "not a shadow cast from the mind. . . . It is the spontaneous life-motive in every organism. . . . It begins where life begins."[86] To be sure, Lawrence's definition of the unconscious is radically different from Freud's—a temporal metaphor for the beginning of consciousness, rather than a spatial metaphor for a psychic substratum of repressed content generally unavailable to the conscious mind. Lawrence's description of the pristine unconscious is emphatically free of sexual connotation, in stark contrast to his hyper-sexualized and gothic representations of the Freudian unconscious. On the other hand, Lawrence's ideal of sexual innocence as a state that can be returned to might be interpreted, according to a Freudian reading, as the very origin of the psychoneuroses. To ameliorate a patient's neurosis through analytic treatment required a greater, rather than a lesser, degree of self-awareness in the patient; it required a loss of innocence, so to speak. If for Freud, the psyche is always already burdened with the seeds of its own pathology—neurosis being the tragic cost of an individual's entry into culture—for Lawrence, the unconscious is a state of primary innocence that marks the origin of our being and offers a model of how to live. Lawrence's imperative to the reader to rediscover such a state of being ("we must"), is of course tempered by the conditional language of doubt ("if we can").

In *The Myth of the Modern*, Perry Meisel adduces both Freud and Lawrence as epitomizing a modernist obsession with the recovery of origins and, in particular, a primal ache for a self that exists outside of culture.[87] In Lawrence's case, this "will to modernity" consists of an effort to recover the innocence and spontaneity he perceives to be lacking in modern culture. Allison Pease has described Lawrence's utopic project as reflecting an urge for an ontological framework of "pure being," "a moment/place of transcendence that is simultaneously purely physical."[88] For Lawrence, discovering the unconscious would be akin to finding a new way to live, a way that was spontaneous, instinctive, and embodied. With its emphasis on "innocence" and the "pristine," the Lawrentian unconscious contains a numinous quality: It is the place where Lawrence's psychology and his faith intersect. Lawrence says in *Fantasia* that in order to discover a "true unconscious" science would have to give up its intellectualist position and embrace the old "religious faculty." He may have challenged Christian doctrine in its orthodox and institutional varieties, but he was highly committed to a mystical notion of the soul as a life-giving, creative force that resists comprehension:

> By the unconscious we wish to indicate that essential unique nature of every individual creature, which is, by its very nature, unanalyzable, undefinable, inconceivable. . . . And being inconceivable, we will call it the unconscious. As a matter of fact, soul would be a better word. By the unconscious we do mean the soul. But the word soul has been vitiated by the idealistic use, until nowadays it means only that which a man conceives himself to be. And that which a man conceives himself to be is something far different from his true unconscious. So we must relinquish the word soul.[89]

Lawrence's conception of the unconscious, or the more religiously inflected soul, is predicated on the limits of epistemological mastery. The unconscious is *unanalyzable* and by implication resistant to psycho*analysis*, or to any kind of intellectual effort. The soul is distinctly non-intellectual, for as he says in *Fantasia*, "We have really no will and no choice, in the first place. It is our soul which acts within us, day by day unfolding us according to our own nature."[90] Lawrence's reified binaries are all too apparent at this point: spontaneity, instinct, and embodiment are used in direct opposition to mentality, abstraction, and the ideal. Lawrence seeks an unalienated origin of pure physical consciousness prior to mentality; but those same abstractions and conceptual languages that he eschews necessarily contaminate his description of this ontology. As Meltzer points out, any description of the unconscious as a metaphor for the unknown must be understood in terms of the known. Ultimately, Lawrence cannot escape the trap that he sets for himself: He cannot evade the analytic or discursive treatment of the unconscious if he is to write about it, just as he cannot situate the body or sex outside of discourse. Writing about the unconscious is always an abstract operation, but Lawrence appears to exhibit little awareness of this double bind, although it can be argued that the almost hysterical level of the attacks against "sex in the head" and "mentality" indicates a displaced awareness of the problem. Lawrence is, after all, constantly having sex in his head and on the page, if not in the body.

Lawrence struggles to locate the pristine unconscious outside of the mind, but he cannot divorce mind from body in the manner he suggests. Critics such as Taylor Stoehr have emphasized the metaphoricity of this construction of the unconscious rather than its pretensions to concreteness.[91] But Lawrence's strategic inversion of Cartesian dualism, by which the body is elevated over the mind as the primary site of consciousness, is not merely a didactic strategy to realign our thinking; it was also, for Lawrence, a deeply held conviction about human experience and human emotion. Contained in Lawrence's philosophy was, for his disciples, a potentially revolutionary prescription of how to live according to the instincts of the body rather than the dictates of the mind. But such confabulations also embed Lawrence back into the world of "mentality" from which he seeks to escape. The "pristine unconscious" is, like Freud's unconscious, an intellectual abstraction and philosophical construct, and Lawrence is condemned to articulating this abstraction through rhetorical tropes—metaphors, similes, and analogies—the very stuff of literary language. Nor can the "pristine" unconscious, constructed out of the materials of the Freudian unconscious, expel the traces of its precursor, for it is already contaminated by this earlier influence.

I would argue that the intensity of Lawrence's diatribes against "sex in the head" and "mentality" in *Psychoanalysis* and *Fantasia* illustrates a disavowed or partial awareness of the challenge he has created for himself in attempting to construct a language for the unconscious free of abstraction. Yet even he is willing to concede that any attempt to rediscover the unconscious requires a degree of "mental recognition . . . to break the limits which we have imposed on the movement of the unconscious."[92] This is a striking deconstructive moment in Lawrence's essay and one of several in which Lawrence suggests that we must use our self-consciousness in order to escape from it. In the words of Elisabeth Ladenson, no one was more "willing to assume seemingly self-annihilating positions"[93] and Lawrence's struggle with his own ideas is especially pronounced in his critique of psychoanalysis. Lawrence's project ultimately affirms the necessity of thinking about consciousness and the unconscious in rational terms—just as Freud attempted—even as he appears to argue otherwise. Lawrence may disavow the discourses that enable his work, but clearly his polemics are dependent on the discursivity and abstraction that they condemn.

2
The Soul under Psychoanalysis
Virginia Woolf and the Ethics of Intimacy

> And the truth is, one can't write directly about the soul. Looked at, it vanishes. . . .
>
> —WOOLF, DIARY, VOL. 3

Both D. H. Lawrence and Virginia Woolf resisted reading Freud's work directly, and distanced themselves from Freud's writing, yet both were crucial in disseminating psychoanalytic ideas to a broader British public: Lawrence through his extensive responses to, and redescriptions of, psychoanalytic ideas, and Woolf through her publication of the International Psycho-analytical Library and the *Standard Edition* of Freud. In a crucial moment of exchange between literary modernism and psychoanalysis that would help to ensure the mutual success of both fields, Virginia and Leonard Woolf became the official English publishers of the International Psycho-analytical Library in 1924. James Strachey had convinced the Woolfs to publish all of Freud's works, past and present, in definitive English translations out of their home-run press at the Hogarth House. The Psycho-analytical Library, and especially Freud's papers, would serve as the press's greatest source of revenue, helping to subsidize the publication of Woolf's novels and other experimental works that would be commercially unviable for larger presses.[1]

The Hogarth Press survived many of its competitors largely because of the profits of the Psycho-analytical Library, which published Freud's *Collected Papers* and the work of Ernest Jones, Melanie Klein, Helene Deutsch, and Karl Abraham. While Woolf was involved in publishing these texts, her letters and diaries suggest a reluctance to view them as anything more than objects to be "handled."[2] As she says in a letter to Marjorie Joad in 1924 on the eve of

Hogarth's adoption of the Psycho-analytical Library: "the psycho-analytic books have been dumped in a fortress the size of Windsor castle in ruins upon the floor."[3] The references to *handling* and *dumping* reflect the distance Woolf preserved from the ideas embedded in these objects, heaped like ruins on the ground. Though Woolf was intimately involved in publishing and popularizing psychoanalysis to an English audience, she remained suspicious of Freud's ideas for over two decades, reading his work only shortly before her death in 1941.[4]

Bloomsbury served as an intellectual enclave for psychoanalysis; several of its figures dabbled in psychoanalytic theory and a few became trained analysts themselves. But Woolf claimed never to have opened a volume of Freud's until the late thirties and stated in a 1932 letter: "I have not studied Dr Freud or any psychoanalyst—indeed I think I have never read any of their books: my knowledge is merely from superficial talk."[5] Virginia Woolf, Roger Fry, and Clive Bell remained vocal adversaries of psychoanalysis, and were especially skeptical of its entanglement with art and literature. As Elizabeth Abel has demonstrated, the literary cast that psychoanalysis acquired through its interactions with Bloomsbury fueled Woolf's intense professional rivalry with psychoanalysis, which she viewed as a disciplinary interloper encroaching upon literature.[6] Still, Woolf's aesthetic and intellectual preoccupations with the nature of selfhood and subjectivity seem inconceivable outside of a psychological culture oriented to the representation and interpretation of interior life. Woolf's layered conception of self—a self that accrues meaning over time through the sedimentation of memory and experience; a self that is often opaque to itself; a self that develops only insofar as it is still tied, both consciously and unconsciously, to childhood experience—seems continuous at many points with Freudian accounts of subjectivity.[7] An example of such kinship is found in Woolf's late essay "A Sketch of the Past," when she declares that "a great part of every day is not lived consciously" and that certain suppressed memories "come to the surface unexpectedly."[8] To affirm the overlap between Woolf and Freud's intellectual and aesthetic projects, however, is not to diminish Woolf's complicated resistance to Freud. It is to highlight the intimate and adversarial qualities of their relation, as well as her quarrels with the medical establishment more broadly.

In what follows, I show how Woolf's discursive battle with Freud was tied to her aesthetic and ethical (albeit secular and modern) defense of the "soul," and to her polemic against medical and psychological authoritarianism—a polemic that reaches its apogee in *Mrs. Dalloway* (1925). Woolf was intimately involved with psychoanalysis in the years she was to plan and write the novel, an involvement that impacted her thinking about the role of fiction in narrating the self, and about the place of the human sciences in managing, studying, and representing psychic life. While neither Freud nor psychoanalysis are explicitly addressed in *Mrs. Dalloway*, it is difficult to disentangle her withering critique of psychoanalysis in her essays, diaries, and letters, from the caricatures of doctors and psychologists in *Mrs. Dalloway*. Her own experience as a woman patient suffering from, and writing about, mental illness and its treatment informed her critique of the medical and psychiatric professions.

Woolf's resistance to psychoanalysis was an aspect of a broader suspicion of scientific authority and masculine intellect: She frequently collapsed distinctions among medicine, psychiatry, and psychoanalysis while insisting on an ethical space for psychical interrogations that were specifically literary. When Woolf discusses psychoanalysis, she hyperbolizes its dangers as a scientific dissection of the soul. In both Woolf and Lawrence's writings, there is a desire to preserve the mystery and ineffability of the soul, and an anxiety about reductive approaches to interpreting it. As Woolf says in her diary, "the truth is, one can't write directly about the soul. Looked at, it vanishes."[9] But, as I suggest later in the chapter, Woolf's use of free indirect discourse as a narrative mode that offers access to the deepest recesses of the self by way of a distant and anonymous narrator, evokes analogous psychological interventions that Woolf rejected in psychoanalysis.[10]

Woolf's resistance to Freud was more than a professional rivalry; it was also a bid for a certain aesthetic, ethical, and rhetorical relationship to the soul, or what she calls the "essential self" and "spirit," in language that seems to resist demystification. The "soul" in Woolf's writings, that essential yet ineffable part of the self, that interiorized space so intimately connected to privacy, sometimes serves as a rhetorical foil to the Freudian psyche. The dialectical movement between private and public, inside and outside, so crucial to her writing about selfhood informed her skepticism of psychoanalysis as a discipline infringing upon the guarded precincts of the self. And yet, as I go on to suggest, Woolf's complicated narrative interventions evoke similar ethical dilemmas to those she raises in relation to psychoanalysis. As Woolf extends imaginatively into the lives of others, as she excavates the thoughts, memories, desires, and fantasies of her characters, does she risk replicating the same invasive practices she condemns? Or does Woolf's fictional project reflect a more ethical model of extension?

Ambivalent Alliances

Woolf's essays and fictional experiments of the 1920s make it increasingly clear that modernism and psychoanalysis were engaged in parallel projects, similarly committed to intimate representations of mental life and to the aestheticization of withheld worlds. Her investments in mental life, memory, and trauma are reflected in her innovative experiments with free indirect discourse and "tunneling," or what she described as the pressure of memory on present consciousness and behavior.[11] In her well-known essay "Modern Fiction" (1919), Woolf identifies an obvious parallel with psychoanalysis by insisting that what distinguishes the "moderns" from their Victorian predecessors and the middle-brow authors of the day, is that the moderns find their "point of interest . . .

> in the dark places of psychology. At once, therefore, the accent falls a little differently; the emphasis is upon something hitherto ignored; at once a different outline of form becomes necessary, difficult for us to grasp, incomprehensible to our predecessors."[12]

In announcing this rupture with her Victorian predecessors, Woolf makes a claim for a novel presentation of psychological subjectivity. "Modern Fiction" gestures to what Raymond Williams describes as a "structure of feeling," a lived experience of the present that is neither firm nor definite, but a kind of social experience "in solution."[13] Woolf affirms the social experience of modernity as the foundation for a new formalism, highlighting the psychic and affective experiences of modernity as access points to the production of innovative fiction. She entreats her fellow moderns to "Look within," to direct aesthetic attention to personal, subjective experience—which is vital if writers are to escape the deadening conventions of plot and genre.[14] But if Woolf identifies an inward turn as the orientation of modern fiction, she is also anxious to preserve "a different outline of form," one that renders human subjectivity mysterious and complex, a subjectivity that cannot be reduced to the fixity or transparency of a structure. This aesthetic value, one that emphasizes indeterminacy over definitiveness at the level of form, is crucial to Woolf's critique of psychoanalysis, which she denounced for its will to demystify. Thus, while Woolf and Freud's directives are both ostensibly to *look within*, "Modern Fiction" presents a language of suggestive mystery about the self that is more akin to mysticism than to the positivism she equates with psychoanalysis, psychiatry, and the medical establishment.

For my purposes, "Modern Fiction" functions in two ways: It affirms the relation between Woolf's modernism and Freud's psychoanalysis, but it also anticipates her critique of the latter as a threatening extension of scientific rationalism into the aesthetic. Her memorable appeal, "Let us record the atoms as they fall upon the mind in the order in which they fall, let us trace the pattern, however disconnected and incoherent in appearance, which each sight or incident scores upon the consciousness," resembles Freud's dictum to his patients to relate everything that enters consciousness, in whatever order these associations emerge.[15] Both Woolf and Freud purport to trace patterns from apparently random phenomena. Woolf praised the fiction of Dorothy Richardson for its ability to discern "unity, significance, or design" in the "helter-skelter of flying fragments."[16] Much like Freud, Woolf saw her role as that of a medium, making connections among seemingly disconnected ideas, impressions, and perceptions, and connecting subjects across psychic and physical boundaries.

As post-war writers, Woolf and Freud were similarly interested in examining the ways in which modern life impinges psychologically on the subject. Not only were both concerned with making psychic pain legible to readers, they were alike in imagining everyday experience as potentially traumatic. Woolf's "Modern Fiction" (1919) and Freud's *Beyond the Pleasure Principle* (1920)—published in English within a year of each other—present ordinary psychic experience as a sensory assault. When placed side by side, their metaphors of consciousness yield surprising continuities:

> Examine for a moment an ordinary mind on an ordinary day. The mind receives a myriad impressions—trivial, fantastic, evanescent, or engraved with the sharpness of steel. From all sides they come, an incessant shower of innumerable atoms; and as they fall, as they shape themselves into the life of Monday or Tuesday, the accent falls differently from of old. . . . Life is not a series of gig lamps symmetrically arranged; life is a luminous halo, a semi-transparent envelope surrounding us from the beginning of consciousness to the end.[17]

Freud's human organism is similarly embattled by forces both internal and external:

> This little fragment of living substance is suspended in the middle of an external world charged with the most powerful energies; and it would be killed by the stimulation emanating from these if it were not provided with a protective shield against stimuli. It acquires the shield in this way: its outermost surface ceases to have the structure proper to living matter, becomes to some degree inorganic and thenceforth functions as a special envelope or membrane resistant to stimuli.[18]

In their respective thought experiments, Woolf and Freud imagine the human organism enveloped in a psychic membrane that is both protective and porous, an envelope that manages the onslaught of external and internal stimuli. Woolf's "incessant shower of innumerable atoms" and her impressions "engraved with the sharpness of steal," and Freud's assaultive "stimulation" and "protective shield" imagine consciousness as akin to an experience of war. In the wake of the First World War, such models of sentience envision the everyday as a stimulus-assault, an incessant whiplash from which the vulnerable organism defends itself.[19]

However resistant Woolf was to Freud's work in the coming years, she expressed similar frustrations with the failure of traditional empirical methods to register psychological disorders with non-organic origins. For both Woolf and Freud, the war provided overwhelming evidence of the existence of invisible wounds: Indeed, Freud credited World War I with putting "an end to the temptation to attribute the cause of [traumatic neurosis] to organic lesions of the nervous system brought about by mechanical force."[20] In *Beyond the Pleasure Principle*, Freud suggested that the existence of injury or wounds on the body mitigated the symptoms of psychological trauma by acting as sites of cathexis; neurotic symptoms were, paradoxically, the result of the absence of physical injury.[21] What emerges in the work of both writers is a problem of legibility: how to make legible psychic pain that is invisible, that resists conventional epistemological frameworks. Woolf's solution to the problem is ultimately formal: she uses free indirect discourse to mediate between private and public realms, to make available for representation the psychic wounds that empirical methods failed to register, but that were central to modernist and psychoanalytic concern. Woolf and Freud both rely on metaphors of surface and depth, exteriority and interiority, consciousness and repression to theorize a model of consciousness that registers the historical forces of trauma.

Such similarities in their approaches to consciousness and psychic trauma notwithstanding, Woolf tended to subsume Freudian psychoanalysis beneath the larger problem of medical tyranny. In 1920, she published an essay entitled "Freudian Fiction" (1920), which satirized what she viewed as the vulgar application of psychoanalysis to literature. "Freudian Fiction" is a review of John Beresford's novel, *The Imperfect Mother*, one of the many book reviews Woolf wrote for the *Times Literary Supplement*.[22] It is also her most explicit critique of Freud and his methods. Woolf begins by ridiculing the Oedipal overtones of Beresford's novel, with its protagonist who is provoked by unconscious impulses, including an "unacknowledged passion for his mother."[23] She then declares that Beresford's "bastard children" (i.e., his characters) are the legitimate children of Freud, Oedipal clichés rather than complex, plausible figures. Woolf deftly manipulates the Oedipal narrative here for the purposes of satire, reinforcing her argument that literary character as an aesthetic category should not be subject to the demystifications of doctors analyzing patients.[24] Enacting a schematic divide between science and literature, she accuses Beresford's novel of an insufficient loyalty to aesthetic values:

> Judged as an essay in morbid psychology, *An Imperfect Mother* is an interesting document; judged as a novel it is a failure. . . . We cannot help adopting the professional manner of a doctor intent upon his

diagnosis. A love scene interests us because something bearing significantly on our patient's state of mind may emerge . . . Yes, says the scientific side of the brain, that is interesting; that explains a great deal. No says the artistic side of the brain, that is dull and has no human significance whatsoever. Snubbed and discouraged, the artist retreats; and before the end of the book the medical man is left in possession of the field; all the characters have become cases; and our diagnosis is now so assured that a boy of six has scarcely opened his lips before we detect in him unmistakable symptoms of the prevailing disease.[25]

In the metaphorical battleground Woolf constructs, the novelist cedes authority to the "medical man," who reduces literary character to a clinical case study, misreading literature as scientific evidence. Characters are flattened into symptomatic subjects suffering from the "prevailing disease." "The triumphs of science are beautifully positive," Woolf continues, "but for novelists the matter is much more complex; and should they, like Mr. Beresford, possess a conscience, the question how far they should allow themselves to be influenced by the discoveries of the psychologists is by no means simple."[26] The transgression, therefore, is not just aesthetic but ethical, insofar as the novel should represent matters of "human significance" that are too fine-grained for the positivist procedures of science. While the more specific target of her polemic is "Freudian" fiction, Woolf constructs a recognizably humanist critique of scientific observation as oversimplifying, dehumanizing, and invasive.[27]

Woolf's central critique is the novel's hermeneutic privileging of explication at the expense of mystery and complexity. Psychoanalysis "pretends to be the key that opens every door": It "simplifies rather than complicates, detracts rather than enriches."[28] The novelistic and the psychoanalytic are configured at cross-purposes: the former deepens, enriches, and complicates, while the latter simplifies, reduces, clarifies. What is perhaps most offensive to Woolf is psychoanalysis's ability to masquerade as literature; her efforts to manage the boundaries between the two suggest an anxiety about the marginalization of literature by psychoanalysis and other scientific discourses: The artist "retreats" and "the medical man is left in possession of the field." What "Freudian Fiction" reinforces, however, is that the commitment to artistic purity in high modernism is already a retrospective gesture at this point, for the purportedly pure space of the novel imagined here has already been transformed by psychoanalytic discourse.

Woolf's eagerness to differentiate the spheres of literature and psychoanalysis as distinct spheres of value forms a reflexive response to an assimilation of psychoanalysis that had already begun to take place in British literature by 1920.

The embrace of psychoanalysis by several of Woolf's family members and her Bloomsbury peers signaled to Woolf not just a disturbing entanglement but an anxiety about literature's loss of authority, which she attributes in part to psychoanalysis. In her polemic, one can hear echoes of Baudelaire's statement on aesthetic autonomy, that "Poetry cannot, except at the price of death and decay, assume the mantle of science or morality; the pursuit of truth is not its aim, it has nothing outside itself."[29] Woolf's call for autonomy in "Freudian Fiction," however, is less a categorical statement about art than a response to the emergence of what Graham Richards calls a "Freudish" culture.[30] Her skepticism of psychoanalysis, with its tendency to simplify and reduce and make case studies of character, informed her approach to psychological subjectivity in Mrs. Dalloway, which oscillates between an impulse to plumb the depths of the self and a reluctance to expose its most profound truths.

Woolf and the Woman Patient

Perry Meisel has identified the uncanny simultaneity of the publication of Mrs. Dalloway and the first volume of Freud's Collected Papers in English: "That the material production of English Freud was a physical labor of Woolf's immediate circle of friends is the last and best historical instance of the very real relation between modern literature and psychoanalysis."[31] But why was Woolf so threatened by a discourse that she herself was helping to disseminate?

Woolf's resistance to psychoanalysis is tied to her complicated relationship to medical and psychiatric treatment, and to the historical realities of being a female patient in the early decades of the twentieth century. As is well known, Woolf suffered acutely with mental illness throughout her life, and she experienced periodic breakdowns which culminated in several suicide attempts, and finally a successful suicide in 1941 at the age of fifty-nine. A victim of almost unrelenting trauma in her early years, Woolf suffered the death of her mother at the age of thirteen, the deaths of her half-sister, father, and brother in subsequent years, as well as years of sexual abuse at the hands of her half-brothers. Her diaries, letters, and essays make reference to anxiety and depression, breakdowns, hallucinations, fatigue, headaches, repeated bouts of influenza, and a reluctance to eat. While critics and biographers have diagnosed her with something akin to bipolar disorder, her biographer Hermione Lee reminds us that "to choose a language for Virginia Woolf's illness is at once . . . to rewrite and represent it, perhaps to misrepresent it."[32] That is, to attach diagnostic labels to her condition may be to commit a problematic presentism while effacing Woolf's own language for representing her illness.

As Lee also points out, there are gaps and inconsistencies in Woolf's accounts of her illness and considerable confusion about the effects of her illness and those of her treatment.[33] Subjected to years of medical treatment, some of it unwanted and coercive, Woolf wrote intermittently of her personal experience with physicians, nerve specialists, and psychiatrists.[34] Perhaps unsurprisingly, the discourses of medicine, psychiatry, and psychoanalysis are not only entangled with each other, they are also narrated in distinctly gendered terms in her writing, and are linked to larger systems of oppression—heteropatriarchy, imperialism, and militarism. In the early years of her marriage, Woolf attributed her anxiety and despair to the medical treatments she was subjected to; most oppressive were the rest cures that denied her the outlets of reading and writing—her preferred therapies.[35] Woolf would later write to her friend Gwen Raverat: "You can't think of what a raging furnace it is still to me—madness and doctors and being forced."[36]

Woolf's resistance to medical authority and more specifically psychoanalysis, as both a set of theories and a therapeutic method, is revealing given her complex role as author, patient, and pioneering critic of heteropatriarchy in an era in which the female subject often figured as a mute object of scientific analysis, and in which female sexuality was theorized as the very locus of pathology. In the words of Elaine Showalter, "the traditions of English psychiatric medicine during the nineteenth century . . . tended to silence the female patient, to make her the object of techniques of moral management or of photographic representation and interpretation."[37] When the female subject did speak, as in Freud and Breuer's analytic encounters with hysterical patients in the 1890s, she was still subject to the expertise of the male scientist who submitted her testimony and bodily language to his reasoned interpretation. Psychoanalysis was partly born out of such gendered epistemologies, in which male expertise and female pathology constituted the uneven structure of scientific knowledge. Feminist critics such as Phyllis Chesler, Elaine Showalter, Sandra Gilbert, and Susan Gubar have emphasized the extent to which psychoanalytic definitions of mental illness were gendered, producing and reproducing the ideological binds that kept women anchored to damaging stereotypes.[38]

Showalter's *The Female Malady* details the ways in which female hysteria was obsessively "presented, represented, and reproduced" in settings such as the public lectures of Charcot's hospital, the Salpêtrière, where the spectacle of female illness, obsessively staged and photographed, lent scientific credence to the idea that hysteria was a constitutionally "female malady."[39] Woolf's life coincided with a transformation, albeit gradual, in attitudes toward the diagnosis and treatment of mental illness, but the suspicion of psychoanalysis in her writing is hard to disentangle from a broader suspicion of masculine scientific authority. Her own psychiatric treatment was mostly overseen by men, including Leonard Woolf, who assumed the role of live-in doctor, supervising feeding times and rest cures and documenting the status of her health in a daily journal, what Lee calls "a careful clinical narrative."[40] It is no coincidence that when Woolf conceded some authority to doctors later in life, they were female doctors with a less authoritarian approach to medicine. And when Woolf finally expressed interest in psychoanalysis after years of resistance, the theorist she embraced was analyst Melanie Klein, who productively challenged the explanatory power of the Oedipal narrative by decentering the male patriarch from his privileged place within the family.[41] It was Klein and British object-relations theorists who brought into focus the maternal origins of subjectivity, which orthodox psychoanalysis had elected to deemphasize.[42] Though speculative and dualistic, Klein's metapsychology was insistently focused on the relational, rather than simply the ego-centric subject.[43]

The displacement of the woman's origins of subjectivity in Freud's evolving narratives of sexual development is merely one dimension of his problematic views on women. While Freud narrated the male subject's entry into culture and morality as a submission to the law of the father, he declared female sexual development to be "more shadowy and full of gaps"—a story without closure.[44] The year Woolf published *Mrs. Dalloway* (1925), Freud asserted in "The Psychical Consequences of the Anatomic Distinction Between the Sexes" that "Women oppose change, receive passively, and add nothing of their own."[45] The centerpiece to his theory of women was that of penis envy; in "Femininity" Freud declares that women's desire "to carry on an intellectual profession—may often be recognized as a sublimated modification" of the repressed wish of "the longed-for penis."[46] At the same time, Freud proclaimed his ignorance of all things feminine, expressing in 1933: "That is all I have to say to you about femininity. It is certainly incomplete and fragmentary and does not always sound friendly. . . . If you want to know more about femininity, enquire of your own experiences of life, or turn to poets, or wait until science can give you deeper and more coherent information."[47] Thus, for Freud, women's desire is elusive and unresolved, but centered on a longing for the phallus, and the presumed power and potency that the phallus signifies.

Woolf allegedly refused psychoanalytic treatment out of fear that it might affect her creativity, regarding the "intervals" of illness in her life as "the most fruitful artistically—one becomes fertilized."[48] Leonard Woolf declared in his autobiography, *Beginning Again* (1964), that "Virginia's genius was closely connected with what manifested itself as insanity . . . here surely is an exact description of genius and madness, showing how they occupy the same place in her mind."[49] Woolf's friend, the psychoanalyst Alix Strachey, feared the effects of analysis on Woolf's creativity, commenting in *Recollections of Virginia Woolf* that "Virginia's imagination, apart from her artistic creativeness, was so interwoven with her fantasies—and indeed with her madness—that if you had stopped the madness you might have stopped the creativeness too. It may be preferable to be mad and be creative than to be treated by analysis and become ordinary."[50]

Upholding a Romantic conception of the author as genius, Strachey expresses an increasingly common opinion that psychoanalytic treatment would denature the artistic impulse—transforming the illness that was the very engine of creativity. Woolf may not have been fully aware of the potential of analysis as a therapeutic method, but she remained suspicious of its benefits: "For my part, I doubt if family life has all the power of evil attributed to it, or psychoanalysis of good."[51] It is equally likely, as Strachey suggests, that Virginia and Leonard had enough knowledge of psychoanalysis to recognize its limitations in the treatment of a condition like Woolf's. If psychoanalysis threatened Woolf's interpretive primacy over "the dark places of psychology," it also threatened the Romantic conception of art wrought through the genius of its creator.

Woolf describes illness as creatively generative, while she also acknowledges that it made writing and deadlines more difficult and left her dependent and vulnerable to medical management. While, in her writing, medicine and psychiatry are often defined by violation and uneven power relations, illness is frequently described as a vehicle to privacy and autonomy, as well as a welcome retreat from social obligations. In "On Being Ill," which she published in T. S. Eliot's journal *The Criterion* in 1926, illness is envisioned as a state of psychic freedom that enables the patient to subvert class and gender norms. For Woolf, there is an implicit freedom achieved in illness: illness is a solitary activity, a necessary retreat from the burdens of shared experience and social conformity, which always imply a surrender of self: "Here we go alone, and like it better so. Always to have sympathy, always to be accompanied, always to be understood would be intolerable."[52] Health is, in turn, associated with the false formalities of a public self, which Woolf associates with "make-believe" or a social disguise.

In "On Being Ill," Woolf represents illness as a catalyst for the kinds of privacy that women were so rarely afforded in domestic spaces. Illness becomes a viable pretext for female seclusion, as well as an alibi for the neglect of domestic and social duties expected of women. As Victoria Rosner suggests, upper-class women of the nineteenth and early-twentieth centuries were left exposed in the social spaces of the drawing room, while their male counterparts had access to the more secret chambers of the house, such as the study.[53]

Woolf's arguments in "On Being Ill" resemble those of *A Room of One's Own*; they contain a similar discourse of privacy, although under different premises. Nineteenth-century women authors, Woolf argues in the latter, were denied access to male retreats like the study and had to produce their work amid constant disruption. Her solution to this inequity is pragmatic and material: Women must be provided with the same conditions of privacy as their male counterparts, "a room with a lock on the door."[54]

Illness and privacy are ineluctably intertwined: Illness both enables and disables privacy, becomes a vehicle to privacy and exposure. Catherine MacKinnon has written: "Privacy is everything women as women have never been allowed to be or have; at the same time the private is everything women have been equated with and defined in terms of men's ability to have."[55] Woolf's logic in "On Being Ill" is as fascinating as it is problematic, for she romanticizes illness at some points and overturns romantic clichés at others. In many ways, her ideas anticipate the theoretical speculations of Michel Foucault and Gilles Deleuze and Félix Guattari, who not only oppose the prerogatives of treatment and cure, but posit, at least in the abstract, madness as a censored form of truth and a potential site of resistance to bourgeois norms. But Woolf, always aware of the double-edged nature of illness, provides a humanizing reminder of the challenges and inhibitions inherent in such an experience: To the abstractions of these theoretical languages she provides the necessary affective, embodied content that is missing.

Woolf's ambivalence about illness derives from her sense of its power as a resource for creative expression and its capacity to both enable and disable privacy. It can yield greater freedoms but also render the subject dependent on others and vulnerable to treatments and interventions. In a letter to Ethel Smyth in 1930, Woolf suggests: "As an experience, madness is terrific. I can assure you, and not to be snigged at; and in its lava I still find most of the things I write about. It shoots out of one everything shaped, final, not in mere driblets, as sanity does."[56] With her signature humor and irony, Woolf builds a case for the value of illness, suggesting that it lends her writing a sense of coherence otherwise absent during moments of sanity. While there were times when she was too ill to write, or prevented from writing as part of her treatment, there were other times when being sent to bed afforded her both the imaginative and the literal space to create—analogous to a room of one's own. But this narrative of creative vision inspired by illness is thoroughly complicated by evidence from her own life: Woolf's sphere of privacy was consistently invaded by clinicians, psychiatrists, nerve specialists, nurses, and by her own husband, who documented and managed her conditions. The enabling fiction of illness as a metaphorical room of one's own was shadowed by the real threat of institutionalization and the loss of privacy and autonomy that followed from illness.

"Madness and doctors and being forced"

Illness retains its ambivalent qualities in Woolf's *Mrs. Dalloway*, connected as it is to poetic inspiration, the defiance of social norms, the vulnerability to medical authority, and the loss of autonomy and privacy. Among other things, Woolf's novel is an indictment of the psychiatric and medical community's response to shell shock during World War I, a portrait of incompetence, cruelty, and complicity with the war machine. It is also a critique of the failure of these regimes to assist in the reintegration of traumatized soldiers into post-war civilian society. In June 1923, Woolf outlined her ambitions for the novel: "I want to give life & death, sanity & insanity; I want to criticize the social system & and to show it at work, at its most intense."[57] The "social system" that forms the object of Woolf's critique in *Mrs. Dalloway* suggests a complex network of social, political, and economic forces responsible for both the war and its repression, the effects of which are located on the mind and body of Septimus Smith. If broadly defined, these forces constitute the aggressive imperialism, militarism, and masculinity that culminated in the slaughter of the Great War, the more explicit objects of critique are the institutions of psychiatry, psychology, and medicine called on during and after the war to manage its effects on the social body. Ever attuned to the complex matrix of forces in which the subject is enmeshed, Woolf integrates the larger structures of nationalism, militarism, imperialism, and the institutions of medicine and law into her experimental study of the lives of a small group of characters in London. Woolf's characters are embedded in a dense web of ideological, institutional, and social relations, but they are also profoundly enclosed in their own private thoughts, desires, memories, and traumatic experiences.

Mrs. Dalloway is famously built on a double design, a narrative structure in which two lives are told in parallel: Clarissa Dalloway, an upper-class society woman hosting a party, and Septimus Smith, a poet, former clerk, and shell-shocked veteran in the throes of a traumatic breakdown. Although Clarissa is the unifying consciousness of the novel, Septimus is her narrative double and bears much of the novel's ethical load. Septimus figures as a thorn in the flesh to the upper-class society that the Dalloways represent, a society whose thriving depends on the repression of the war it helped catalyze. Septimus bodies forth the psychic and social consequences of the war, while also undercutting the normative claim issued by the narration in the novel's opening passage, that "The War was over."[58] Septimus returns from the war and cannot assimilate into post-war British society. He moves about the streets of London reading the unfamiliar codes of the new world as evidence of an underlying horror. When a car engine backfires on the street and attracts a crowd of spectators, Septimus views the event as a sign of world-wide destruction: "This gradual drawing together of everything to one centre before his eyes, as if some horror had come almost to the surface and was about to burst into flames, terrified him. The world wavered and quivered and threatened to burst into flames."[59]

The motorcar episode turns on the problem of perception; Septimus's exacerbated consciousness, with its Paterian impressionism ("wavered" and "quivered"), is juxtaposed with the observations of other spectators, who wonder, for example, if the car contains the queen going shopping. The backfiring car is ultimately a cipher available for symbolization, an event that knits together the dispersed perspectives of a range of social types of post-war London. Woolf's supple free indirect style showcases an ability to move among distinct points of view; between an intensely isolated consciousness, like Septimus's, and a more public consciousness mediated by objects and events.

Scholars of free indirect style emphasize its ability to offer the intimacy of a first-person perspective while retaining the distance of an observer. Franco Moretti sums up the style as "Emotions, plus distance," while D. A. Miller describes it as "the paradoxical form of an impersonal intimacy."[60] Herman Rapaport underscores these contradictions by describing free indirect discourse as "interiorized and private, though it appears objective and sharable enough."[61] Woolf's free indirect style permits us to enter the linguistic and psychological reality of Septimus, a shell-shocked soldier, while preserving the omniscient voice that can enlarge the frame, offer more objective description, and shift to other points of view. When we first encounter Septimus, we are offered a distant, generalizing description that becomes increasingly specific: "aged about thirty, pale-faced, beak-nosed, wearing brown shoes and a shabby overcoat, with hazel eyes which had that look of apprehension in them which makes complete strangers apprehensive too."[62] From the outside, Septimus looks "queer," dressed in a "shabby overcoat," staring into the distance, and mumbling to himself. Septimus's queerness suggests a lack of fit with his surroundings, a dissonance that engages issues of sexuality, class, and disability, while also reinforcing society's rejection of his war experience. As the narration turns inward through the machinations of free indirect discourse, the reader is exposed to Septimus's tormented inner landscape with its haunting images of persecution: "The world has raised its whip; where will it descend?"[63] Septimus's interiority, dominated by refrains of poetic ecstasy and agony, is filled with hallucinations ("faces laughing at him, calling him horrible disgusting names, from the walls, and hands pointing round the screen"), and delusions, as Septimus thinks of himself as a prophet "called forth in advance of the mass of men to hear the truth."[64]

The linguistic descriptions of his hallucinations and delusions, and the lyrical prose attributed to his thought, suggest the construction of a self-conscious and poeticized shell shock rather than a fidelity to clinical accounts of the condition. Septimus's alienation is a poetic construction: He is described as "an outcast who gazed back at the inhabited regions, who lay like a drowned sailor, on the shore of the world."[65] Because his experience at war is incommensurable with that of other characters in the novel, and because he is thoroughly distanced from the ruling-class ideology represented by the Dalloways and their clique, Septimus is positioned as the novel's most penetrating social observer. As Rebecca Walkowitz points out, there is a tacit analogy between Septimus's symptoms (hallucinations, delusions, linguistic slips, sarcasm, poetic language, disordered thoughts) and the tactics of social critique that Woolf mobilizes.[66] Ulysses D'Aquila observes that Septimus's "moments of lucidity are revealed to be more penetrating and observant than the duller awareness of his wife and doctors."[67] Septimus is positioned as an observant outsider who has lost the ability to communicate with those on the inside.

The parallels between Woolf's life and Septimus's are intriguing, and Woolf scholars have looked to *Mrs. Dalloway* for the reflections on illness and trauma that are missing in her diaries and letters. Some of her biographers have viewed the doctors in *Mrs. Dalloway* as satirical assemblages of the doctors Leonard consulted about Virginia's mental health, namely George Savage, Theo Hyslop, Henry Head, and Maurice Craig.[68] Like the doctors in *Mrs. Dalloway*, many of these figures were conservative and authoritarian, and reluctant to empathize with their patients.[69] But despite the autobiographical overtones of the novel, we can also recognize the generic and historical specificity of its representation of war trauma. If *Mrs. Dalloway* measures the status of madness as modernist trope, it refers to a historically specific traumatic illness produced by the war and to a heightened literary madness adapted to the formal and thematic concerns of the modernist moment. It is an illness irreducible to Woolf's own experience and one that must be treated on its own terms, as well as in relationship to other cultural representations of shell shock that appeared during and after World War I. Like other modernists, Woolf identified war trauma as a crucible for investigations of consciousness; she is reputed to have visited Siegfried Sassoon after the war and modeled Septimus's experiences on Sassoon's. Several writers of Woolf's acquaintance, including Sassoon and Rebecca West, pre-empted Woolf in the formal representation of shell shock, but Woolf's well-known battles with mental illness have tended to efface a critical awareness of the extent to which she was writing within an emerging subgenre of literature. Mrs. Dalloway is the clearest example of Woolf's engagement with mental illness as formal subject, and it is also her most forceful indictment of the medical establishment and the modern practice of psychiatry.

The doctor-patient dynamics in Mrs. Dalloway are structured by stark asymmetries of power. Dr. Holmes is a general practitioner averse to psychological understanding, who, as part of the machinery of repression, tells Septimus that there is nothing the matter with him and that he must take an interest in things outside himself: "he brushed it all aside—headaches, sleeplessness, fears, dreams—nerve symptoms and nothing more, he said."[70] Dr. Holmes encourages distractions, such as trips to the music hall, and reminds Septimus that mental health is "largely a matter in our own control," a statement that condenses turn-of-the century moralistic attitudes to mental illness.[71] Holmes shifts responsibility from social and institutional factors onto Septimus, whom Holmes accuses of malingering. Dr. Holmes' dismissal of Septimus's psychic pain—"there was nothing the matter with him"—becomes an incantatory refrain of the narrative, paired in ironic juxtaposition to overwhelming evidence of Septimus's suffering. The narration emphasizes the disproportionality of Septimus's and Holmes' perspectives: While Septimus internalizes responsibility for his role in the war, considering "the sins for which human nature had condemned him to death," Holmes assesses the worth of Septimus's belongings, presumably to assume control of the estate once Septimus has been forcibly incarcerated. Holmes is figured as predatory, "the repulsive brute, with the blood-red nostrils," the incarnation for Septimus of the dark human instincts that produced the war.[72] The refrain "Holmes is on me" metaphorizes Septimus's perceived powerlessness in relation to Holmes, whose very name evokes the threat of institutionalization.[73]

Septimus is sent next to the Harley Street nerve specialist Sir William Bradshaw, "the priest of science," a pompous bullying figure and member of the upper class who attributes Septimus's symptoms to "a lack of proportion."[74] Both Holmes and Bradshaw become disciplinary figures within the narrative, concerned with efforts of normalization and regulation, part of a professional field of psychological governance rooted in the figure of the expert—a figure Woolf subjects to withering scrutiny. Bradshaw "ascertain[s] in two or three minutes" the severity of Septimus's condition and explains to Septimus's wife that he must be sent to a "home" for a rest cure:

> It was merely a question of rest, said Sir William; of rest, rest, rest;
> a long rest in bed. There was a delightful home down in the country

where her husband would be perfectly looked after. Away from her? She asked. Unfortunately, yes; the people we care for most are not good for us when we are ill. But he was not mad, was he? Sir William said he never spoke of "madness"; he called it not having a sense of proportion. But her husband did not like doctors. He would refuse to go there. Shortly and kindly Sir William explained to her the state of the case. He had threatened to kill himself. There was no alternative. It was a question of law. He would lie in bed in a beautiful house in the country.[75]

Bradshaw's unwillingness to name Septimus's illness or its connection to the war suggests an adherence to comfortable meanings that deliberately obscure the root causes and affective intensities of Septimus's experience. With predictable evasiveness, Bradshaw describes his treatment for Septimus in the euphemistic language of English upper-class domesticity. As Rebecca Walkowitz observes, Sir William's discourse is dominated by euphemism, which "translates intense experiences into language that is habitual and therefore invisible"; thereby making "words mean as little as possible."[76] The fact that Sir William's asylum cannot be represented—that euphemism marks the limits of its representation—does not mitigate the impact of its disciplinary and carceral force; on the contrary, Bradshaw's account of his asylum as a "delightful home down in the country" belies a reality linked to other forms of oppression represented in the novel. Indeed, the "beautiful house in the country" is hardly a comforting space for Clarissa, who is haunted by hazy flashbacks of her adolescent home at Bourton. Through Clarissa's memories, we see Bourton lorded over by a domineering father and an aunt whose predilection for pressing flowers beneath dictionaries suggests an atmosphere of repression, especially for women. A symbol of the violence of heteropatriarchy rather than the romance of the pastoral, the country house is where Clarissa's erotic bond with Sally Seton is prematurely ruptured and where Clarissa's sister dies from a falling tree, seemingly due to the neglect of the father. Bourton's eventual entailment upon a male relative reinforces its status as a site of masculine privilege.

Sir William Bradshaw's "beautiful house in the country" implicitly reterritorializes bourgeois norms by reproducing the family structure, a structure in which Bradshaw is father and authority figure and Septimus is obedient child. The "beautiful house in the country" is symbolic of the "prestige of patriarchy" that Foucault describes in *Madness and Civilization*, a patriarchy that disciplines and orders, and of a compulsory heterosexuality against which Septimus and Clarissa attempt to rebel.[77] Rather than offer lines of escape from social pressures and obligations, Bradshaw's asylum reinforces social hierarchies by placing unruly members of society under the thumb of patriarchal authority. With its power to segregate the sane from the insane, the conforming from the deviant, and to subject those deemed unfit or "queer" to the normalizing pressures of the dominant culture, Bradshaw's asylum figures as the institutional equivalent of his theory of "proportion," another euphemism that strategically masks the disciplinary effects of his power.

When Rezia tells Sir William Bradshaw that Septimus will refuse the asylum, Bradshaw threatens compulsory confinement and evokes the full disciplinary power of the law: "It was a question of law" the narration tells us, in Bradshaw's voice. Septimus fights for British law abroad and then returns, traumatized, and is threatened as a potential lawbreaker—which effectively occludes the state's role in his condition. Bradshaw's imperatives are short and declarative and highlight the discourse of authority ("he must be taught to rest"). The narration then shifts to a more distant and ironic mode to accomplish a withering critique of Bradshaw: "Worshipping proportion, Sir William not only prospered himself but made England prosper, secluded her lunatics, forbade childbirth, penalized despair, made it impossible for the unfit to propagate their views until they, too, shared his sense of proportion. . . . Sir William with his thirty years' experience of these kinds of cases, and his infallible instinct, this is madness, this sense; his sense of proportion."[78]

The long sentences here, different in quality from the short declarative sentences of the previous quotation, are satirical in their effect: Bradshaw's list of accomplishments (excessive and brutal) give the sense of someone losing their grip. If the term "proportion" suggests a kind of rational or balanced approach to the problem of mental health, the narration reveals it to be a euphemism for a regime of punishment against the socially "unfit," from whom he profits. As a social theory, proportion implies normativity, rationality, order, uniformity; it demands compliance and submission from those deemed unfit. As Molly Hite points out, Bradshaw's law of proportion connotes a type of "assimilation into socially restricted, 'normal' classifications of thought and feeling," of which Bradshaw, as the man of science and reason, is the supreme embodiment.[79] For Rebecca Walkowitz proportion is a "system of representation" that denies "individuality and antagonism" and polices the boundaries of thought.[80] Proportion's narrative equivalent is the official time of Big Ben, which disrupts the fluid internal experience of the characters with its insistence on official time: "The clocks . . . counseled submission, upheld authority, and pointed out in chorus the supreme advantages of a sense of proportion."[81] As a means of excluding competing perspectives, Bradshaw's law of proportion is antagonistic to Woolf's strategies of representation, which privilege a multiplicity of perspectives that overlap, qualify, and ironize one another. With its perspectival complexity and decentered point of view, Woolf's narration undermines Bradshaw's creed of absolutes to make way for a more nuanced and flexible portrait of human experience. Walkowitz is correct to point out that while Woolf constructs a critique of euphemism, such as that perpetrated by Bradshaw, she also critiques literalism, "which proposes that there is only one, objective experience to present."[82] The German-American tutor Miss Kilman, whom Clarissa loathes for her influence over her daughter, provides a qualification to Bradshaw's absolute views: "there were people who did not think the English invariably right. . . . There were other points of view."[83] While initially defined through Bradshaw's perspective, "proportion" is reabsorbed by the narration, which works outward, expanding its definition:

> But proportion has a sister, less smiling, more formidable . . . in the heat and sands of India, the mud and swamp of Africa, the purlieus of London. . . . Conversion is her name and she feasts on the wills of the weakly, loving to impress, to impose, adoring her own features stamped on the face of the populace. At Hyde Park Corner on a tub she stands preaching; shrouds herself in white and walks penitentially disguised as brotherly love through factories and parliaments; offers help, but desires power; smites out of her way roughly the dissident, or dissatisfied.[84]

Through this extended metaphor, Woolf makes it clear that Bradshaw's social theory has its complement in imperialism, religious conversion, and reform—which she views as analogous modes of domination that are more subtle and cunning. Woolf genders "conversion" female to suggest that the work of moralizing, Christianizing, and converting so often assigned to women are underestimated as forms of power. Instead, the ironic narration exposes the egotism and lust for domination beneath the façade of social uplift. Woolf's critique becomes more abstract and complex as it creates connections among Bradshaw's version of psychiatry and the civilizing mission and social reform Britain practices at home and abroad.

The novel ultimately suggests that psychiatry and psychology are part of a larger patriarchal and militaristic regime that restricts dissent and promotes uniformity of thought and behavior. Rather than mitigate the effects of war, such apparatuses perpetrate a second form of warfare by encouraging soldiers to repress their experiences: It is no coincidence, therefore, that the encounters with doctors in *Mrs. Dalloway* are described as military operations, as invasions from which Septimus must defend himself. The doctors in *Mrs. Dalloway* care little for the enclosures that delimit private space: They burst through doors and topple Septimus's wife to get to him. If Woolf romanticizes illness at times, she also positions the shell-shocked Septimus as the character most vulnerable to social control, the figure whose autonomy is most compromised. The more Septimus resists the authority of doctors and nerve specialists, the more these figures enlarge their sphere of influence.

Critics have cited Foucault as a useful context for interpreting Woolf's writings, despite the obvious anachronism, differences in methodology, and Foucault's contested historiography. Foucault's work suggests that modern psychiatry creates docile subjects, by refusing to acknowledge the validity of mad speech or by reducing madness to silence.[85] In *Madness and Civilization* (1964), Foucault argues that in the modern era madness becomes the target of intervention of certain kinds of power; under the sign of humanitarian treatment of mental illness, insanity is forced to yield to the truth of its unreasonableness. In Foucault's terms: "Health must lay siege to madness and conquer it in the very nothingness in which the disease is imprisoned."[86] Such language resonates with Woolf's descriptions of medical and psychiatric intervention: Both Foucault and Woolf analogize medical treatment and warfare—the medical apparatus not only derives its power from the state, it also borrows the military tactics of warfare in attacking its own citizens as internal enemies.[87]

Holmes and Bradshaw receive the full force of Woolf's critique with little of the complexity she reserves for other figures. The narration preserves the maximum distance from the points of view occupied by these two figures, for neither of them possess the complexity or emotional depth that are, for Woolf, the hallmarks of character. Bradshaw rivals Holmes in his snobbery and ruthlessness, and desire to "impress" his will on others. The description of Bradshaw as a predatory bird captures the dynamics of uneven power: "Naked, defenseless, the exhausted, the friendless received the impress of Sir William's will. He swooped: he devoured. He shut people up."[88] The swift brutality of the sentences highlights Bradshaw's brutality toward the most vulnerable using the weapons of his profession and class; he both suspends freedom and stops communication in its tracks: "He shut people up." Bradshaw profits from confining patients to the asylums he runs, invoking law as a coercive measure. The scathing portrait of Bradshaw expands to encompass the economic logic of psychiatry and institutionalization, as Bradshaw's exploitation of the mentally ill is connected to national prosperity: "Sir William not only prospered himself but made England prosper."[89]

Bradshaw's brand of eugenic psychiatry, the kind to which Woolf herself was subjected, emphasizes segregation of the mentally ill ("secluded her lunatics"), and compulsory sterilization ("forbade childbirth"), as forms of social hygiene. Rather than view mental illness as existing on a continuum of human experience, Bradshaw enforces a discontinuity model, enacting a rigid divide between sanity and insanity. The novel dramatizes the way both doctors invalidate Septimus's perspective on his own illness. The cruelty of their brute scientific opinion is echoed in Septimus's ironic refrain, conveyed to us through free indirect discourse—"One must be scientific, above all."[90] Like an introjected command, the statement emerges as a check on Septimus's more dissident impulses, while underscoring the failure of sympathy and comprehension on the part of his doctors. In his most agentive yet self-destructive act, Septimus takes his life before he can be committed against his will by Holmes. Septimus and Rezia destroy Septimus's writings before they can be used as evidence for institutionalization and as a final attempt to preserve the authorial act and the intimate space of the soul from the violations of the clinical gaze.

In the middle of her party Clarissa learns of Septimus's suicide. She is unnerved by the irruption of death, which seems inappropriate to the nature of the event and threatens to destabilize her social poise. Clarissa is a society hostess giving a party, yet she intuits Septimus's suffering better than the trained professionals in her midst. To Holmes, the suicide is an act of cowardice, but to Clarissa it is an act of resistance: "A thing there was that mattered; a thing, wreathed about with chatter, defaced, obscured in her own life, let drop every day in corruption, lies, chatter. This he had preserved. Death was defiance. Death was an attempt to communicate."[91] Clarissa's attempt to communicate with Septimus across the boundaries of class and gender, life and death, sanity and insanity, offers a vivid contrast to Bradshaw's efforts to "shut people up." Clarissa identifies the loss of something essential in herself with what Septimus has preserved through death.[92] The ambiguity of the "thing" to which she alludes, signals, at one level, the incommensurability of thought and language, and on another level, the dissonance between one's essential self and the self that is constructed from outside by others, "wreathed about with chatter." Woolf prioritizes linguistic vagueness here not only to reinforce the limits of what can be articulated about the self, but to affirm something irreducible and unknown about it that neither language nor narrative can resolve.[93] Woolf's efforts to render the self mysterious in language reflects not only an urge to protect the vulnerable private self but also a hesitation about the capacity of the self to be fully represented.

The reader may speculate about what defiance might mean for Clarissa: the repudiation of marriage and domesticity, the rejection of ruling-class privilege and its attendant forms of blindness, the surrender of the persona of the "perfect hostess," the resumption of the kinds of queer passions that motivated her youth. But broader forms of defiance are also implied in the dilations the novel makes: the defiance of patriarchy, dogma, blind patriotism, national triumphalism, and official truths of all kinds. In an act of sympathetic extension not unlike authorship itself, Clarissa intuits Septimus's motivations for suicide:

> Or there were the poets and thinkers. Suppose he had had that passion, and had gone to Sir William Bradshaw, a great doctor yet to her obscurely evil, without sex or lust, extremely polite to women, but capable of some indescribable outrage—forcing your soul, that was it—if this young man had gone to him, and Sir William had impressed him, like that, with his power, might he not then have said (indeed she felt it now), Life is made intolerable; they make life intolerable, men like that?[94]

Clarissa suspects that Septimus has ended his life to protect his soul from the violations of Sir William Bradshaw. Where Bradshaw and Holmes have been indifferent to Septimus's suffering, Clarissa, an untrained yet sympathetic observer has managed a feat of sympathetic imagination with a person she has never met: "she felt somehow very like him—the young man who had killed himself."[95] Once again, the terms of the problem are distinctly gendered: Medicine and psychology are affiliated with a domineering patriarchy and a chauvinism that refuses to allow for different points of view, whereas Clarissa's consciousness has the power to recognize commonality across difference. This is not to say that Clarissa has not been blind to difference before: Her class horizons and ideology of femininity have prevented her from empathizing with a figure like Miss Kilman. But at moments in the novel, Clarissa's interiority expands to assimilate the thoughts and feelings of other characters. Through the machinations of Woolf's aesthetic, Septimus and Clarissa merge the distant spheres of war and home, male and female, madness and sanity, upper and lower class. Clarissa's ability to empathize with Septimus provides an ethical model of attention that challenges the vertical and violating interactions between Septimus and his doctors.

Defending the Soul

Intuiting the foul play behind Septimus's suicide, Clarissa suspects Bradshaw of committing "some indescribable outrage—forcing your soul, that was it."[96] Here the "soul" connotes a private realm of selfhood that might be called interiority, with its implied spatial connotations, that if *forced* (forced open? as Dr. Holmes does Septimus's bedroom door) renders the subject vulnerable, exposed, violated. Woolf understands the soul to be the most profound and essential part of the self, and it is something quite different from what she calls "personality," the outer shell of a person that is shaped by social expectations and pressures. For Woolf, reductive and totalizing approaches to the soul were typical of a masculine "intelligence" that insisted upon the rational analysis of complex emotional experience.

Reviving the antiquated, spiritualized signifier—the soul—constitutes one tactic in Woolf's resistance to the assaultive masculine stratagems of the human sciences. Woolf presents the soul as embattled, encroached upon by the forces of modernity; but she imagines for literature a more aestheticized and less ethically suspect approach to the soul. In place of the psychical apparatus designated by Freud, Woolf revives and repurposes the soul as that which resists analysis. I use the word "soul" intentionally, rather than psyche, personality, subjectivity, or consciousness, not because "soul" has more semantic stability—indeed it seems to have less—but because of its strategic use by Woolf and Lawrence, who find in it a less reductive, more spiritualized remnant of a tradition in which the self was less vulnerable to demystification. Woolf and Lawrence use the term in a quasi-spiritual, yet modern secular fashion to challenge what William James called the "medical materialism" of psychology. In his rival version of the unconscious, which he opposes to the cauldron of repressed energies that is the Freudian unconscious, Lawrence demonstrates his commitment to a mystical tradition of the soul by defining it as a life-giving, creative force that resists comprehension. For Lawrence, the soul is synonymous with the unconscious; it is "the essential unique nature of every individual creature, which is, by its very nature, unanalyzable, undefinable, inconceivable."[97] The repetition of negative modifiers performs the work of defending the soul from the positivist procedures of analysis that he identified with psychoanalysis.

In Woolf's essay "The Russian Point of View" (1925), the soul becomes a rich source of metaphor. She uses tropes of liquidity and flooding to capture the "mixed" and mingling nature of the soul and its inability to be "restrained" by language or the body: "Whoever you are, you are the vessel of this perplexed liquid, this cloudy, yeasty, precious stuff, the soul. The soul is not restrained by barriers. It overflows, it floods, it mingles with the souls of others. . . . Out it tumbles upon us, hot, scalding, mixed, marvelous, terrible, oppressive—the human soul."[98]

The soul here is something not just intra- but also inter-psychic, in that it provides a figure for the transpersonal exchanges and boundary crossings that unite individuals into a broader human continuum. Woolf imagines an intersubjective consciousness that undermines Enlightenment ideas of a bounded, coherent subject. The soul evokes a collective sense of being with otherness, rather than a representation of the egoistic subject fortified by boundaries, real or imagined.

The soul is therefore a terrain on which Woolf's dispute with Freudian psychoanalysis is waged, insofar as Woolf purports to defend the sanctity of the inner life, as well as the soul of the aesthetic, from the interventions of psychoanalysis and psychiatry. Both Woolf and Freud presuppose at some level a transcendent or ahistorical soul. For Michel Foucault, however, the modern "soul" is far from an uncontaminated essence or *a priori* identity, but the very product of those discourses of enlightenment—medical, psychological, juridical, sociological—that have secured its domination. Far from its mystical nature, the soul is, for Foucault, "the effect and instrument of a political anatomy; the soul is the prison of the body."[99] The soul is the locus of the operations of discrete, non-corporal, forms of discipline and punishment:

> It would be wrong to say that the soul is an illusion, or an ideological effect. On the contrary, it exists, it has a reality, it is produced permanently around, on, within the body by the functioning of a power that is exercised on those punished—and, in a more general way, on those one supervises, trains and corrects, over madmen, children at home and at school, the colonized, over those who are stuck at a machine and supervised for the rest of their lives. This is the historical reality of this soul, which, unlike the soul represented by Christian theology, is not born in sin and subject to punishment, but is born rather out of methods of punishment, supervision and constraint.[100]

To Clarissa's horror at the methods of modern medicine and psychiatry, "forcing your soul, that was it," Foucault would respond that the soul is *always already* forced, that it does not preempt the modern disciplines like psychoanalysis and psychiatry but rather comes into being through the very technologies of these disciplines. In *The History of Sexuality*, Foucault argues that psychoanalysis constructs and governs the soul by way of its therapeutic practice of extracting knowledge through confession. Interestingly, Foucault attributes to modern literature a similar disciplinary function when he describes it as "ordered according to the infinite task of extracting from the depths of oneself, in between the words, a truth which the very form of the confession holds out like a shimmering image."[101] Modern literature is simply one extension of "our modern confessing society," where the confession reflects a search for the fundamental relation to the true.[102] While many early twentieth-century writers yearned to differentiate their work from psychoanalytic ideas, Foucault sees little distinction between the two, as both he claims are invested in a process of confession in which buried truths await their extraction.

We might use Foucault's argument about the similarities between the modern disciplines and modern literature to locate other affinities between Woolf and Freud. Woolf is eager to preserve the integral mystery of the soul from the invasive practices of the modern disciplines, especially psychoanalysis and psychiatry. Yet she is also reliant on formal strategies that access submerged parts of the self. For example, the spontaneous flow of sympathy between Clarissa to Septimus after Septimus's death, an ethical extension across psychic and bodily boundaries, is central to Woolf's structural and ethical vision for the novel. The moments of overlapping consciousness between Clarissa and Septimus evoke Freud's uncanny, which he describes at one point as "the spontaneous transmission of mental processes from one of these persons to the other—what we would call telepathy—so that the one becomes co-owner of the other's knowledge, emotions, and experience."[103] *Mrs. Dalloway* is clearly interested in the problem of other minds; yet such acts of sympathetic extension rely on a narrator who, among other feats, can manipulate the borders of consciousness and lay bare the exquisite interiorized pain of a character like Septimus. Through the machinations of free indirect style, the narrator enters the mind of the character and reports the character's thoughts in the character's own language. In his reading of the novel, J. Hillis Miller describes Woolf's narrator as a "state of mind" which exists outside of the characters and of which the characters are unaware. This "state of mind . . . surrounds them, encloses them, pervades them, knows them from within."[104] Anna Snaith points out: "Although Woolf's narrators have access to the characters' private thoughts, they rarely reveal their own. Her narrators are public in their anonymity."[105] Woolf's narrators illuminate characters from within, reveal inner thoughts and feelings, and excavate memories and desires, while remaining invisible themselves—a structural position not unlike that of the psychoanalyst. Indeed, with their simultaneous capacity for intimacy and distance, Woolf's narrators frequently display the asymmetrical dynamics of the analyst. But an important distinction remains: Woolf's narrators do not seek to resolve the mystery of the characters they describe, as the analyst might decipher the mystery of the patient's psychoneurosis. Rather, Woolf's free indirect style offers a glimpse of the deep psychology of its characters without mastering it, as psychoanalysis attempted.

Hillis Miller refers to Woolf's narration as a "disquieting mode of ventriloquism . . . a strange one-way interpersonal relationship."[106] When the narrator tells us that Clarissa, "had the oddest sense of being herself invisible; unseen; unknown" we experience a sense of intimacy with a character at her most isolated.[107] The line also has an ironic charge given that the narration allows us to *see* and *know* Clarissa on an intimate level without her knowledge of us. In Hillis Miller's view, Woolf's narrator penetrates the surface, surveils, ventriloquizes, and comments on the thoughts, beliefs, attitudes, and perceptions of characters who are otherwise unaware of the narrator's presence. While the stakes are certainly different in the world of the novel, we might note the resemblances between Woolf's narrator and Freud's analyst as figures who are both intimate and anonymous, proximate and distant. We recall Freud's statement that "for the patient the doctor should remain, opaque, and, like a mirror surface, should show nothing but what is shown to him."[108]

Mrs. Dalloway establishes an interpersonal (indeed inter-psychic) exchange between Clarissa and Septimus that challenges the vertical interactions of doctor and patient, even though her narration produces, on a formal level, some of the asymmetries of the psychoanalytic scenario, namely an uneven distribution of knowledge among narrator, character, and reader. Woolf's narrator is like the analyst in being the figure most *knowing* and the least *known*; but the narrator does not attempt to solve the complexity of a figure like Clarissa, and indeed Clarissa remains somewhat of a mystery, while the same might not be said of the patients of Freud's case studies. Woolf's struggle to defend the sanctity of inner life was consonant with her efforts to model imaginative sympathy across psychic and bodily boundaries; yet she struggled with how to represent intimacy with others in ethical ways.

Rapprochement and Revision

In 1936 Woolf appeared to surrender her twenty-year resistance to Freudian psychoanalysis by helping to collect the signatures of writers and artists presented to Freud as an eightieth birthday gift, a gift that paid tribute to his influence on art and literature. Thomas Mann, who offered a speech at the event, declared it "the first official meeting between the two spheres," a belated "acknowledgment and demonstration of the relationship" between literature and psychoanalysis.[109] Three years later, in January of 1939, Virginia and Leonard Woolf would visit Freud at his house in north London, where he was living with his daughter, Anna, after fleeing Nazi-controlled Vienna. This was the first time the Woolfs had met Freud after years of publishing his works with the Hogarth Press.[110] Freud famously gave Woolf a narcissus, a gesture that has generated endless speculation about what Freud assumed about Woolf's character.[111]

A month prior to this encounter, we learn from Woolf that she is "gulping up Freud," surprising language given her prior renunciations.[112] Rather than handling Freud's manuscripts, or dumping them on the floor, she begins to incorporate his ideas—a much more intimate relation. The concept Woolf is most eager to embrace at this point in her life is "ambivalence," which she applies to her conflicting emotions about returning to London: "Two days in London: a great distraction; leaving my mind in a torn state, which I record, being all of a muzz . . . I dislike this excitement, yet enjoy it. Ambivalence as Freud calls it."[113] The concept is not new to Woolf, and it seems to characterize much of her thinking at the time about war and death, and her relationship to a discourse that she had long perceived as alien to her work as an author. She records her ambivalence to Freud in her diary: "Freud is upsetting; reducing one to whirlpool; & I daresay truly. If we're all instinct, the unconscious, what's all this about civilization, the whole man, freedom &c? . . . The falseness of loving one's neighbours. The conscience as censor. Hate . . . But I'm too mixed."[114] She says in a contemporaneous passage in *Moments of Being*, "It was only the other day when I read Freud for the first time, that I discovered that this violently disturbing conflict of love and hate is a common feeling; and is called ambivalence."[115]

The texts Woolf selects as her belated introduction to Freud, *Future of an Illusion, Civilization and Its Discontents, Group Psychology and the Analysis of the Ego,* and *The Ego and the Id,* have explanatory power for her as she struggles to come to terms with the resumption of war and the aggressive instincts that lay behind it. As Sanja Bahun points out, such reading would have underscored that human nature is marked by ambivalence and the human subject is fragmented and heterogeneous with itself.[116] We can see this concept make its way into Woolf's 1927 novel *To the Lighthouse*, specifically in Lily Briscoe's complex feelings toward the Ramsays: "Such was the complexity of things. For what happened to her, especially staying with the Ramsays, was to be made to feel violently two opposite things at the same time."[117] Yet Woolf is distressed by Freud's theory that we are ruled by unconscious forces, a view very much at odds with the forceful claims she makes the same year in *Three Guineas*, in which she declares that "men and women, here and now, are able to exert their wills; they are not pawns and puppets dancing on a string held by invisible hands. They can act, and think for themselves."[118] Woolf wants to replace instinct and drive with those conscious habits of reason and deliberate action that could disrupt the machinery of war; but as her diary suggests, she is also contemplating humankind's fascination with its own destruction as compelling evidence of a ghost in the machine.

In the early 1920s Woolf satirized psychoanalysis as an invasive method of reading the subject and a discourse threatening to reduce the complexity of fictional character to a clinical case study; but by the late 1930s she would come to acknowledge its affinities with her own creative process. In her autobiographical essay "A Sketch of the Past" (1939), Woolf admits that *To the Lighthouse*, as a fictional tribute to her late parents, resembled the narrative of the psychoanalytic patient who has purged emotion through personal testimony:

> Then one day walking round Tavistock Square I made up, as I sometimes make up my books, *To the Lighthouse,* in a great, apparently involuntary, rush. One thing burst into another. . . . I wrote the book very quickly; and when it was written, I ceased to be obsessed by my mother. I no longer hear her voice; I do not see her.
> I supposed that I did for myself what psycho-analysts do for their patients. I expressed some very long felt and deeply felt emotion. And in expressing it I explained it and then laid it to rest."[119]

Acknowledging the therapeutic potential of fiction, Woolf sees the novel's completion as a catharsis. *To the Lighthouse* (1927), with its narrative remediation of the Oedipal triangle and its therapeutic reworking of traumatic memories, might be considered a fiction of the sort she condemns in "Freudian Fiction." As Julia Briggs reminds us, both Freud and Woolf "would draw on their memories of life in nineteenth-century, educated, middle-class, patriarchal families as a way of understanding themselves and their society."[120] In its opening pages, *To the Lighthouse* plunges its reader into the vexed dynamics of family life, which as many critics have remarked, evoke the Oedipal tensions that Freud described as the "nucleus of all neuroses."[121] Father and six-year-old son are in an emotional standoff over a trip to the lighthouse while mother tries to mediate between the two opponents. James, the son, longs for a phallic weapon to challenge his all-powerful father: "Had there been an axe handy, a poker, or any weapon that would have gashed a hole in his father's breast and killed him, there and then, James would have seized it. Such were the extremes of emotion that Mr. Ramsay excited in his children's breasts by his mere presence. . . ."[122] In Lacanian terms, Mr. Ramsay's stark "No" to his son, James, could be viewed as an invocation of the law of the father, while the mother's "Yes" evokes the son's unconscious longing for unity with the mother, which is seemingly ruptured in this dramatic scene. In the third section of the novel, the Oedipal triangle reassembles for the next generation, with Cam taking her mother's place as a mediator in the father-son rivalry. Such fraught dynamics are framed by a narrator who sounds at times distinctly like an analyst explaining a son's rivalry with his forbidding father and a daughter who assumes the role of surrogate mother and struggles with her own gender difference. Time and distance allow for subtle shifts in perspective, but the agon between James and Mr. Ramsay continues as James, once a rebel against tyranny, comes to assume the phallic authority of the father. Clearly, Woolf and Freud were aligned in viewing the experiences of childhood as vital to subject formation and in viewing parental relationships as models for future relationships. The episode that takes place between James and his mother in part one of the novel, "The Window," could be read as staging, in Lacanian terms, the desire for "oneness" or unity with the mother (who is "fringed with joy," like James's cut-outs) and whose future absence in part three, "The Lighthouse," signifies a loss of oneness that is also an entry point into the symbolic order.

As a novel of recollection, reworking, and revision, *To the Lighthouse* reveals its structural and thematic affinities with psychoanalytic theory. While part one contends with the nuanced dynamics of family life; part three follows the return of the characters to the house ten years after Mrs. Ramsay's death to reckon with her ghost. In the words of Maud Ellmann, the Oedipal crisis that Mrs. Ramsay's death produces forces the characters "to realign their own positions in relation to the absent mother."[123] Each of the characters attempt to rework and reframe the past and wrestle with its hold on the present. Mr. Ramsay takes his children to the lighthouse in a belated tribute to his late wife; Lily recreates her painting and finally completes it as she reimagines her relationship to Mrs. Ramsay. The novel's temporality is recursive: the past is never fully past, only reworked and repeated. Though Woolf denied reading psychoanalysis before writing the novel, we might argue that a "Freudish" culture had worked its way into the text.

The potency of psychoanalysis in the early twentieth century palpated its way into the most reluctant modernists, but Woolf and Auden were clearly wrestling with its legacy in complex ways. Woolf, ever reluctant to master the souls of her characters, made it narratively possible to access the depths of character while preserving the elusive core of the self. The chapter that follows shows Auden wrestling with the normalizing pressures of the medical establishment and orthodox psychoanalysis, challenging the objectification of dissident sexualities. By the early 1930s, Auden turns to a more heterodox model of lay analysis, which envisioned a future in which subjects were liberated from the scourge of repression. As with Woolf, Auden does not categorically dismiss Freud's theories as idiosyncratically reimagined them.

3

The Heterodox Psychology and Queer Poetics of Auden in the 1930s

> if often he was wrong and at times absurd,
> to us he is no more a person
> now but a whole climate of opinion,
> ... under whom we conduct our different lives ...
> —AUDEN, "IN MEMORY OF SIGMUND FREUD" (1939)

> What do you think about England, this country of ours
> where nobody is well?
> —AUDEN, THE ORATORS (1932)

Convinced that he inhabited a culture of illness—one rooted in war, fascism, a tyrannical conformism, and heteronormativity—Auden flirted with psychoanalysis and Marxism in the late 1920s and 1930s as potentially liberatory discourses, but was never fully convinced of the curative potential of either. Auden shared with Freud a passion for diagnosis, a passion no doubt fueled by the psychological and medical frameworks newly available for self-interrogation, those that, as Michel Foucault and Eve Kosofsky Sedgwick argue, had implications for homo/heterosexual definition in an era in which knowledge and sex had become conceptually inseparable from one another.[1] In his struggle to theorize his sexuality, which took place most pointedly at the level of his lyric poems, Auden engaged in a complex dialogue with available therapeutic discourses, including psychoanalysis, which he adopted with vigor in the 1920s as a critical hermeneutic. Critics such as Randall Jarrell, Richard Davenport-Hines, and Richard Bozorth have emphasized Freudian psychoanalysis as a context for interpreting Auden's prose and poetic production of this era, and for good reason: By his teens Auden was reading Freud and Jung and imagining a future career as an analyst.[2] By his college years he was assimilating psychoanalytic theory into his art, using its tropes of concealment and repression to construct encrypted high modernist poems. But by the late 1920s, after graduating from Oxford, Auden would discover other, rival psychologies that would become just as, if not more, influential to his own improvisational theories of illness, sexuality, and desire.[3]

During his ten-month visit to Berlin from October 1928 to July 1929—a watershed year for the young poet—Auden was introduced to a group of heterodox psychologists who offered him a new relationship to therapeutic discourse—at once unstable and idiosyncratic—which yielded novel ways of making sense of his sexuality. If psychoanalysis had informed both Auden's self-understanding and his poetics in his early years, he came to grasp its limitations as a mode of diagnosis and a vehicle to psychic, social, and sexual liberation. We can observe this shifting relationship to psychoanalysis in the aphoristic fragments of his 1929 Berlin journal: "The trouble with Freud is that he accepts conventional morality as if it were the only one."[4] It was in Berlin that Auden encountered the idiosyncratic teachings of John Layard, Homer Lane, and Georg Groddeck, thinkers who were, to varying degrees, influenced by and critical of psychoanalytic doctrine. The experience in Berlin expanded Auden's views, especially because it provided him a fuller range of psychological frameworks and vocabularies than those he had access to in England. Moreover, Weimar Berlin, with its thriving gay sub-culture and homophile activism, offered a context for recognizing the possibilities of gay self-affirmation and sexual pleasure.

Critics have viewed Auden's engagement with the psychologies of Lane, Layard, and Groddeck, and his earlier influence, D. H. Lawrence, as a passing idiosyncratic phase on the way to more serious and mature pursuits. The two primary influences, Lane and Layard, are treated intermittently and anecdotally in Auden criticism. For example, Peter Firchow burlesques Auden's "naïve" and "uncritical endorsement" of these figures as illustrative of Auden's penchant for the "silly" and the "not-so-good."[5] Peter Porter enjoins the reader of Auden "if not to ignore, then at least to discount the influence of such healers, early on, as Homer Lane and John Layard" with the explanation that the poet "knew how much trust to place in ex-cathedra rulings."[6]

We might wonder why Auden turned to the resources of psychology to articulate a nascent queer consciousness, especially as turn-of-the-century psychology has frequently been associated with the pathologization, stigmatization, and disciplinary management of queer subjects. But Auden's attraction to the views of these figures was fueled by their relative marginality and by the challenges they posed to conventional morality. Auden discovered in these amateur psychologists, situated outside the medical and psychiatric establishment, an enabling set of ideas that helped defamiliarize the codes of English sexual morality. Foucault's discussion of "reverse" discourse in *The History of Sexuality* is relevant to the way Auden repurposes psychological and psychoanalytic theories for a discourse of gay self-affirmation. Homosexuality, Foucault suggests, "begins to speak on its own behalf, to demand that its legitimacy or 'naturality' be acknowledged, often in the same vocabulary, using the same categories, by which it was medically disqualified."[7]

The dismissal of Lane, Layard, Groddeck, and Lawrence as eccentric thinkers or charlatans obscures the extent to which Auden's early poetics were inspired by the heady intellectual atmosphere that Berlin and these figures provided. John Layard, an English anthropologist living in Berlin for psychological treatment, would catalyze Auden's interest in these new psychologies, preaching an ethic of pleasure without guilt while advancing the commitment of his mentor, Homer Lane, to the curative power of uninhibited sexual expression. Lane's views were partly underwritten by the theories of Georg Groddeck, "that wild rebel in the Freudian camp,"[8] who practiced an extreme form of psychosomatic medicine based in the conviction that all physical maladies, from stomach pain to cancer, were caused by psychic and sexual inhibition. Auden also returned to the writings of D. H. Lawrence, who polemicized the dangers of excessive "mental consciousness" and directed his readers to live from their spontaneous centers of bodily consciousness. By the early 1930s Auden had assembled a group of relatively marginal psychologists who represented, in the words of Randall Jarrell, the "risky, sometimes unscientific, fertile and imaginative side of modern psychology."[9] Borrowing the cultural capital of Freud, these theorists promoted revisionist strains of psychoanalysis that challenged what Michael Warner calls "the ethics of sexual shame."[10]

By effacing the influence of these thinkers at this particular moment of Auden's self-fashioning as a gay poet, I argue, Firchow and Porter have perpetuated the practice of reading his poetry in a "universalizing" mode, of evacuating its queer content.[11] As Penny Farfan points out, "queer" in the modernist period could serve as a placeholder for the many ways one could be "odd or at odds" with the dominant culture.[12] Auden used "queer" as synonymous with gay and homosexual, while also deploying other coded and stigma-inflected terms, such as "crook" and "bugger" to refer to homosexuals.[13] But Auden's thirties poetry, I argue, anticipates some of queer theory's more contemporary registers, as it oscillates between a subversive critique of bourgeois sexual morality; a rejection of social, institutional, and disciplinary forms of homophobia; and a consciousness of queer experience as inflected by loss, stigma, and pathologization.[14] Reflecting the disjunctions and contradictions at the heart of understandings of same-sex desire, Auden's poetry of the late twenties and early thirties represents a crucial moment in queer history in which discourses of psychopathology comingle with an emergent queer critique of heteronormativity.

Auden's attempts to transpose the psychologies of Lane, Layard, Groddeck, and Lawrence into a politics of resistance and a discourse of queer legitimation finds expression in four of his poetic and prose experiments on which I will focus: the sonnet "Petition" (1929), the four-part pastoral poem "1929" (1929), the fragmented long poem in prose and verse, *The Orators: An English Study* (1932), and the extended light verse epistle "Letter to Lord Byron" (1937). Especially in "Letter to Lord Byron" Auden develops what he calls an "intuitive" and "homeopathic" poetics that challenges the "certain diagnosis" and "expertise" that he identified with the modern psychological disciplines. I read Auden's transitional modernist style of the 1930s as a turn toward a strategically amateurish mode of poetic commentary that preempts the need for expert critical intervention. Auden's contribution to queer literary history is not a progressive or reparative narrative, but an ongoing engagement with the stigmatizing discourses that helped shape his experience as a gay man.

Circumventing the Censor

Auden's early poems, composed between 1927 and 1933, are often painfully resistant to interpretation. Such resistance goes hand in hand with an encoding of queer desire and with a modernist poetics of difficulty that Auden carefully cultivated, and that was shaped, in part, by an interest in the hermeneutical methods of psychoanalysis. But unlike the promise of revealed meaning made possible through psychoanalytic interpretation, Auden's early poetry revels in ambiguous rhetorical situations and fugitive meanings. His comments on *The Orators*, generally regarded as his most obscure modernist production, are revealing in this light: "The spirit naturally chooses the difficult rather than the easy. It is so much more interesting. . . . This also accounts for the success of repression. Half the mind enjoys the difficulty of censoring, the other half of circumventing the censor."[15]

Auden articulates the libidinal pleasure generated for the poet both in censoring his meanings and evading the censoring gaze—and here censorship is invoked in a double sense: in the psychoanalytic context of a mechanism of psychic repression, and in the literary context of a prohibition against certain forms of disclosure. Auden's strategies of indirection may be a signature of queer poetics. But there is an excess difficulty in his lyrical and narrative poetry that goes beyond the strategies of indirection necessary for a coding of queer desire—an excess that speaks to a bravura play with symbol, syntax, and reference that Auden claims is so much more "interesting."

Auden's "games of knowledge"[16] with the reader include a refusal of return on the promise of secure meaning. Such refusal is part of the subversive strategies of his queer poetics. Rather than offer the reassurance of hermeneutic stability or secure diagnosis, the early poems generate an open-ended interpretive struggle that is intellectually and affectively unsettling. Read in the light of Sedgwick's theories of the closet, what she calls "the defining structure for gay oppression in this century,"[17] we can interpret such forms of poetic indirection as "pointed and performative,"[18] reliant for their charge on an equally potent and colluding ignorance demanded by the larger culture. In the early poetry, with its lexicon of coded figures and obscure allusions, same-sex desire is invisible to some readers and insistent to others. F. R. Leavis described Auden's early poetry as "immature" for its performance of excess difficulty; but such difficulty was arguably generated as much by social, cultural, and legal injunctions to conceal same-sex desire as it was by modernist aesthetic impulses. Nor are such impulses mutually exclusive: The urge to be difficult and oppositional gestures pointedly to the influence of queer thought and experience on modernism, and to the influence of modernism on queer thought and experience. As Heather Love has suggested, there is a historical fit between the emergence of modern categories of sexual identity and of literary modernism, for "the indeterminacy of *queer* seems to match the indeterminacy, expansiveness, and drift of the literary—particularly the experimental, oblique version most closely associated with modernist textual production."[19]

Reading modernist and queer modes of expression together, Piotr Gwiazda suggests that the attraction of poetic impersonality for queer poets such as Auden illustrates the difficulties of queer self-assertion in a homophobic culture.[20] For Gwiazda, the self-effacement or "egolessness" which comes across in Auden's early poetry reflects the rhetorical constraints on the queer poet in establishing a public poetic persona. While hardly reticent about sexuality to friends and acquaintances, Auden did not address same-sex desire openly in his early poetry. But readers conversant with the codes he deploys to represent same-sex desire will recognize, despite the frequent absence of the lyrical "I," a set of highly autobiographical references to Auden's own sexuality. The dedication to Stephen Spender, one of the figures in Auden's coterie, at the beginning of *The Orators* suggests the careful manipulations of secrecy and disclosure, the "balancing subterfuge"[21] that Auden performed in his poetry: "Private faces in public places / Are wiser and nicer / Than public faces in private places."[22] The punning epigraph not only constructs an audience with privileged access to the personal messages and double-meanings embedded in the poem, it functions as a set of instructions on how to read *The Orators*, as a poem that is not only *about* subterfuge, but is itself an extended form of subterfuge.

In his 1929 poem "A Free One," the queer subject is described as "poised between shocking falls, on razor-edge," having to perform a "balancing subterfuge / Of the accosting profile, the erect carriage."[23] The self-conscious poem both references and performs the subtle maneuverings required for the queer subject to pass. Auden's poetry likewise performs such "balancing subterfuge" to bypass the constraints of moral and legal censure. Full of doublespeak and obscurity, freighted with tropes of subterfuge and spying and an atmosphere of war and paranoia well suited to an interwar political climate in which queer subjects were frequently imagined as national subversives, the early poetry stages an incredibly sly art of encoding. The figure of the spy or secret agent, ubiquitous in Auden's early work, becomes an allegory not just for the poet who slips in and out of different contexts for the purposes of observation, but also for the queer subject whose only freedom lies in their ability to remain invisible. Or, if viewed as a composite figure in the Audenesque imaginary, the queer poet / secret agent is one who is deft both at reading and writing in code, although the trick is to be able to read and write in code without being read. The spy is always on the wrong side of the territorial border or is treated as an enemy within. He is alert to signals and signs that others fail to register.

Auden's unrhymed sonnet "Control of the passes" (1928), later titled "The Secret Agent" for the 1945 *Collected Poems*, constellates these various themes of subterfuge and loyalty, knowledge and ignorance, around a set of signs that the reader may or may not recognize as related to sexuality. The poem can be read as a meditation on queer experience, and more specifically, on the difficulties of communication for the queer poet:

> Control of the passes was, he saw, the key
> To this new district, but who would get it?
> He, the trained spy, had walked into the trap
> For a bogus guide, seduced by the old tricks.
>
> At Greenhearth was a fine site for a dam
> And easy power, had they pushed the rail
> Some stations nearer. They ignored his wires.
> The bridges were unbuilt and trouble coming.
>
> The street music seemed gracious now to one
> For weeks up in the desert. Woken by water
> Running away in the dark, he often had
> Reproached the night for a companion
> Dreamed of already. They would shoot, of course,
> Parting easily two that were never joined.[24]

As is the case with much of Auden's early poetry, "The Secret Agent" is available to both a minoritizing reading of same-sex desire and to a universalizing interpretation that is more conventionally modernist. The painfully unspecific content of the poem, including a reference to an ambiguous "Greenhearth," registers the kind of indeterminacy that is both a signature of modernist style and of queer writing. In a more conventionally modernist reading of the poem, Edward Mendelson describes it as "a masterpiece of dry foreboding" and emphasizes its themes of alienation. De-emphasizing the sexual overtones of the final verses describing parted lovers, he insists that "the division it concerns is not only sexual: it is *any* separation from unity or satisfaction."[25]

"Seduced" by a "bogus guide," the "trained spy" follows his instincts and is tricked into operating against his own best interests—such is "the trap" he finds himself in. The "trap" evokes Sedgwick's description of the closet as a "system of double binds systematically oppressing gay people, identities, and acts by undermining through contradictory constraints on discourse the grounds of their being,"[26] and the "erotic double binds that structure the infinite blackmailability of Western maleness through the leverage of homophobia."[27] This infinite danger of blackmail is reflected in the omnipresence of an enemy who is everywhere and nowhere at the same time. In the second quartet, the spy suffers the abandonment by his own side: "They ignored his wires." The verse describes failed communication, a particular concern for the poet who cannot communicate effectively to an audience. The third stanza is perhaps most revelatory of sexual desire, as the poetic speaker dreams of a companion but imagines the consequences of his actions: "They would shoot, of course / Parting easily two that were never joined." John Fuller's attention to the allusion made in these final verses to an Old English poem "Wulf and Eadwacer," which describes the "monologue of a captive woman addressed to her outlawed lover (she is on one island, he on another)" renders even more compelling a queer reading, given the intertextual echoes of an impossible love besieged by a hostile "they" willing to annihilate the lovers for an outlaw desire.[28]

Themes of intrigue, subterfuge, and encrypted desire in Auden's poetics must be viewed in connection to the forms of suppression and censorship that early twentieth-century gay poets confronted. Same-sex acts were criminalized by British authorities until 1967 and prosecuted in England beyond that date; the Wilde trial in England was succeeded by similar high-profile trials in Germany. The years when Auden composed the poetry that would be published first as a private edition by Stephen Spender in 1928 and then in commercial form by Faber in 1930 were also the years that saw the infamous *Ulysses* trials and the prosecution of Radcliffe Hall's *Well of Loneliness* (1928) for obscenity.[29] Auden could not print the word "bugger" in early editions of *The Orators*, where it appeared as *****. Such censorship may have even carried over to the most material aspects of composition, for the inscrutable nature of Auden's handwriting gestures to the resistive writing strategies he deployed. Scholars eager to plumb Auden's largely unpublished Berlin notebook to reconstruct the activities and ideas that preoccupied him during the time will be hard pressed to string together full sentences and will likely defer to Edward Mendelson's helpful transcriptions of brief sections of the notebook in *The English Auden*. As Gregory Woods puts it, Auden was sexually frank but also "aware of the need for strategic discretion."[30]

Auden's 1953 poem, "The Truest Poetry is the Most Feigning," with its Wildean paradox in the title, offers instructions for the poet on how to discuss same-sex desire while bypassing the constraints of the censor: "Be subtle, various, ornamental, clever, / And do not listen to those critics ever."[31] Such verses suggest that the poetry in which queer subjects dare to talk about desire and love is by necessity the most dissimulating. To read these poems with the consciousness of censorship is, as Bozorth points out, to acknowledge that "meaning is initiated and elaborated in social networks and institutions where truth is very much a matter of what is speakable."[32]

Self-Diagnosis and Resistive Reading

In "Sexual Culture" (1994) Edmund White writes, "No homosexual can take his homosexuality for granted. He must sound it, palpate it, auscultate it as though it were the dead limb of a tree or the living but tricky limb of a body; for that reason all homosexuals are 'gay philosophers' in that they must invent themselves."[33]

White's call for an obligatory gay philosophy, described cleverly in the language of the scientific method, suggests the simultaneous difficulty of generating self-knowledge for gay subjects, who are endlessly subject to the damaging and prescriptive narratives of institutions and disciplines. As Richard Bozorth points out, few writers have embodied so thoroughly in their work as Auden has the cultural and intellectual effects of the phenomenon Foucault describes in the *History of Sexuality* as the "medicalization" of homosexuality.[34] Foucault's insistence that medical, psychiatric, and sexological discourses were responsible for the invention of the modern personage of the homosexual—a contested argument in recent queer scholarship, and one that Didier Eribon suggests Foucault himself challenged in the 1970s[35]—seems compelling in Auden's case nonetheless, considering the extent to which his self-interrogations were shaped by the psychosexual models offered by Freud and his psychologist and sexologist contemporaries. In *The History of Sexuality*, Foucault insists that homosexual identity has been constructed through and by homophobic narratives that have come down through the taxonomic categories of medicine, psychiatry, language, and law. These homophobic discourses are embedded in the very texts through which queer subjects struggle to negotiate their self-identities in a culture that insists upon a binarizing of identity according to sexual object choice.

In struggling to theorize same-sex desire and his own sexual identity, Auden exhibited in his work a heightened awareness of the volatility of diagnosis. His tendency to subject his sexuality to the pathologizing narratives of psychology, psychiatry, and medicine in the late 1920s and early 1930s finds striking illustration in his Berlin journal, in which chaotic theorizations on poetry and politics as well as references to Berlin rent boys are juxtaposed with pathologizing accounts of same-sex desire. Part testament to Auden's awakening sense of sexual freedom in Berlin, part artifact of his own ambivalence about same-sex bonds, the journal identifies Auden's persistent view of homosexuality as a regressive stage of sexual development and a larger symptom of cultural degeneration.

Figurations of backwardness are everywhere in Auden's early poetry and prose—"backward love" being one of his consistent codes for same-sex desire. Such figurations suggest both the poet's melancholic reckoning with loss tied to the difficulties of same-sex love and his lingering sense of his sexuality as deviant and regressive. Auden's reliance on the trope of "backward love" is helpfully contextualized by Heather Love who, in *Feeling Backward*, reminds us of the ideological nature of backwardness as an account of queer life as well as the lived reality of backwardness for many queer subjects: "Not only do many queers . . . feel backward, but backwardness has been taken up as a key feature of queer culture."[36]

Auden was convinced that he would live a life of ostracism and loneliness and that same-sex love would always be provisional and insecure. As he says in his poem "Too Dear, Too Vague," "Love is not there / Love has moved to another chair."[37] In 1927, Auden wrote to an Oxford companion, "There still lingers in my mind the idea of something indecent in a mutual homosexual relation."[38] During his final years at Oxford, he vacillated between unabashed sexual experimentation with men and periods of celibacy in which he attempted to control his instincts through powerful acts of will.

One of Auden's earliest sources of authority on homosexuality was Freud, who largely rejected the equation of homosexuality with hereditary degeneracy and acknowledged the flawed perception of homosexuality as pathological. Freud refused to treat patients for their homosexuality alone, and mocked the militant moralizing of American psychoanalysts who saw homosexuality in explicit opposition to a "normal, well-adjusted" sexuality.[39] In his well-known 1935 letter to an American mother of a gay son, Freud reassures her that her son's homosexuality is "nothing to be ashamed of, no vice, no degradation, it cannot be classified as an illness, we consider it to be a variation of the sexual function produced by a certain arrest of sexual development."[40] Opposed to the criminalization and stigmatization of homosexuality and to its depiction as vice, illness, or moral failing, Freud viewed it instead as a universal human potential in that "all people are capable of making a homosexual object-choice and have in fact made one in their unconscious."[41] Freud's progressivism, as Tim Dean and Christopher Lane suggest, was to universalize same-sex desire by locating its ubiquity in the unconscious.[42]

Auden may have found liberating Freud's proposition that all individuals house at the unconscious level both hetero- and homosexual libidinal attachments. And yet, as someone who was clearly ambivalent about his sexual identity and about the significance of same-sex bonds in modern culture, Auden found early on that Freudian psychoanalysis undercut the affirmative side of such ambivalence, hovering as it did between tendencies to universalize same-sex desire and to cast it in evolutionary terms as an arrested development or infantilism. In a text that illustrates some of these contradictions, *Three Essays on the Theory of Sexuality* (1905), Freud proposes continuities between heterosexuality and homosexuality, between "perverse" and "normal" behavior, and between genital and non-genital sex. In the first essay, Freud defends the existence of a varied human spectrum of sexual object choices and aims, disentangling sexuality from its assumed relationship to reproduction. But in the second, Freud relies on a more teleological framework in which proper sexual development leads to a heterosexual object choice with coitus as its final aim. Freud's psychosexual model of development presumes an elementary stage of polymorphous perversity, but it also suggests that this disposition should be transcended as the subject proceeds through successive stages of development—a schema, Sedgwick reminds us, in which "heterosexist and masculinist ethical sanctions found ready camouflage."[43] Auden's own idiosyncratic reading of Freud emphasizes the links between homosexuality, an excessive attachment to the mother, and a failure to resolve the Oedipus complex.

Sedgwick's discussion of the productive contradictions at the heart of homosexual definition is useful in framing Auden's contradictory investments in self-diagnosis and his parody of diagnostic frameworks. In the 1920s, Auden adopted the view that homosexuality constituted a regressive stage in a developmental schema, a stage that could be surmounted with the help of psychoanalysis.[44] In 1928, en route to Berlin, he stayed briefly in Spa Belgium where he worked with a psychoanalyst on "curing" his homosexuality, a trip that highlights his equation of psychoanalysis with the project of heteronormativity. Auden's own remarks at the time make this equation explicit: "I wish to improve my inferiority complex and to develop heterosexual traits."[45] But whether the "cure" to the perceived illness was psychoanalysis or the subsequent trip to Berlin is unclear. Auden may have viewed Berlin as a cure for psychoanalysis, just as he had previously viewed psychoanalysis as a remedy to his sexuality. Both possibilities are suggested in a poem Auden wrote in Berlin:

> Sir, no man's enemy, forgiving all
> But will his negative inversion, be prodigal:
> Send to us power and light, a sovereign touch
> Curing the intolerable neural itch,
> The exhaustion of weaning, the liar's quinsy,
> And the distortions of ingrown virginity.
> Prohibit sharply the rehearsed response
> And gradually correct the coward's stance;
> Cover in time with beams those in retreat
> That, spotted, they turn though the reverse were great;
> Publish each healer that in city lives
> Or country houses at the end of drives;
> Harrow the house of the dead; look shining at
> New styles of architecture, a change of heart.[46]

Written shortly after his failed psychoanalytic "change of heart," the sonnet reflects Auden's simultaneous investment in, and increasing ambivalence about, therapeutic intervention. Characteristic of his early compressed, elliptical style, the sonnet—with its syntactical and structural irregularities—unsettles straightforward appeals to healing and enlightenment. The poem emphasizes Auden's understanding of poetry as a mode of cultural diagnosis and self-diagnosis. But what seems initially like a supplication to a god-like healer to provoke a "change of heart" in those "with the intolerable neural itch," proves less an interrogation of same-sex desire than a satire of the therapeutic endeavor. The healer is asked to take increasingly draconian and absurd measures to identify and root out deviant subjects, who are humorously characterized as "spotted." These subjects are identified through a series of disorders—"neural itch," "ingrown virginity," even "negative inversion"—that function, like Sedgwick's "nonce taxonomy," as inventive remakings of psycho-medical categorization. Laced with innuendo, the poem evokes the healing effects of sexual pleasure—a "sovereign touch" as a cure for "neural itch"—an idea that Homer Lane endorsed and Auden considered central to his "change of heart." Here as elsewhere, Auden's theorizations of same-sex desire are contradictory and unstable, replicating the moralistic, psychoanalytic, and psychosomatic definitions of homosexuality he had assimilated, while offering humorous parodies of those very definitions. Auden was still restlessly searching for healing in Berlin, but his "change of heart" would take another form from that of a conversion to heterosexuality.

A Change of Heart

Auden's efforts to "develop heterosexual traits" through psychoanalysis seem ironic given that his next healing venture was into a world of sexual tourism. "Is Berlin very wicked?" he asked a friend before his trip,[47] knowing full well that it was. Auden arrived in Berlin in the fall of 1928 and stayed for approximately ten months, during which time he openly flouted the protocols of English upper-middle-class sexual morality. In Edward Mendelson's words, Auden experienced Berlin as "an amusement park for the flesh," engaging in casual liaisons with working-class locals in exchange for food and financial gifts.[48] He indulged fully in the sexual permissiveness and diversity of late Weimar Berlin, which he described as "the bugger's daydream."[49] To fully immerse himself in the city's offerings, he moved from his initial residence with a family in a middle-class suburb to a working-class district close to Berlin rent bars such as the Cosy Corner café, Auden's favorite spot for pick-ups and a pivotal setting for Isherwood's Berlin stories. Berlin offered Auden and his circle a gay subculture with access to male partners, as well as an intellectual and artistic bohemia. Berlin was the cosmopolitan center of a new international modernism that was taking place across the arts, richly diverse and self-consciously hybrid, borrowing heavily from popular art forms while retaining its avant-garde credentials.

Berlin's thriving gay subculture was nourished by the activism of Magnus Hirschfeld, regarded as the founding father of the German gay rights movement.[50] Auden was familiar with Hirschfeld's Institute for Sexual Science and introduced Isherwood to it when his friend arrived in Berlin. While an earlier generation of modernists sought refuge in the international cities of Paris and London, the Auden circle looked to German culture, with its rich philosophical traditions and its distinctly non-English milieu, to aid its artistic, intellectual, and sexual development. No doubt Auden's affection for German culture constituted a subversive challenge to an English national identity, as it marked the beginning of his cultivation of a dissident identity in exile from his home nation.

Auden's self-described "promiscuity" during the Berlin period was no less intellectual than sexual, restless as he was in search of new ideas and commitments. The teachings he imbibed fueled his energetic sexual interactions.

In the first part of "1929," a poem written against the backdrop of this new milieu, Auden uses the allegory of the Easter story to account for a sense of spiritual, aesthetic, and sexual awakening:

> It was Easter as I walked in the public gardens,
> Hearing the frogs exhaling from the pond,
> Watching traffic of magnificent cloud
> Moving without anxiety on open sky—
> Season when lovers and writers find
> An altering speech for altering things,
> An emphasis on new names, on the arm
> A fresh hand with fresh power.[51]

The tone of this opening stanza is romantic and easeful, a stunning contrast to the anxious, paranoid, and moody intonations of many of his early poems. The lyrical "I," generally absent from all but a handful of poems from the period, makes a surprising appearance, as if the speaker is more comfortable inserting himself as subject in this milieu. As Patrick Deer suggests, Berlin in "1929" "provides the stage both for a modernist redescription of the world and a liberating reinvention of the self."[52] It is a "Season when lovers and writers find / An altering speech for altering things." Not only is a new speech available—a new poetry—but a new love: "A fresh hand with fresh power."[53] Although many of Auden's poems contain obscure autobiographical references, "1929" exhibits an unusually strong authorial presence at some remove from the poetic impersonality of his earlier poems. As biographers have noted, Easter of 1929 was the day Auden met Gerhart Meyer, the most significant of his lovers during his time in Berlin. Meyer is referenced in the poem not explicitly as a lover but as a symbol of sexual liberation, a "truly strong man" with "an absence of fear." Like the clouds moving without anxiety upon the open sky, Meyer signifies an absence of the anxious self-consciousness about sexual identity that typifies many of Auden's early poetic performances.

Norman Page identifies Easter 1929 as the "turning-point at which Auden definitively recognized his sexual identity and chose his own future."[54] But the final two sections of "1929," written after Auden's return to England, point to a darker configuration of same-sex desire. The poem's reworking of the languages of psychopathology, those that endeavored to make homosexuality both known and knowable and to render it strategically invisible at the same time, is evident in part three of "1929" in which the speaker describes the insecurity of love in language that associates same-sex love with uncertainty, illness, and degeneracy:

So, insecure, he loves and love
Is insecure, gives less than he expects.
He knows not if it be seed in time to display
Luxuriantly in a wonderful fructification
Or whether it be but a degenerate remnant
Of something immense in the past but now
Surviving only as the infectiousness of disease[55]

Insecure about the promise of love—"love" itself hangs precariously at the end of the first verse in a pointed enjambment—the speaker wonders if his love will bear fruit, "be seed in time to display / Luxuriantly in a wonderful fructification," or if it will degenerate into something like "the infectiousness of disease." Earlier, a description of "intercepted growth" emerges as a counter-image to this figure of "fructification." Auden joins turn-of-the-century discourses of degeneration—with their associations of sexual deviance with disease, crime, and addiction—to a more personal language of regression, in which the psychic past obstructs future development and fulfillment. However obliquely, the poem plays on two related strains of degeneration theory—the widespread fear about the degenerative effect of sexually transmitted disease (Auden had just returned from a world of sex tourism and might have been concerned about such things), and cultural anxieties about homosexuality's link to the degeneration of the social body. In his popular book *Degeneration* (1895), Max Nordau associates degeneration with virtually any sexual practice that did not submit to the imperative of reproduction, including homosexuality, masturbation, and prostitution. Auden deploys such degenerative discourses slyly and idiosyncratically in "1929"; yet he was admittedly troubled by the non-reproductive nature of homosexuality, which adds meaning to the poetic speaker's anxiety over whether his love will "bear fruit."

The temporality of desire is crucial to "1929." The four-part poem begins on Easter day, with its promise of newness and rebirth, and follows the changing seasons of a single year, until winter, with its attendant imagery of death and decay, offers a morbid conclusion to life and love. The speaker pronounces the universal condition of death as the ineluctable termination of Eros: "We know it, we know that love / Needs more than the admiring excitement of union, / . . . Needs death, death of the grain, our death."[56] And yet, the language in the previous stanza of degeneration and disease, of maturation and growth, of addiction and infection, invokes a more specific cultural semiotics allied to discourses on homosexuality. The final images of the poem—hallucinatory and paranoid—are darkly suggestive of the alliance between intrapsychic conflict and the external social and political terror exercised against queer subjects. The fact that the nature of the enemy is left deliberately ambiguous suggests the mutual reinforcement of psychic and social persecution:

> Orders are given to the enemy for a time
> . . .
>
> To haunt the poisoned in his shunned house,
> To destroy the efflorescence of the flesh,
> The intricate play of the mind, to enforce
> Conformity with the orthodox bone
> With organized fear, the articulated skeleton.[57]

Rhetorically ambiguous in situation and subject, the final stanza nonetheless evokes the "organized fear" of a fascistic state, which "destroys the efflorescence of the flesh" and the "intricate play of the mind" (foreshadowing, perhaps, the ascendancy of the Nazis and their campaigns of racial and sexual purity).

"1929" is remarkable in both inviting and refusing diagnostic readings. Auden's pursuit of homosexual self-definition frequently made aesthetic use of the very discourses that conflated homosexuality with degeneracy, disease, deviance, and sin—an appropriation that disrupts any straightforwardly affirmative reading of this or other poems in relation to queer critical projects. "1929" echoes what Heather Love has described as the dark side of queer representation, the side that exposes the losses, melancholy, and self-loathing in many early twentieth-century queer texts. It is telling that the poetic speaker's burgeoning love is set in Berlin in the spring, while the doomed and pathologized portrait of same-sex desire is set against the backdrop of a return to England, to the Oedipalized constraints of the home nation and family relations.[58] The speaker imagines the return to England and to the Oedipal family as a regression both psychic and cultural, as both are configured as "enforce[ing] conformity with the orthodox bone."

Mentorship

If Berlin represented a provisional space of sexual freedom for Auden, it was in part because his sexual experimentation found legitimacy and affirmation in the dissident analysts whose work he encountered there. In the autobiographical fourth section of "Letter to Lord Byron" (1937), Auden assembles his archive of mentors from this period, their names absorbed into the allusive, citational structure of the verses:

> Then to Berlin, not Carthage, I was sent
> With money from my parents in my purse,

And ceased to see the world in terms of verse
I met a chap called Layard and he fed
New doctrines into my receptive head.

Part came from Lane, and part from D. H. Lawrence;
Gide, though I didn't know it then, gave part.
They taught me to express my deep abhorrence
If I caught anyone preferring Art
To Life and Love and being Pure-in-Heart.
I lived with crooks but seldom was molested;
The Pure-in-Heart can never be arrested.[59]

As a poetic bildungsroman, the poem celebrates the renunciation of "Art" for a philosophy of life and love in Berlin. Such lessons carry specific inflections within the realms of sexual politics. If Auden was to pursue "Life and Love" in Berlin, it was partly because the lessons he assimilated enabled a refreshing *art-lessness* in relation to romantic love and a new ethical code, one that Auden and Isherwood would call the "Pure-in-Heart."[60] This spiritual ethic would reflect a convergence of gay self-affirmation with a Christian ethic of tolerance. With characteristic wit, Auden plays on the verbal tension between being "Pure-in-Heart" and living with "crooks"—one of Auden's codes for homosexuality and an allusion to its criminalization. If homosexuality was criminalized in both England and Germany in the early twentieth-century and homosexuals were vulnerable to "arrest," Auden articulates a discourse of ethical purity that is defiant and playful: "The Pure-in-Heart can never be arrested."

An understanding of Auden's accession to the ethical, political, and aesthetic stance embodied in "Letter to Lord Byron" requires a deeper knowledge of his mentors. John Layard, the charismatic English student of anthropology who became one of Auden's lovers in Berlin, prompted Auden's enthusiastic new investigations of psychology, introducing him to Homer Lane, André Gide, and Georg Groddeck, among others.[61] Layard had been living in Berlin since 1926 to receive treatment for "psychosomatic" illness and had met Auden soon after the latter's arrival. Layard had been a student of medieval and modern languages at King's College, Cambridge, and, after graduating, made a trip with the psychologist and anthropologist W. H. R. Rivers to the island of Malekula in the New Hebrides to conduct fieldwork. After returning to England to publish his research, he suffered a nervous breakdown and sought treatment with the American psychologist Homer Lane, becoming a dedicated preacher of Lane's message, which Auden at his most "receptive" was eager to hear.

As an amateur psychologist and future educator, Auden was particularly struck by Lane's radical views on education. Lane was the headmaster of the

Little Commonwealth School in Dorset, which he had founded as a utopian experiment in the reformation of delinquent children. Progressive in character, Lane's institution rejected the punishment found in most reformatory schools in favor of the cultivation of "love," "freedom," and "self-government."[62] Convinced that coercion and punishment were the very cause of delinquency in children, Lane viewed his commonwealth as an organic society freed from the tyranny of arbitrary authority. Lane left little behind in the way of a textual corpus, but his one published work, *Talks to Parents and Teachers* (1928), offers a clear condensation of his thought. In this collection of essays, Lane encourages parents and teachers to look to the child himself to "initiate the methods that govern his development," and to abstain from imposing moral prohibitions.[63] Such views are easy to assimilate to modern practices in education; but among the more controversial of Lane's ideas was an erasure of the line between authority figure and child. Lane was eventually exiled from the Little Commonwealth School due to charges of sexual misconduct with students, and the school closed in 1918. The charges were never proven and Lane was deported from England on a more technical infraction; but Auden made it clear in his poem "Get there if you can" (1930) that he felt Lane was unjustly victimized by British authorities because of his radical views.

Layard was an enthusiastic follower of Lane, but Layard's theories were more radical and eccentric than Lane's. Layard had developed a metaphysical system by which "God" constituted physical desire—the inner law of our own nature—and the "Devil" resided in the conscious control of instinct.[64] Inspired by D. H. Lawrence's creative inversions of Christian morality in *Fantasia of the Unconscious*, in which the original sin of civilization is its fall into self-conscious awareness, Layard proposed that sin was not giving in to individual instinct, but rather the betrayal of it, and that instinct should be followed at all costs. Auden had already read Lawrence's *Fantasia of the Unconscious* in college, but it acquired new meaning in Berlin, as a manifesto for the liberation of the body from the dictates of the mind. Other major influences on Layard included André Gide, who insisted that "humanity should act without the restraint of accepted morality,"[65] and the German psychologist and father of psychosomatic theory, Georg Groddeck, who declared that the price of denying God (i.e., our own instincts), was physical illness.[66] Developing his concept of the "It," an antecedent to Freud's "Id," Groddeck saw all illness as a physical manifestation of psychic conflict, as well as a symbolic expression of the unknown forces of the "It."[67] For Layard, Lawrence, and Groddeck, human instinct represented the infallible law of human health. If instinct in Auden's earlier poems, such as "The Secret Agent," renders queer subjects vulnerable to entrapment by a coercive culture, it is recast in Auden's Berlin jottings as that which must be expressed lest its suppression cause psychic and physical illness. Auden would go so far as to suggest that social morality develops when individuals are permitted to express their instincts fully.

The idea that the health of a society can be calibrated according to how much it allows for the expression of human instinct is a view considerably at odds with Freud's discussions in *The Future of an Illusion* (1927) and *Civilization and Its Discontents* (1930). If Freud exhorted a neurotic culture to acknowledge the pathological effects of its own repression, he nonetheless accepted repression as constitutive of the social fabric—a necessary social good. In his *Introductory Lectures*, Freud declares, "Society believes that no greater threat to its civilization could arise than if the sexual instincts were to be liberated and returned to their original aims."[68] In *Civilization and Its Discontents*, he depicts civilization as a march of progress dependent upon ever-higher degrees of repression, a tragic formulation in which the aims of society and those of the individual are necessarily in conflict. Although Freud highlights the dangers of excessive repression, he insists on the social value of sublimation and other forms of psychic containment and displacement. As he says in *Civilization*: "the intention that men should be 'happy' is not included in the plan of Creation."[69] Auden's increasing skepticism toward such views is reflected in his Berlin journal, in which Freud is (perhaps unfairly) recast as an agent of repression rather than liberation: "Freud you see really believes that pleasure is immoral, ie, happiness is displeasing to God."[70]

Lane's theories bore certain resemblances to Freud's in their attribution of neurotic illness to sexual repression; but Auden found in Lane a different approach to human instinct. Richard Davenport-Hines suggests that Auden's sexual adventures in Berlin were encouraged by Lane's belief that uninhibited sexual expression was curative.[71] If, for Auden, Freud projects an unyielding social environment onto the panorama of human instinct and action, one in which human beings learn to repress or sublimate their instincts, Lane suggests a more harmonious relation between human instinct and the social order. Lane represents the expression of human instinct as not only therapeutic but morally desirable—an unequivocal social good: "Only through self-expression can the instinctive tendencies be developed, and their demands thus lived through, outgrown and carried up to a higher level."[72] This is of course a developmental narrative but one based in expressive, rather than repressive, goals. Through the prism of such theories Auden began to redirect his pathologizing focus from same-sex desire to the social, political, and legal sanctions against its expression.

While Lane practiced psychoanalysis, and lectured widely on the subject, he did so without official training and with expressed hostility to established psychoanalytic practice, bound as he thought it was by outmoded attachments to authority. As dependent as Lane was on depth psychology and on the developmental models of selfhood articulated by Freud, he was committed to distinguishing his techniques, insisting that while Freud clung to an idea of man's original sin, he believed in man's "original goodness." Building on the work of Nietzsche and Lawrence, Lane argued that "human nature is innately good," and that "unconscious processes are in no way immoral."[73] Lane shared with Groddeck the idea that the repression of natural instincts led to psychosomatic illness. He offered psychic etiologies for various physical ailments: Syphilis was the direct result of sexual guilt; impotence, of sexual inhibition; cancer, of foiled creativity.[74] In these disorders, human instincts have been perverted by the mechanisms of shame, guilt, and disapproval, and psychically transformed into physical disease, an etiology derived from Freud's theories of the psychoneuroses. But whereas Freud articulated such etiologies to explain the origin of the psychoneuroses and the necessary human costs of civilization, Lane used them to endorse a theory of individualism that justified uninhibited sexual expression.

Auden's diagnostic and prognostic writings of the early 1930s, newly directed toward legitimizing pleasure and sexual experimentation, were energized by such speculations. In his Berlin journal, Auden writes, "To those brought up on repression, the mere release of the unconscious is sufficient to give a sense of value and meaning to life."[75] Following Lane, Auden developed an idiosyncratic set of taxonomies that linked sexual inhibition to illness. In one section of the journal he diagrams a series of "Hatreds" and their corresponding ailments: "Hatred of the flesh," "Hatred of other people," and "Hatred of physical love" are arrayed on one column, while "Boils. Skin diseases. / Infectious diseases. / Influenza," are arrayed on the opposite column.[76] Cause and effect, psychic conflict and somatic response, are visually graphed for the reader, but elaboration and explanation are noticeably lacking. However bizarre such correlations may appear, they suggest an attempt to confront the hatred of same-sex "physical love." To grapple with the relationships among psychic, somatic, and social effects of homophobia and repression, Auden generates his own etiology of illness, one that interprets hatred of the body, hatred of others, and hatred of physical love as pathologies in their own right. Generated in the spirit of an emergent anti-normative inquiry, such taxonomies reflect Auden's efforts to put psychopathology to different use by making sexual inhibition, rather than sexual expression and behavior, the object of inquiry. Through the development of such unsystematic "nonce" taxonomies, Auden began to cognitively map "the possibilities, dangers, and stimulations" of a liberated desire.[77]

Social Diagnosis

Lane's progressive views on sexuality, child development, and education permeate *The Orators* (1932), "The Liberal Fascist" (1934), and "Letter to Lord Byron" (1937). Looking back on his boarding school education at Gresham, Auden declared in "The Liberal Fascist," using a language inflected by Lane's ideas, that students educated on such a code tended to leave school either "frozen and undeveloped, or else, their infantilized instinct suddenly released, they plunge into foolish and damaging dissipation."[78] English boarding schools were highly conducive to same-sex intrigues, and yet Gresham's honor code was designed to compel students to confess sexual feelings and behaviors to instructors and administrators. Indicting liberalism as a false politics of freedom in which subjects are trained to police themselves and each other, Auden equates boarding school with a fascist state, a community united around fear, furtiveness, and coercion.

Auden often drew analogies between his own education in conformity and the kinds of brutal coercion practiced under fascism. The prose-poetry experiment, *The Orators*, which Richard Davenport-Hines has called "the great creative sequel to these months [in Berlin],"[79] features a revolutionary protagonist who tries to expose the fascist underside of English liberalism. Like many of Auden's earlier poems, *The Orators* uses tropes of militarism and espionage as codes for queer experience, although the ambitious poetic experiment gestures beyond this experience as it builds an unstable caricature of liberalism, education, and militarism. Such linkages were not specific to Auden: Part of what united the Auden group was its fascination with the war they had missed, and a warlike imagination that gave meaning to their experiences as gay men living in the 1930s. The group's obsessive deployment of wartime imagery offered a commentary on 1930s queer experience, which given the legal and cultural prohibitions on homosexuality, was literally a dangerous engagement with the enemy.

Valentine Cunningham describes the Auden group's pursuit of German boyfriends as a fraternization with the enemy that formed an imagined approximation of wartime experience. The rough trade element of the sexual subculture in Weimar added additional danger: One could get injured in the encounter.[80] Christopher Isherwood described the rectal fissure that afflicted Auden in the 1930s as "a wound got in the homosexual trenches."[81] Auden described it as "the stigmata of Sodom,"[82] a quasi-humorous, yet moralizing blazon of his own sense of sinfulness. For Auden, the "stigmata" was psychic and corporeal, marking him as psychologically and physically damaged by sexual transgression. But equally notable in the punning description is the evocation of sainthood, as if that which marked Auden as deviant also identified him as spiritually exceptional. In "Letter to a Wound," a short discursive fragment at the end of Part I of *The Orators*, the speaker addresses a wound from his "undercarriage" as if it were an intimate lover or friend: "Do you realize we have been together now for almost a year?"[83] The speaker reminisces about considering suicide after the wound was shown to be inoperable, but he goes on to describe his gradual acceptance of it as a permanent part of himself: "And now, here we are, together, intimate, mature." The speaker's secret devotion to his wound reinforces the linkage between suffering and exceptionalism.

Auden opens *The Orators*, his madhouse study of England, with a pointed rhetorical question: "What do you think about England, this country of ours where nobody is well?" The poem is littered with psychic and somatic symptoms and conflicts—wounds, illnesses, neuroses, as well as offenses and transgressions within the realm of sex. Auden surveys interwar British culture and assesses the ailments of its social body—its rigid social hierarchies and class-bound history; its patent sense of malaise tied to its lost pre-war grandeur; its lack of collective identity, with individuals isolated, self-interested, and unable to connect politically or personally; its post-industrial landscape of abandoned machines and factories, a loss of tangible progress attached to the machine age; and most of all, its tyrannical conformism. As in Auden's earlier poetry, there is a restless search for healers and heroes, for the "tall unwounded leader" or "truly strong man." The landscape of *The Orators* is peopled not by heroes and healers, however, but by enemies, traitors, secret agents, spies, and revolutionaries—protagonists of a post-war modernity in which people are bound neither by nation, state, family, nor clan, nor by the emotional bonds of love, trust, and compassion. The cast of traitors and spies, constituted by uncertain loyalties and secret agendas, invokes one of the most enduring of themes of homophobic discourse: the gay subject as national traitor.[84]

Book I, "The Initiates," opens with "Address for a Prize-Day," a parody of an English public school oration that is delivered to a group of airmen recruits. Psychiatric and psychosomatic ideas saturate the speaker's discourse, as he commands the recruits to be on the alert for "abnormals" among them: "Take a look around this hall, for instance. What do you think? What do you think about England, this country of ours where nobody is well?"[85] The speaker then goes on to taxonomize distinct types of abnormals according to their defective relationships to desire: The first type is the narcissist, the "excessive lovers of self," "habituees of the mirror, famous readers" who leave behind "diaries full of incomprehensible jottings";[86] the second is the "excessive lovers of their neighbors. Dare-devils of the soul, living dangerously upon their nerves"; the third type is the "defective lover" with his "barrowful of unacted desires," who is "anaemic, muscularly undeveloped and rather mean"; and the fourth are the "perverted lovers," the "Last and worst" who have "lost their nerve" and thus "end in hospitals as incurable cases . . . the hard death of those who never have and never could be loved. . . . These are they who when the saving thought came shot it for a spy."[87] The orator warns the recruits that abnormals can be anyone, "a rich man taking the fastest train for the worst quarters of eastern cities; a private school mistress in a provincial town,"[88] and that the recruits should seek them out, gain their trust, and work to expose them. The poem constructs an unstable discourse of deviance and illness in which the putatively gay or queer—described as psychically damaged and characterologically flawed— are identified as potential subversives who must be classified, diagnosed, and reeducated, if not shot "for a spy." As Douglas Mao points out, the Prize Day orator's catalogue is so unsettling because it "seems to demonize every possible adherence to norms as well as every possible deviation from them. . . . By the time it concludes, virtually everyone has been rendered queer and dangerous."[89] The speech ends with the orator's harrowing command: "Quick, guard that door. Stop that man. Good. Now boys hustle them, ready, steady—go."[90]

The oration offers a parodic version of the specification of individuals that Foucault describes as the relationship of sexual taxonomies to modern forms of power. However, it is unclear whether the oration endorses these taxonomies and their psychosomatic explanations or subverts them through parody. Such taxonomies recall the various "hatreds" Auden associates with sexual inhibition in the Berlin notebook. The extreme specificity of each individual type verges on absurdity; yet some of the sentimentalized descriptions of queer experience and its relationship to suffering and stigma suggest a vicariousness in the speaker, as if he knew too much about queer experience to not be queer himself. As an example of Sedgwick's analysis of gay mutual recognition, "It takes one to know one," there is an essential asymmetry in this type of rhetorical positioning, as the speaker uses the projective attributions of homosexuality as a cloak of invisibility.[91] There is also an asymmetry in the reader's own interpretive mastery over the speaker, who is exposed as a closeted homosexual, "the violence of rendering his closet, in turn, as spectacle."[92] The oration ultimately draws our attention to the rhetorical and performative power of these categories and descriptions, in spite of (or perhaps because of) their incoherence. As David Halperin has argued, homophobic discourse does not have to be coherent for it to wield explanatory and performative power over the lives of gay or putatively gay people.[93] Auden's poetic taxonomies can be understood as a counter-discourse to these phobic constructions of homosexuality. And yet the fact that the central figure of the poem, the airman, is brought down by a perceived wound or character flaw, suggests once again the contradictions in Auden's queer philosophy and the impossibility of resolving its contradictions.

What is also clear from *The Orators* and its Foucauldian investments in power is the reversibility or instability of power, which can also come from below. The airman, whose diary constitutes part II of *The Orators*, is a quasi-fascist leader of a revolutionary insurgency whose aim is to topple British society, in part for the casual way it sends men into war, "thoughtlessly and light-heartedly as we would send off a team for a cricket match."[94] As a secret agent, the airman personifies the reversibility of power, for it is never entirely clear whose side he is on. He is also arguably one of the subversives the first orator identifies, his homosexuality suggested by a litany of signifiers including a strong identification with a gay uncle who motivates the airman's rebellion, and repeated evocations of a boyfriend described only with the initial "E." The airman worries that his one weakness, his love of men, will be discovered and used against him either by the enemy or by one of his co-conspirators: "Does Derek suspect? He looked at me very strangely at dinner. No; no one must ever know. If the enemy ever got to hear of it, my whole work would be nullified."[95] As the poem progresses it becomes increasingly apparent that the revolutionary aims of the airman also lie within the realm of sex: The airman's same-sex desire is at once a primary motivation for his subversion and a "flaw" that might blow his cover as a loyal airman.

As Douglas Mao, Edward Mendelson, Richard Bozorth, John Fuller, and Peter Firchow have all pointed out, the airman's journal alludes to two ethnographic papers Auden read by Layard. Layard had conducted fieldwork with W. H. R. Rivers in 1914–15 on the "flying tricksters" of Malekula in the New Hebrides, and the airman is modeled on the tribal trickster of Layard's ethnographies. According to local legend, which Layard recounts in his papers, the "flying tricksters" or Bwili were thought able to fly and assume disguised forms to kill their enemies and play practical jokes on their friends.[96] Similarly, Auden's airman dons various disguises to demonstrate his loyalty to England, while contriving schemes to outwit the enemy. Among the rituals of the Bwili that Layard recounts and Auden assimilates are the ability to fly, the playing of practical jokes, and the initiation of the candidate by a maternal uncle. The airman describes his own "counter-attacks" as "complete mastery of the air—ancestor worship—practical jokes."[97] Layard discusses the Bwili initiation ritual of anal penetration of the candidate by the Malekulan ghost; he goes on to speculate that homosexuality fits Bwili culture because, like the infantile pranks of the Bwili, homosexuality is a form of regressive behavior. Basing his sect in a theory of "ancestor worship," and specifically in the transmission from matrilineal uncle to male child, Auden's airman avers: "The true ancestral line is not necessarily a straight or continuous one."[98] Like the Bwili, the airman's own initiation to the subversive sect is through his maternal uncle. After meeting his uncle at the age of sixteen, the airman "knew who and what he was, my real ancestor."[99]

As the charismatic leader of a militant sect, the airman relies on weapons that are mostly rhetorical: sexual innuendo, wordplay, practical jokes, and schoolboy slang. The airman's diary is composed of disordered fragments in various rhetorical forms: prose, poems, lists, pictures, itineraries, acrostics. As the poem progresses, the forms of rebellion suggested by the airman in his hallucinatory jottings seem more like schoolboy pranks than violent revolution: They consist of obscene phone calls to non-combatants, crude graffiti on the blackboards of "Form-masters," banks making payment in "fairy gold," boys drinking grape soda and peeing into ink-pots, "girl-guides, nocturnally simulated, mob vicars at the climax of their sermons."[100] Such antics may constitute a particular form of liberation, but is it the liberation that Auden's psychologist mentors proposed? As the poem devolves into a parody of revolution—a schoolboy fantasy of endless pranks against authority figures—the radical potential of revolution is nullified.

The Pure-in-Heart

Auden's poetry produced both during and after the Berlin period remains attached to depictions of queer suffering. Auden continued to represent same-sex love as ephemeral, unsatisfied, or foreclosed by the "intricate ways of guilt,"[101] in verses that achieve performative and rhetorical force through such tortured formulations. We might say that the transitional poems of the early and mid-1930s mark the gap between the aspirational and the actual, between the urge for psychic and social transformation fueled by his unorthodox mentors and the climate of late Weimar Berlin, and the sobering recognition that the wounds of queer history are not so easily remedied. But his critique of expertise and its relationship to the objectification and disciplining of queer subjects, combined with his affirmative nods to eccentricity and pleasure, offer prescient examples of queer critical commitments to come.

Although Auden remained interested in self-diagnosis in the mid-1930s, he became increasingly attuned to diagnosing the social. More specifically, he became less inclined to diagnose homosexuality (as regressive, infantile, degenerate), and more focused on diagnosing cultures of conformity and heteronormativity. In "Letter to Lord Byron," Auden satirizes the English boarding school as a coercive institution that "straightens out" sexually deviant subjects: "The aim is training character and poise, / With special coaching for the backward boys."[102] The poetic speaker declares: "I hate the modern trick, to tell the truth, / Of straightening out the kinks in the young mind, / Our passion for the tender plant of youth / Our hatred for all weeds of any kind."[103] Here, as elsewhere, Auden's tropes of backwardness and crookedness conjure associations of gender and sexual deviants; but the poem satirizes the disciplinary targeting and compulsive orienting of these subjects toward heteronormativity. Auden plays on the dual connotation of cultivation as both the promotion of growth (of plants, etc.) and the development of character and mind by way of education; the weed becomes a metaphor for the queer subject who refuses heteronormative development. Satirizing the "modern trick"—the disciplining of children who exhibit signs of sexual deviance—the poem performs its own trickery through rhetorical strategies of wit and inversion designed to reverse the valence of pathologizing discourses whereby straightness is valorized in relation to backwardness, crookedness, and experience—those tropes closely aligned with queerness. The poem is yet another example of Auden's unstable use of queer categorization, for it appropriates stigmatizing cultural signifiers in the service of a queer poetics.

After condemning the hetero-normalization of children through the discursive and social practices of modern education, the poem expands its indictment through a more generalized satire of normativity:

> Goddess of bossy underlings, Normality!
>   What murders are committed in thy name!
> Totalitarian is thy state Reality,
>   Reeking of antiseptics and the shame
>   Of faces that all look and feel the same.[104]

"Normality" is personified here as the goddess of "bossy underlings," while "Reality" is personified as a totalitarian dictator coercing subjects into hygienic conformity. Deeply suspicious of the standardization wrought by modern liberal institutions, the speaker eventually turns to "neurosis" as itself a possible refuge of individuality, eccentricity, and non-normativity: "Let each child have that's in our care / As much neurosis as the child can bear."

In the final verses, psychosomatic theories are repurposed yet again for a discourse of gay self-assertion and an ethics of tolerance:

> He's gay; no bludgeonings of chance can spoil it,
>   The Pure-in-Heart loves all men on a par,
> And has no trouble with his private toilet;
>   The Pure-in-Heart is never ill; catarrh
>   Would be the yellow streak, the brush of tar;[105]

Not only is a gay identity explicitly affirmed, albeit deferred to a third person, it is recognized as a positive and unalterable identity that cannot be "spoiled," a narrative opposed to Auden's accounts of homosexuality as symptomatic of arrested development. Through a clever inversion, Auden liberates homosexuality from its pathological taint and transfers his diagnostic focus to the shame-inducing mechanisms of homophobia. Those who fail in the ethical obligation to love and accept are tarred, brushed with the "yellow streak," which, given the syntactic ambiguity of the verse, refers cleverly to both cowardice and "catarrh" (catarrh also playfully echoes tar). The lyrical inversion works effectively because Auden plays upon, and reverses, negative tropes associated with same-sex desire: being tarred by its brush, painted as cowardly, or afflicted with illness. Being "Pure-in-Heart" or loving all men "on a par" is an ethical call for acceptance (not assimilation), and an affirmation of being gay and loving men.

By presenting himself as a modern heir to Byron, a figure who was also deft at literary "passing" and the author of *Don Juan*, a non-normative character motivated by a voracious sexual appetite, Auden self-consciously inserts himself into a tradition of gay male poets, and indulges, in a playful and provocative way, his own personal quest for pleasure and erotic exchange. Bozorth offers a compelling reading of Auden as a modernist heir to both Byron and Wilde, having fashioned a career that consists of "a staging of public and private selves through a range of codings of queer desire."[106] But in "Letter to Lord Byron," Auden gestures toward expanded forms of pleasure that don't necessitate coded references. Libidinal pleasure is found in the poem's daring avowals of same-sex desire and in the playful and provocative inversions of the usual tropes: "'No, I am that I am, and those that level / at my abuses reckon up their own. / I may be straight though they, themselves, are bevel."[107] Citing Shakespeare, the speaker uses a queer tropology to transfer the shame onto those who practice shaming. Auden's direct address to Byron as a proto-gay literary ancestor and his affirmative descriptions of same-sex desire suggest a self-conscious effort to position himself as a modern gay poet.

Yet the poem is not simply affirmative; it also recognizes through its intertextual identification with Byron the pressures on the gay poet to occupy a certain self-abnegating role, to remain "anonymous, observant, / A kind of lab-boy, or a civil servant."[108] Such anonymity is understood as one of the costs of criminalization, for the poetic speaker acknowledges the need for reticence: "I've no wish to go to prison."[109] Of course, neither Byron nor Auden occupied the minor position suggested by these analogies, but the affective charge of diminishment and self-effacement is poignant. The verse reflects anxieties about the expectations placed upon poets in a modern administered world: The poem's indulgence in autobiographical detail, mundane observation, and eccentricity constitutes a challenge to critics who demanded from Auden in the 1930s a more politically direct aesthetic. Auden's subversion of these expectations in "Letter" forms part of an ongoing negotiation of how to be a public gay poet.

Adopting the light verse form that Byron made famous, Auden explores questions of authorship and gay identity with an "airy manner," a negation one might say of the high modernist aesthetic with which Auden's early poetry was associated. Indeed, Auden's efforts to participate in a queer literary tradition required receptiveness to generic, as it did to sexual, diversity: "Only on varied diet can we live. / The pious fable and the dirty story / Share in the total literary glory."[110] In its deliberate campiness, its mixture of the mundane and the melancholy, and its valorization of popular verse forms, "Letter" exhibits a hybrid modernist aesthetic that is expansive, eclectic, and still able to share in the "total literary glory." In part III of the poem, Auden evaluates the aims of his poetic practice, namely its status as a critical and analytic endeavor:

> In setting up my brass-plate as a critic,
>   I make no claim to certain diagnosis,
> I'm more intuitive than analytic,
>   I offer thought in homeopathic doses
> (But someone may get better in the process).
> I don't pretend to reasoning like Pritchard's
> Or the logomachy of I. A. Richards.[111]

In this stanza, Auden manages a pointed jab at the modern disciplines and their human representatives: analysts, philosophers, and literary critics. Attempting in this section to distance his poetics from the work of experts, those charged with administering "certain diagnosis," Auden describes his qualifications, much as Lawrence does, through the language of intuition. Lawrence, one of Auden's eccentric mentors, celebrated amateurism over psychoanalytic expertise and promoted personal intuition as a more direct vehicle to knowledge about the self. By distancing himself from expert knowledge, Auden makes claims to another kind of authority: The poet will not only offer "thought" instead of "diagnosis," and intuition instead of expertise, he will offer a queer perspective with more authority than the authoritative discourses about homosexuality produced by "experts." Indeed, it is difficult not to locate the double meanings embedded in "homeopathic." Auden's increasing unease with the pathologizing and demystifying protocols of disciplines such as psychiatry and psychoanalysis can be discerned in his attempt at an "intuitive," "homeopathic," or queer poetics. But if expertise is delegitimized here, poetry is reinstated as a potential remedy: *someone may get better in the process.*

4
Nabokov and the Lure of Freudian Forms

All my books should be stamped Freudians, Keep Out.
— NABOKOV, FOREWORD TO *BEND SINISTER* (1963)

While Auden and Woolf wrestled with Freudian psychoanalysis in nuanced and complex ways, Nabokov responded to Freud with explicit rejection and critique, and with an unparalleled rancor that makes him an appropriate bookend to this project, opposite D. H. Lawrence. As with Lawrence, the intensity with which Nabokov sought to distance himself from Freud is a telling indicator of the power psychoanalysis exerted over him and his fictions. Nabokov famously used his literary forewords to anticipate and fend off Freudian readings of his novels. In the foreword to *The Eye*, for example, he writes: "My books are not only blessed by a total lack of social significance, but are also mythproof: Freudians flutter around them avidly ... stop, stiff, and recoil.[1] The foreword to *Bend Sinister* is even more direct: "All my books should be stamped: Freudians, Keep Out."[2] Such para-textual gate-keeping reinforces one of the key arguments of this study: that modernists resisted the reduction of their works to psychoanalytic metanarratives, as well as the reduction of themselves to neurotic beings who could be analyzed through their art.

Nabokov's disavowals are also acknowledgments of a haunting, for the ghosts of Freud appear everywhere in his fiction, consistently present in their stated absence. Nabokov's books can seem decidedly post-Freudian in their rejection of Freudian "myths" about the self, and in their mockery of psychoanalytic methods—the fanatical surfacing of hidden depths, the obsession with sexual secrets, the insistence on the privileged knowledge of the analyst-interpreter. But Freudian forms are so entangled with the texture of Nabokov's fiction that they become inescapable frameworks for interpretation. In *Lolita*, the narrator, Humbert, manipulates his audience through a dependence on Freudian forms, appropriating concepts of childhood trauma and sexual repression as exculpatory evidence for his crimes. But as I go on to illustrate, a critical reading of *Lolita* that does not deploy suspicion of these Freudian forms would fail at an ethical reading. That is, a mere surface reading of Humbert's lyrical praising of Lolita as "nymphet" would amount to a form of ethical complicity with Humbert and his abuse. To put it another way, the ethical necessity of reading deeply and critically for the muted suffering of Dolores Haze, suggests an important affinity between Nabokov's fictions and the system of investigation that Nabokov so despised.

Nabokov's famously fraught engagement with psychoanalysis often took the shape of imitation and parody, which reveal an intimacy with psychoanalysis and a thorough knowledge of its source material. No literary figure has taken Freudian parody to such a pitch, and no figure is more synonymous with anti-Freudianism.[3] Geoffrey Green calls Nabokov's treatment of "Freudianism," "the grandest and most extravagant contempt for psychoanalysis known in modern literature;"[4] Jeffrey Berman refers to Nabokov's "unprecedented war on psychoanalysis"; while Michal Oklot and Matthew Walker emphasize Nabokov's "excessive, almost neurotic, obsession with Freud."[5] Joanna Trzeciak's keenly observes that Nabokov turns "Freud" into a Nabokovian construction—part caricature, part straw man—while short-circuiting the potential of psychoanalysis as an interpretive framework through parody, travesty, and pastiche.[6]

Nabokov's decades-long polemic against Freud could be dismissed as the idiosyncratic obsession of a notoriously cantankerous author, but I hope to show how indebted Nabokov was to psychoanalysis as a psychological discourse and theory of the self, and how consistently he engaged with psychoanalytic themes, rhetorical structures, genres of writing, and methods of interpretation. Nabokov's polemic against Freud, whom he labelled "The Viennese witchdoctor" and the "Austrian crank," exemplifies the secret sharing and discursive rivalry that this book details, revealing a dialectic of resistance and dependence that is not unlike D. H. Lawrence's famously vexed relationship to Freud.[7] One cannot take Nabokov's blanket dismissal of psychoanalysis at face value, particularly as his writings are structurally, rhetorically, and epistemologically reliant on the very discourse it rejects. And although Nabokov announced in the foreword to *Bend Sinister*, "All my books should be stamped Freudians, Keep Out," his books obsessively invite them in, enlisting Freudians as characters, narrators, readers, antagonists, and foils.

As in the other rivalries detailed in this book, Nabokov's rivalry with Freud is rooted in intimacy. Both were known for their attunement to language and wordplay, for their heightened attention to wayward details (Nabokov quipped that readers "should notice and fondle details"),[8] and for their interest in the unruly paths of consciousness, memory, and desire. Their personal lives furnish important parallels as well: both Freud and Nabokov escaped the advance of the Nazis and sought refuge in the United States, where they experienced a profound sense of exile and dislocation. Nabokov's brother died in a concentration camp, and Nabokov and his family would have risked the same fate had they stayed in Europe. Both held Europe in high esteem and viewed the United States as vulgar, commercial, moralistic, and lacking in authentic culture.[9] Paradoxically, Nabokov's resistance to Freud can be understood as a rejection of midcentury America's obsession with Freud, during what Nathan Hale called, "The golden age of popularization."[10] John Burnham writes that by the late 1940s and early 1950s "Freud's ideas had become a conspicuous—indeed, unavoidable—part of the American cultural landscape."[11] The migration of European psychoanalysts during the interwar years helped to ensure that psychoanalysis would become a flourishing discipline in the United States with its own clinics, practitioners, body of literature, and publishing apparatuses.[12] Nabokov's antipathy to psychoanalysis was not exclusively a response to Freudian psychoanalysis but to an American cultural landscape heavily shaped by Freud—what Auden called a "climate of opinion" and what Nabokov described more cynically as a "prison of thought."[13]

Asked in a 1964 *Playboy* interview to discuss his views on psychoanalysis, Nabokov responded with typical irascibility:

> The ordeal itself is much too silly and disgusting to be contemplated even as a joke. Freudianism and all it has tainted with its grotesque implications and methods, appear to me to be one of the vilest deceits practiced by people on themselves and on others. I reject it utterly, along with a few other medieval items still adored by the ignorant, the conventional, or the very sick.[14]

Psychoanalysis is characterized as faddish and medieval, conventional and grotesque—something too silly and disgusting to be contemplated (though Nabokov engages it obsessively). Probed in another interview about why he so despises Freud, Nabokov responded along similar lines: "I think he's crude, I think he's medieval, and I don't want an elderly gentleman from Vienna with an umbrella inflicting his dreams upon me."[15] In the hands of Nabokov, Freud becomes more than a set of suspect ideas; he becomes a metonym for a culture's "vilest deceits," like a confidence trick played on a grand scale. The humorous image of an old man with an umbrella towering over Nabokov's bedside, suggests Nabokov's distaste for ready-made ideas, which have saturated culture so thoroughly that they have invaded our dreams.

Like Lawrence, Nabokov insists that psychoanalysis did not so much discover the truth of the self, so much as offer a set of appealing narratives that modern culture accepted as truth. In the opening pages of *Speak, Memory* (1951), Nabokov describes his "mnemonic" quest to "steal into realms that existed before I was conceived" and how it prompts an inventory of his "oldest dreams for keys and clues."[16] The impulse to inventory his dreams for clues to the past unleashes another diatribe against the "vulgar, shabby, fundamentally medieval world" of Freud's thought, "with its crankish quest for sexual symbols" (something like searching for Baconian acrostics in Shakespeare's works) and its bitter little embryos spying, from their natural nooks, upon the love life of their parents."[17] Seeking to distinguish his own way of reimagining the past from Freud's, Nabokov dismisses as "vulgar" the obsession with dream symbolism and its sexual subtext, as well as Freud's understandings of infantile sexuality played out in the primal scene. In a comical misreading, Nabokov exchanges children for "bitter little embryos," already forced into the primal scene in utero. He also manages a pointed jab at the psycho-biographical craze for reading Shakespeare's works for signs of dubious authorship and attributions to other authors, such as Francis Bacon. Nabokov's contradictory epithets— he offers the same ones repeatedly—suggest that psychoanalysis is both faddish and antiquated, a vulgar form of belief and a crude hermeneutic sheltering under the cover of enlightenment. *Speak, Memory* is invested in reconstructing the past and exploring its relationship to the present; and it chafes against the deterministic narratives of psychoanalysis, which reduce human experience to the same set of myths.

Nabokov enlists psychoanalytic theory primarily to diffuse its authority over literature; yet such "strong opinions" obscure the ways in which his fictions engaged, often seriously, with the hermeneutic and thematic elements of psychoanalysis. While the exact degree of Nabokov's knowledge of psychoanalysis is unknown, he coyly admitted to a "bookish familiarity," critics agree that he must have read a considerable amount of Freud's work in English translation. Nabokov's biographer, Andrew Field, suggests that he was "well acquainted with Freud's work in English translation and that his quarrel with Freudianism dates back nearly forty years."[18] Jenefer Shute points out that Nabokov's writing betrays a "circular indebtedness and mutual absorption" of psychoanalysis that is difficult to discount.[19]

In what follows, I turn my attention to Nabokov, because (a) he is an especially strident and explicit critic of Freud, despite being a studious reader of Freud's texts; (b) he is writing at the historical culmination of psychoanalysis's popularization in Europe and the United States and, arguably, at the nadir of literary modernism; and (c) his fiction illuminates my broader argument about the inescapability of psychoanalysis for modernists, who parody, misread, and reinvent psychoanalysis for their own aesthetic and intellectual projects. If critics have tended to emphasize Nabokov's explicit discrediting of psychoanalysis, I am more interested in the dialectic of refusal and dependence that characterized Nabokov's response. Of the four authors in this study, Nabokov illustrates just how difficult psychoanalysis is to dislodge and how wedded it became to midcentury American fiction. As I go on to show, *Lolita* repurposes the psychoanalytic case study and wrestles with Freudian forms, simultaneously dismissing its hermeneutic while enlisting it as an ethical orientation towards its subject matter.

American Psychoanalysis and Literary Criticism at Midcentury

Nabokov's intimate battle with Freud seems fitting for an era in which popular Freudianism had become fully entrenched as a literary critical discourse, attractive to U.S. writers and intellectuals as varied as W. E. B. Du Bois, Sylvia Plath, J. D. Salinger, Ralph Ellison, Allen Ginsberg, Saul Bellow, and Philip Roth. Ellison's *Invisible Man* (1952), published three years before *Lolita*, is filled with dream states, slips of the tongue, double speak, and other breakthroughs from the unconscious and uses its underground setting in the prologue and epilogue to illustrate both the narrator's internalized invisibility and his unconscious rage before it surfaces in spontaneous acts of resistance. Like Nabokov, Ellison uses psychoanalytic parody to comic and political ends; for example, in the portrait of Mr. Emerson, the wealthy white son of the school donor, who seeks confirmation of his white superiority in Freud's *Totem and Taboo*. Ellison combines Oedipal theory and the discourse of primitivism in the Trueblood episode, in which the black sharecropper describes having sex with a white boss's wife while he rapes his own daughter. In this scathing social critique, Ellison illustrates how in a white supremacist culture, father-daughter rape and interracial sex are deemed equally taboo. A decade earlier, W. E. B. Du Bois would draw on a combination of psychoanalysis and behaviorism in his autobiographical collection of essays, *Dusk of Dawn* (1940). Du Bois argues that irrationalism is central to white supremacy, and that human actions are "not rational and many of them arise from subconscious urges."[20] In trying to examine the brutal excesses of anti-black racism that go beyond the mere construction of racial capital for whites, Du Bois asserts: "The present attitude of the white world is not based solely upon rational, deliberate intent. It is a matter of conditioned reflexes; of long followed habits, customs, and folkways; of the unconscious trains of reasoning and unconscious nervous reflexes."[21] What follows is a distinct pessimism about the possibility of resolving racial antagonism when whites are not only re-enacting "long followed habits" but deriving unconscious sources of gratification from the sadism they inflict on black subjects.

By the time Nabokov writes *Lolita* psychoanalysis had become a fully established idiom of the American middle and upper classes, one instantly recognizable in literature, advertising, and on stage and screen. As Mary Esteve observes, after World War II "knowledge of psychoanalysis became compulsory in realms as diverse as market research and advertising, academic literary criticism, and national security."[22] Analysts were recruited as highly paid consultants for Hollywood films, and women's magazines were using psychoanalytic jargon to empower women to express their feelings of frustration and dissatisfaction.[23] The literary and cultural critic, and disciple of Freud, Alfred Kazin, worried that psychoanalysis would be reduced to a tool of psychic manipulation by commercial advertisers and PR executives.

In his fiction, as in his interviews, Nabokov's contempt for psychoanalysis mingles with his contempt for U.S. culture in general. Psychoanalysis resembles the painting of Van Gogh's "Arlesienne" on the wall of the Haze household: "a banal darling of the arty middle class,"[24] a commodified reproduction of a foreign culture that confers the illusion of worldliness and good taste. The caricature of psychoanalysis in *Lolita* is not unlike the caricature of Charlotte Haze, who is described as a trashy derivative of a European prototype, "a weak solution of Marlene Dietrich."[25] In *Lolita*, Nabokov assembles a collage of American vulgarity that includes psychoanalysis, American Christianity, magazine culture, tourist attractions, motor lodges, parenting manuals, summer camp, and middlebrow book clubs. But American vulgarity is epitomized in its hunger for the faddish pseudo-science of psychoanalysis, which, as Nabokov saw it, offered a superficial and consumerist culture the veneer of intellectualism and psychological depth.

Nabokov's intimate combat with Freud was also bound up with his distrust of professional literary criticism, which had assimilated a psycho-biographical style of interpretation as well as the archetypical criticism of Carl Jung, Maud Bodkin, Joseph Campbell, and later Northrop Frye. Though an academic himself, Nabokov consistently mocked the reduction of individual texts to "standardized symbols" and mythic archetypes, and lays much of the blame at the feet of literary critics. When asked about his hatred of Freud's "standardized symbols" and how his contempt seems to extend to literary criticism more generally, Nabokov responded: "Beware of the modish message. Ask yourself if the symbol you have detected is not your own footprint. Ignore allegories . . . Rely on the sudden erection of your small dorsal hairs. Do not drag in Freud at this point."[26] The set of injunctions is meant to underscore undesirable reading practices, including the use of symbol and allegory and the projection of one's own ideas onto literary texts. Much like Susan Sontag and other anti-hermeneutical thinkers, Nabokov appeals to a transforming aesthetic experience that is embodied and sensuous, over the imposition of ready-made ideas and values.

Will Norman points out that Nabokov was highly skeptical of the psychoanalytic literary criticism that emerged within the American academy at midcentury, "in which readers positioned themselves as analysts, interpreting narrative as raw psychoanalytic data, in order to be able to reconstruct the unconscious of either individual characters, or the author."[27] It is no coincidence that the 1950s were also the peak of Freud's popularity among American college students, the era in which Nabokov was teaching at Cornell.[28] Psychoanalysis had been adopted by a range of midcentury literary critics, including Lionel Trilling, Herbert Read, Edmund Wilson, Van Wyck Brooks, Ernest Kris, Kenneth Burke, and Jacques Lacan, and expressed itself in biographical, structuralist, and textualist modes. This is the era in which Kenneth Burke based his theories about the production and reception of rhetoric on the Freudian unconscious and in which Lionel Trilling declared in "Freud and Literature" (1940) that Freudian psychology was "the only systematic account of the human mind which, in point of subtlety and complexity, of interest and tragic power, deserves to stand beside the chaotic mass of psychological insights which literature has accumulated through the centuries."[29] In the following decades, Lacan would begin his dramatic poststructuralist revision of Freudian psychoanalysis, destabilizing Freud's humanist and empiricist conceptions and offering a more linguistic conception of how subjects enter into the social order. Nabokov believed that psychoanalysis, both as an influence internal to the work of art and as a form of literary criticism, reduced the rich interpretive possibilities of literature to a set of predictable formulas and "standardized symbols." Psychoanalytic literary criticism thus becomes a foil to Nabokov's aestheticism, which privileged the expressive autonomy of the artist and the idiosyncratic singularity of the artwork over a critical or theoretical approach to texts.

In "The Idea of a Psychoanalytic Literary Criticism," Peter Brooks writes that "psychoanalysis is imperialist, almost of necessity. Freud works from the premise that all that appears is a sign, that all signs are subject to interpretation, and that they ultimately tell stories that contain the same dramatis personae and the same narrative functions for all of us."[30] Such relentless pursuit of the sign in the service of interpretation and the subjection of the sign to the same narrative patterns and character arcs, are central to what Nabokov found offensive in psychoanalysis. In *Strong Opinions*, he proclaims:

> Why should I tolerate a perfect stranger at the bedside of my mind? . . . I've no intention to dream the drab middle-class dreams of an Austrian crank with a shabby umbrella. . . . The Freudian racket looks to me as much of a farce as the jumbo thingum of polished wood with a polished hole in the middle which doesn't represent anything except the gaping face of the Philistine who is told it is a great sculpture produced by the greatest living caveman.[31]

In this memorable scene, Freud returns with the umbrella, imposing his second-order dreams onto the artist. Nabokov ridicules the "Freudian racket" with its clichéd and predictable formulas, and mocks the Freudian impulse to probe for deeper meanings, especially sexual meanings, in the most uninspiring objects—in this case a "jumbo thingum of polished wood." Here Nabokov mocks multiple audiences at once: the bourgeois modernists with their "primitivist" tastes, who elevate the work of the "caveman" to the status of high art, as well as the middle-class consumers of such art who fuel the Freudian racket with their hunger for psychotherapy.

Leland de la Durantaye suggests that Nabokov was most offended by psychoanalysis's determinism, its tendency to suspend the rich multiplicity of meanings in favor of a singular—generally sexual—meaning. Nabokov went so far as to align psychoanalysis with totalitarianism for its capacity to neglect the "rich singular instance in favor of a dangerously hollow generality."[32] In *Speak, Memory*, Nabokov refers to the "Viennese Quack" and his followers as the creators of a "police state of sexual myth": "what a great mistake on the part of dictators to ignore psychoanalysis—a whole generation might easily have been corrupted that way!"[33] Teckyoung Kwon observes that Nabokov viewed psychoanalysis as a totalitarian ideology on the order of Soviet communism or Nazism.[34] Nabokov equates psychoanalysis with the thought control of totalitarian regimes, calling it, "A disgusting racket. La psychanalyse a quelque chose de bolchévik: la police intérieure [Psychoanalysis has something of the Bolshevik about it: the internal police]."[35]

In his late novel *Ada, Or Ardor: A Family Chronicle* (1970), the narrator Van Veen, though a psychologist himself, eventually flees his homeland after it becomes overrun with therapists, as if it were a totalitarian state dominated by analysis. Indeed, the Freudian figures in *Ada* have the flavor of dictators, including Dr. Froid, "one of the administerial centaurs" who uses the "therapistic device" of "a 'group' feeling," and Dr. Sig Heiler, whose name plays on the "Sig" in Sigmund Freud. Such comparisons of analysts to Nazis mingle the punning with the reactionary and offensive, and are especially unsettling given Freud's Jewishness and his escape from the Nazis after Hitler's annexation of Austria. Both *Ada* and *Lolita* feature narrators who dabble in psychology or are psychologists themselves. Van Veen is a psychologist, philosopher, and writer of science fiction, who works at the "Department of Terrapy" and treats mentally ill patients. Van writes treatises on *The Texture of Time, Suicide and Sanity*, and "The Farce of Group Therapy in Sexual Maladjustment," which we are told nearly gets him sued by "the Union of Marital Counselors and Catharticians."[36] Both Van and Humbert are obsessed with the incipient sexuality of pre-pubescent girls or "nymphets" and both use enchanting lyrical prose as a diversion from their taboo desires and dubious ethical behavior. Although what follows will focus on *Lolita*, both novels present an unstable satire of psychoanalysis with narrators who play a double game—ironizing Freudian psychoanalysis while speaking in its idioms.

Lolita and Psychoanalysis

Lolita is the apotheosis of Nabokov's enduring parody of psychoanalysis, unfolding like a bogus case study replete with sexual confessions, taxonomies of deviant behavior, and a trove of Freudian clichés about perversity, arrested development, childhood trauma, incest, and the Oedipus complex. Humbert and Freud are positioned as twinned charlatans in the novel, exotic European exports who work a perilous magic on unrefined Americans (and readers). Humbert Humbert, the protagonist and first-person narrator, purports to be telling his story as an unrevised confession begun in a psychiatric hospital and finished in a prison, and drafted over the course of fifty-six days. He chronicles his infatuation with the "nymphet" Lolita (i.e., Dolores Haze), whom he eventually abducts after the death of her mother and holds in captivity in a paranoid road trip across the United States. Lolita eventually flees with another pedophile: Humbert's rival, the playwright and pornographer, Clare Quilty.

In the fictional foreword to *Lolita*, the psychiatrist John Ray Jr., tells us that Humbert is a psychiatric patient on trial for a crime, but of course John Ray sounds distinctly Humbertian. Part of the text's double game lies in Humbert's questionable sanity: Humbert makes reference to his own madness but also identifies as a "manqué" psychoanalyst, taking obvious pleasure in impersonating psychoanalysts and psychiatrists and exposing their gullibility and lack of sophistication. He discovers "an endless source of robust enjoyment in trifling with psychiatrists: cunningly leading them on; never letting them see that you know all the tricks of the trade,"[37] while boasting of his ability to outwit them through his invention of "elaborate dreams" with "fake 'primal scenes'" for the "dream extortionists"[38] who misdiagnose him as impotent or gay. Humbert tells us that the psychoanalytic treatment he receives in the asylum does nothing to reroute his perverse desires, it merely "wooed me with pseudoliberations of pseudolibidoes" (18), offering fraudulent liberations from fraudulent impulses.

From the outset, Humbert baits the reader with psychoanalytic explanations, using his backstory as a psycho-history to justify his obsession with underage girls. He insists that his obsession for nymphets is a consequence of his unconsummated passion for the young Annabel Leigh, an obvious pastiche of Poe's prepubescent poetic muse and a literary precedent for Humbert's taboo eroticism. Annabel, like her poetic counterpart, dies tragically in her youth, frozen metaphorically in a *nymphic* state. Playing the part of both analysand and analyst, Humbert grafts Freud's trauma theory onto what he calls his "tortured past," claiming that his thwarted sexual experience with Annabel constitutes the origin of his sexual perversity. The scene in which the young Humbert and Annabel are interrupted in their attempted lovemaking by two older men, the Hemingway-esque "old man of the sea and his brother,"[39] playfully enacts Freud's argument in *The Interpretation of Dreams* that "coitus interruptus" is one of the "aetiological factors in the development of neurotic anxiety."[40]

By using his childhood to frame his story of sexual abuse of children, Humbert draws on Freudian ideas that would have been familiar to midcentury readers: that his own unhappy childhood is the source of his current behaviors and that, in Freud's words, "The events of [a child's] first years are of paramount importance for his whole later life."[41] For context we might turn to Alfred Kazin's *New York Times* essay, "The Freudian Revolution Analyzed" (1956), published one year after *Lolita*, which declares that "the greatest and most beautiful effect of Freudianism is the increasing awareness of childhood as the most important single influence on personal development."[42] Adopting Freud's argument that adult mental illness is a symbolic expression of repressed childhood experiences, Humbert suggests that his unconsummated desire for Annabel Leigh is the source of his stalled sexual development as well as his obsessive search for Annabel's substitute. Freud writes in *Three Essays on the Theory of Sexuality* that "the very impressions we have forgotten have nonetheless left the deepest traces in our psychic life, and acted as determinants for our whole future development."[43] Humbert draws on Freud's ideas in the same essays that the lingering perversions in adulthood signify an arrested sexual development, and that the neurotic is compelled to play out, however unknowingly, repressed conflicts of childhood.[44] As Freud articulates in "Remembering, Repeating and Working-Through" (1914), "the patient does not remember anything of what he has forgotten and repressed, but acts it out. He reproduces it not as a memory but as an action; he repeats it, without, of course, knowing that he is repeating it. . . . The part played by resistance, too, is easily recognized. The greater the resistance, the more extensively will acting out (repetition) replace remembering."[45]

In ironic fashion, Humbert enacts Freud's theories of compulsive repetition and childhood sexuality in crafting his abortive tale of romantic love, but in a way that is conscious and crafted rather than unconscious. As Alfred Appel reminds us in his annotations to *Lolita*, Humbert undercuts the legitimacy of this traumatic backstory "by projecting it in fragments of another man's verse," in this case Edgar Allan Poe's.[46] By conflating his traumatic past with Poe's "Annabel Lee" and embroidering this backstory with passing allusions to Hemingway and other authors, Humbert reveals that he, like psychoanalysis, is mostly a tissue of literary and cultural references with questionable depth.

Nabokov positions Humbert and Freud as twinned charlatans in the novel, exotic European exports who work a perilous magic on unrefined Americans (and readers). Humbert's tricks are primarily literary and rhetorical, diverting us from the literal events of plot through dizzying acts of wordplay, wit, allusion, and alliteration. Trading on the verbal echoes between *rapist* and *therapist*, for example, and the idea that one could be concealed within the other, he boasts that "the child therapist in me, (a fake, as most of them are—but no matter) regurgitated neo-Freudian hash and conjured up a dreaming and exaggerating Dolly in the 'latency' period of girlhood."[47] Part of Humbert's double game is that he plays the part of analysand—detailing his memories, desires, fantasies, and dreams—as well as analyst—observing and classifying Lolita's developmental stages, dubbing himself "King Sigmund the Second." He performs this double movement by dangling psychoanalytic readings before the reader while rendering them suspect. Humbert even enlists psychoanalysis as a legal defense by suggesting that his crimes against Lolita are mitigated by his traumatic (yet fabricated) backstory, alluding to the growing popularity within the American legal system of using psychological explanations to reduce criminal sentences. Nabokov found this practice contemptible, complaining in *Strong Opinions* of the "dangerous ethical consequences" of psychoanalysis, "such as when a filthy murderer with the brain of a tapeworm is given a lighter sentence because his mother spanked him too much or too little—it works both ways."[48] Humbert attempts to convince the imagined "ladies and gentlemen of the jury," his imagined readers, that he is helplessly playing out a script from childhood; and yet we are asked to see through this sham form of exoneration, to read against his appropriation of psychoanalysis for exculpatory ends.

Psychoanalytic theory operates on multiple levels in *Lolita*: as a hermeneutic that lures us with the promise of access to Humbert's psychology; as a rhetorical device Humbert uses to manipulate us; as a trap that forces us back onto our own habits of reading. Humbert frames a backstory dominated by traumatic events—a dead mother in infancy, an absent father—who is, among other things, Austrian—a first love who dies tragically in her youth. But the lack of detail afforded these events from an author given to *detailism* points to the hollowness of their explanatory power. The hilarious economy with which the mother's death is treated, she "died in a freak accident (picnic, lightning)"[49] and the absence of retrospection the death affords (nothing exists "save for a pocket of warmth in the darkest past, nothing of her subsists within the hollows and dells of memory"),[50] render a psychoanalytic reading of trauma highly suspicious. A similar event occurs in *Ada*, in which the protagonist's father dies in a freak airplane accident, and the pathos is diffused almost immediately. We come to learn that the father was also an obstacle to the siblings' incestuous relationship, so his death is viewed as fortunate, as if the law of the father were suspended. Humbert subverts the traumatic tale of parental death by telling us he grew up in a "bright world of illustrated books," a "whitewashed cosmos" with women who coo over his "cheerful motherlessness."[51] The manipulation of psychoanalytic formulas for exculpatory ends serves to hollow out the explanatory power and moral credibility of psychoanalysis. Such traumatic scenarios are laced with irony and humor, and the joke is apparently on us if we fall for the trick.

Jenefer Shute sees such Freudian devices as traps wired to explode, preemptive strikes whose signifying power is dismantled before they can signify. Such strikes preempt the reader who would apply a psychoanalytic reading to Humbert's narrative. Addressing the psychiatrist/psychoanalyst as the imagined reader of his case history, Humbert declares:

> The able psychiatrist who studies my case—and whom by now Dr. Humbert has plunged, I trust, into a state of leporine fascination—is no doubt anxious to have me take my Lolita to the seaside and have me find there, at last, the "gratification" of a lifetime urge, and release from the subconscious obsession of an incomplete childhood romance with the initial little Miss Lee.
>
> Well, comrade, let me tell you that I *did* look for a beach, though I also have to confess that by the time we reached its mirage of gray water, so many delights had already been granted me by my traveling

companion that the search for a Kingdom by the Sea, a Sublimated Riviera, or whatnot, far from being the impulse of the subconscious, had become the rational pursuit of a purely theoretical thrill.[52]

Humbert ridicules the psychiatrist who is hypnotized (and aroused) by this tale of compulsion and repetition, who wants the tale to confirm the thesis; yet Humbert is conscious of his compulsion to repeat and does it anyway—a reliance on Freudian temporalities that is also a mockery. The novel ridicules psychoanalysis as philistine, reductive, and immoral; yet it also performs its cultural power, pressing psychoanalytic theories into the service of parody, grafting its cultural clichés onto a self-consciously "perverse" story of love and desire.[53]

Lolita as Case Study

Ultimately, Nabokov appears to disarm psychoanalysis by forcing his loathsome protagonist to hew to its logic. Humbert's discourse is so saturated with psychoanalytic language that it becomes our exclusive means of access to the world of *Lolita*. Nabokov's greatest weapon against Freud is to put psychoanalysis into the mouth of a narrator who is not only unreliable but morally bankrupt, a character we come to recognize as guilty of serious crimes against Lolita. We are left with Freudian forms as the dominant framework for interpreting the novel, whether they be the novel's proliferating symbols, its puns and wordplay, its imitation of the case study, or Humbert's recognizably psychoanalytic afflictions—his stalled sexual development, his compulsion to repeat the past, his interpretive paranoia. Just as Humbert professes to have "nothing but words to play with," the reader has nothing but Freudian forms to interpret with. Humbert's reliance on Freudian forms to justify his solipsism and abuse compels us to recognize these as unethical narrative choices, and thus to view psychoanalysis as not only reductive but immoral.

Jenefer Shute sees Nabokov's polemic against Freud as reflective of larger tensions within the twentieth-century novel, more specifically, "the fictional text's struggle against an encroaching hermeneutics."[54] We see such struggle emerge in *Lolita*'s parody of one of the signature genres of psychoanalysis: the psychological case history. *Lolita* is shot through with ambivalence toward psychoanalysis: In its parodic and playful style it imitates Freudian forms while attempting to diffuse their authority. But parody, as an ironic imitation, makes use of both intimacy and difference, just as its Greek root *para* signifies both *alongside* and *counter to*. It is a doubling structure that conjures its predecessor through an act of repetition while it also stresses difference. Parody is thus an ambivalent mode that "cannot help inscribing and granting authority to what it parodies, even if it aims to challenge it."[55] Rather than deploy a more straightforward response to Freud, Nabokov relies on parody as if to better sustain the rivalry. The novel's secret sharing is as much about proximity and familiarity as it is about irony and difference.

To prepare for writing *Lolita*, Nabokov read case histories and newspaper stories on pedophilia and, like an anthropologist in the field, travelled on school buses to observe the speech patterns and mannerisms of American school girls. The boundaries between case history and fictional narrative blur in the unstable, metafictional world of *Lolita*, as Nabokov illustrates the parallels between the conceits of the case history and those of realist fiction—both invested in narrating subjectivity, both sensational and titillating, both professing to be truthful accounts. *Lolita* begins with a fictional foreword in which John Ray Jr. PhD, a psychologist and prize-winning author of a treatise on "morbid states and perversions," tells us that *Lolita, or the Confession of a White Widowed Male*, will become a classic in psychiatry circles. The foreword frames *Lolita* as a criminal-madman's self-narrated case history, the true confessions of a "demented diarist."[56] As a parodic introduction, *Lolita* mocks the pretentions to expertise and authenticity announced by the case history: John Ray Jr. is supposedly an expert in psychology, but many of his stylistic flourishes are distinctly Humbertian, which produces an authorial vertigo. Is this Nabokov's impersonation of Humbert's impersonation of a psychologist? As it manipulates the genres of case history, first-person confessional narrative, and realist novel, the foreword burlesques the case history's pretentions to facticity and objectivity, as well as its titillating promise of intimacy with the "'real' people behind the 'true' story."[57]

The foreword is awash in comic flourishes, including references to fictional experts like Dr. Blanche Schwarzmann (white black man), who testifies to the prevalence of pedophilia among American adult males, and suspiciously normalizes it. The foreword teases us with the promise of lurid details about taboo desires, pedophilia, madness, and criminality while condemning the reader for a prurient interest in these subjects. While a spoof, it also functions as a defense against censorship, legitimating (however satirically) the moral and pedagogical value of its subject matter, shifting responsibility from the content of the book to the dubious morals of the reader. Indeed, the foreword evokes Nabokov's very real fears about the reception of *Lolita* as an immoral or pornographic text, fears that were exacerbated by the difficulties he had in finding a publisher and its eventual publication by Olympia Press, best known for its publication of erotic fiction.

Although *Lolita* does not make explicit reference to Freud's "Dora: An Analysis of a Case of Hysteria," there are numerous parallels between the novel and the iconic case study. Both *Lolita* and *Dora* tell the stories of young adolescent women thrust into erotic entanglements with self-serving and abusive adults. Nabokov exploits the parallels between Humbert's taboo "nympholepsy" and the illicit relations between adult men and young women depicted in "Dora." Lolita is twelve when she first meets Humbert, and Dora is thirteen when she is first propositioned by Herr K. As narrators and analysts (amateur in Humbert's case), Freud and Humbert are consumed with the early sexual development of young women who are imagined to be full of repressed sexual yearnings: Humbert's obsession with Lolita's "nymphancy" echoes Freud's latency, although Humbert distinguishes his poetic descriptions from dry scientific classification—"the fey grace, the elusive, shifty, soul-shattering, insidious charm." Like a psychologist or psychoanalyst, Humbert offers detailed descriptions of the tastes, fantasies, and behaviors of "nymphets," a sub-species of young girl that he claims only an artist can appreciate: "You have to be an artist or a madman, a creature of infinite melancholy,"[58] once again using his enraptured self-portrait to shroud his deeds.

Freud offers his case study of Dora as a window into the "intimacies of psychosexual life," a revelation of his patient's "most secret and repressed wishes,"[59] as well as an illustration of his theories of the psychoneurosis. Not unlike John Ray Jr., Freud condemns in advance physicians, psychologists, and other readers who receive his study of hysteria as "a *roman à clef* designed for their private delectation."[60] He announces that sexual questions "will be discussed with all possible frankness" while shaming the prurient reader: "it would be the mark of a singular and perverse prurience to suppose that conversations of this kind are a good means of exciting or of gratifying sexual desires."[61] In a parody of this double move, John Ray Jr. defends Humbert's narrative from charges of obscenity by assuring the reader that the case study's primarily values are scientific and ethical: Those "very scenes that one might ineptly accuse of a sensuous existence of their own, are the most strictly functional ones in the development of this tragic tale tending unswervingly to nothing less than a moral apotheosis."[62] Whether the tale culminates in a moral apotheosis, whether Humbert has any remorse, is doubtful. The foreword appeals to the reader's desire for the perversely titillating, while ending with a moralizing cliché that is another game with the reader: *Lolita* "should make all of us—parents, social workers, educators—apply ourselves with still greater vigilance and vision to the task of bringing up a better generation in a safer world."[63]

Dora, whose real name is Ida Bauer, is taken against her wishes to Freud to be treated for depression, suicidality, fainting spells, repetitive coughing, and the recurrent loss of her voice. Freud proceeds like a detective, methodically unravelling her tangled narrative, which reveals to him an erotic attachment to her father and an intense rivalry with her mother. But the conflicts go much deeper than the Oedipal scenario, as Dora's family is entangled with another couple, Herr and Frau K., whom they had met years before at a resort where Dora's father was seeking treatment. Dora becomes aware early on that her father and Frau K. are having an affair, and that she has been positioned as a potential sexual surrogate and surrogate mother for Frau K. and Herr K.'s children. Over the course of the affair, Herr K. makes a series of sexual advances to Dora, which she rejects, while Dora's father looks the other way, which leads her to conclude that her father has handed her over as a consolation prize to Herr K. in exchange for his tolerating the affair between Dora's father and Frau K. Dora's insight about being handed over, echoes Freud's observation that Dora's father "handed her over to me for psychotherapeutic treatment."[64]

Pamela Thurschwell makes the compelling suggestion that Freud becomes "part of the chain of powerful adults who treat Dora as an object of exchange."[65] Freud is most sympathetic to Herr K. and reads Dora's refusals of Herr K.'s sexual advances as unmistakable signs of her pathology, rather than as healthy responses to the manipulations and solicitations of adults. Freud insists that a "healthy" young woman would have received such advances as pleasurable, and that the best outcome for everyone would be for Dora to accept Herr K. in marriage. Freud's prejudices and limitations are manifest in his sympathies with Herr K. and in his inability to scrutinize the self-serving and abusive behaviors of the adults surrounding Dora. Freud does not so much highlight the adults' misdeeds as try to convince Dora that she harbors suppressed romantic feelings for each of them—by turns her father, Herr K., and Frau K. In the words of Stephen Marcus, "the 'reality' that Freud insists upon is very different from the 'reality' that Dora is claiming and clinging to."[66]

Lolita and "Dora" are similar in their portrayal of male narrators who dominate the narrative discourse and claim to speak on behalf of young women. Humbert and Freud are notoriously self-conscious and controlling as narrators, devoting much of their discourse to managing how their narratives will be received. Freud spars with his "narrow-minded critics" and is ruthlessly on guard against intellectual resistance, which he attributes to the accuracy of his interpretations—like the "no" from the unconscious that indicates a suppressed "yes." Humbert flatters, cajoles, and insults a group of imagined readers, whom he calls his jury, the men and women who will decide his fate. Both narrators insist on the trustworthiness of their accounts while they announce their anxieties about the record being "not absolutely—phonographically—exact," to borrow Freud's words.[67] Humbert asks us to imagine that his detailed accounts are transcribed from a previously destroyed pocket diary that he can reproduce perfectly from memory. "I am no poet. I am only a very conscientious recorder," he says, after insisting earlier that he is a poet and madman.[68]

For Freud, the hysteric is an unreliable narrator unable to tell a coherent narrative about her life. Freud sees his role as that of the expert, carefully demystifying Dora's tangled testimony, taking her back to the origins of her symptoms. But Freud is an unreliable narrator himself, over-identified with Herr K. and his sense of rejection, incapable of understanding his own role in Dora's failed treatment. Freud is not only blind to his counter-transference, he is self-conscious about the incompleteness of the analysis, which Dora breaks off prematurely in what Freud perceives as an act of betrayal. Freud is also self-conscious about the genre itself: in *Studies on Hysteria*, he acknowledges that his case histories read like short stories and seem to "lack the serious stamp of science": "I must console myself," Freud says, "with the reflection that the nature of the subject is evidently responsible for this, rather than any preference of my own."[69]

Both works are similar, then, in presenting older men locked in intellectual combat with precocious young women. Freud attempts to convince Dora that she is a prisoner of her unadmitted sexual desires, which in turn provokes her resistance.[70] He turns Dora's resistances into affirmations, neutralizing her objections through recourse to the unconscious; as he says at one point, every no from the unconscious conceals a suppressed yes. Critics have highlighted Freud's self-authorizing maneuvers, his branding of all forms of intellectual resistance from both inside and outside the analytic session as pathological symptoms of repression. But, as the case of Dora illustrates, resistance can also be a healthy non-compliance with a pathological environment and a legitimate protest against injustice. Dora abruptly ends treatment as her final objection to Freud, while Lolita escapes Humbert's captivity for a similarly egregious paramour, which reveals the poverty of options.

Ultimately, what unites Freud and Humbert as narrators is their inability to produce reliable accounts of their subjects: Humbert's idealizing vision of Lolita as an enchanted nymphet in a fairy tale blinds him to any knowledge of her reality: "were we both plunged in the same enchanted mist?"[71] he says after abducting her. Freud's obliviousness to his counter-transference and his unmistakable sexism are similarly disqualifying to his roles as analyst and narrator. And yet, the brilliance of both works is that we glimpse Lolita and Dora's suffering *despite* our dependence on limited narrators; just as we can gain some understanding of Lolita in *Lolita*, we gain something of Dora in *Dora*. We catch glimpses of Lolita's personality through the mesh of Humbert's perspective: flashes of her lively wit, hints of moodiness and despair, and glimmers of nostalgia for an adolescence she never had. Although Humbert speaks in obfuscating euphemisms, Lolita, when we hear her, is stunningly direct. Humbert tells us that Lolita can "load a question with violent significance" and lob "accusatory innuendos" his way.[72] When Humbert tells her that his affections toward her are paternal and protective, Lolita replies: "The word is incest."

Humbert insists that Lolita is not an innocent victim but a knowing, corrupt, and complicit seductress, who has been depraved by "modern co-education," "juvenile mores," and "the campfire racket."[73] He invokes Freud's theories of childhood sexuality to exonerate himself of the charges of child abuse, to reverse the order of seduction; but we are invited to see this as a willful misreading and dubious ethical maneuver. Casting himself as innocent victim, Humbert proclaims: "I was still under the impression that whatever went on among those brash brats, went on at a later age. . . . I should have understood that Lolita had already proved to be something quite different from innocent Annabel, and that the nymphean evil breathing through every pore of the fey child that I had prepared for my secret delectation would make the secrecy impossible, and the delectation lethal."[74]

Humbert goes on to describe Lolita as "the body of some immortal daemon disguised as a female child" and invokes her sexual experimentation at camp as evidence that he has not defiled her.[75] But we should see through such self-serving deployments of psychoanalysis, just as we should see through Humbert's alternately idealizing and demonizing portrayals of Lolita. Although Nabokov often championed an art that is above morality, *Lolita*, insists on an ethics of reading critically, one that attends to the hidden subtext of Dolores's suffering, and by extension the suffering of other young girls and women whom Humbert's perspective diminishes.

Symbol Hunting and Suspicious Reading

Nabokov ridiculed the suspicious style of the Freudians—the pursuit of a mystery that will eventually be unveiled—but he structures *Lolita* around two genres of detection—the case history and the detective story. Both genres highlight the misleading nature of appearances and cultivate a wariness on the part of the reader. In his introduction to Freud's "Dora," Philip Rieff brings these two genres together, describing Freud as "the spiritual detective hired by Dora's worried father," who "catches up with her fugitive inner life."[76] Rita Felski argues that "The detective serves as the prototype of a science of suspicion that developed in the nineteenth century, functioning as an expert reader uniquely able to decipher hidden strata of criminal activity."[77] As many critics have noted, the genre of the detective story also bears resemblances to the writings of Freud, who as Paul Riceour observes, looked upon consciousness as partly false consciousness and helped develop a "hermeneutics of suspicion," whereby the meanings the patient gives for his actions are in conflict with the real meanings of the actions revealed by the analysis.[78]

Freud himself recognized the parallels between the detective and the analyst, describing the latter as "accustomed to divine secret and concealed things from unconsidered or unnoticed details, from the rubbish heap, as it were, of our observations."[79] Freud's attunement to wayward details aligns him with a long tradition of literary critics and theorists, including Althusser, Barthes, Macherey, Jameson, and D. A. Miller who view the text as a tissue of details that can be analyzed for occulted meanings. As a self-described psychoanalyst "manqué," Humbert fancies himself a master of detection, and yet his rival Quilty eludes him, as does Lolita when she escapes. If the first half of the novel draws heavily on the genres of romance and fairy tale to embroider Humbert's one-sided love affair, the second half descends into cold war crime drama and detective fiction to highlight Humbert's intensifying paranoia. We see this generic shift shortly after Humbert abducts Lolita and takes her to the Enchanted Hunters. Humbert drugs Lolita and retreats to the lobby to let the sleeping pill kick in, at which point he is approached by a man in a cloud of smoke who asks questions about Lolita. While in retrospect the reader recognizes the episode as Humbert's first encounter with Clare Quilty, it is left ambiguous at the time whether Humbert has been discovered or whether he is surfacing guilty feelings about his crimes. Nonetheless, the episode is playfully indebted to Freud, with its externally dramatized inner conflict and its use of wordplay and slips of the tongue.

Nabokov takes every opportunity to lampoon the psychoanalytic frenzy for decoding the "standardized symbols of the psychoanalytic racket."[80] Nabokov writes in the afterword to *Lolita*, "I detest symbols and allegories (which is due partly to my own feud with Freudian voodooism and partly to my loathing of generalizations devised by literary mythists and sociologists)."[81] Humbert breathes disdain for the facile hieroglyphs of the Freudians, in which every "fountain pen" signifies a patient who is a "repressed undinist."[82] The reductive and generalizing nature of the Freudian symbol is a Nabokovian obsession, yet Nabokov's writings are flush with symbols that invite decoding, even as they become unstable sites of Freudian caricature. Moreover, Nabokov ridiculed the sexual symbolism of psychoanalysis but was a master of sexual suggestion himself. In Humbert's first erotic dream about Lolita, which occurs on the eve of a promised outing to a lake, the lake is "glazed over with a sheet of emerald ice, and a pockmarked Eskimo was trying in vain to break it with a pickaxe." Lolita and her mother are both on horseback yet Humbert rides nothing but air, "one of those little omissions due to the absent-mindedness of the dream agent."[83] Musing on the obvious sexual symbolism, which evokes themes of sexual frustration and impotence, Humbert concludes, "Dr. Blanche Schwarzmann would have paid me a sack of schillings for adding such a libidream to her files."[84] Humbert's dream is dutifully Freudian in both its disguised wish-fulfillment and its anxieties (the frozen lake, the absent horse), and maybe too transparent to require decoding. The very name of the fictional analyst, "Blanche Schwarzmann," or *white black man*, takes another stab at psychoanalysis for interpreting reality in black and white. Humbert later invokes another fictional psychoanalyst, Melanie Weiss (*black white*), Blanche's inverse double, to the same effect.

Dream interpretation was a crucial feature of Freud's case studies and was pivotal to his comprehension of the psychoneuroses; he described dreams as disguised wish-fulfilment and detours "by which repression can be evaded."[85] Not only is *Ada*'s Van a psychologist and dream analyst in his own right, but his chronicle includes a full chapter on dream interpretation that sounds uncannily like a pastiche of Freud and Proust: "All dreams are affected by the experiences and impressions of the present as well as by memories of childhood; all reflect, in images and sensations, a draft, a light, a rich meal or a grave internal disorder."[86] There are several dreams and scenes of dream interpretation in *Lolita*.[87] Toward the end of the novel, after Lolita escapes, Humbert dreams of kissing Lolita as she shape-shifts into Charlotte and Valeria, Humbert's first wife. Evoking mechanisms of condensation and displacement, Humbert's dream captures his terror of time and his recognition that Lolita has shed her precious "nymphancy" for the disappointing banality of adult womanhood. Humbert calls this a "dream disorder of auctioneered Viennese bric-à-brac," as if the loss of Lolita has ruined his artistry, precipitating a "dream disorder" of second-hand Freudian symbols.

Humbert's horror of "neo-Freudian hash" and "Viennese bric-a-brac" circles back to his contempt for the generic and the derivative. Humbert fashions himself an artist and iconoclast with exquisite taste; yet the joke is also on him, for he idealizes the most conventional subject of all—the modern American adolescent.[88] Humbert assures the reader that "Lolita had been safely solipsized,"[89] that is, transmuted into a pure work of art, as if solipsism were something that could be done to a person; but such heightened prose merely conceals the depths of his abuse. Insisting on his innocence after masturbating to Lolita, Humbert claims: "What I had madly possessed was not she, but my own creation, another fanciful Lolita—perhaps, more real than Lolita; overlapping, encasing her; floating between me and her, and having no will, no consciousness—indeed, no life of her own."[90] The implication is that Lolita's subjectivity and innocence are still intact, and more perversely, that Humbert is protecting them from his own instincts. The abuse will only intensify as the novel progresses, but Humbert will claim later that he is protecting Lolita's innocence by drugging her. Humbert says repeatedly that there is no "real" Lolita but only his artistic rendering of her. Such telling admissions afford us a critical interpretation of Humbert from inside his own discourse: his refusal to recognize Lolita's difference from his "solipsized" version of her, his violent erasure of her subjectivity.

Though Humbert ridicules the incessant symbol hunting of the Freudians and their lust for hidden meanings, he becomes the suspicious reader *par excellence*. After Humbert and Lolita move to Beardsley, Humbert notices shifts in Lolita's behavior and is certain that her theatre lessons and friendship with Mona Dahl are making her a proficient deceiver. The references to infidelity and duplicity proliferate as Humbert imagines Lolita in the guise of Mr. Hyde, and then as Emma Bovary. Increasingly anxious about losing her, Humbert senses "instinctively that toilets—as also telephones—happened to be . . . the points where my destiny was liable to catch."[91] His suspicion is not unfounded, for as we learn later Lolita has been in contact with Quilty since their stay at the Enchanted Hunters. In a metafictional aside, Humbert remarks that this is not "one of those honest mystery stories where all you have to do is keep an eye on the clues."[92]

Paranoia dominates Humbert and Lolita's second journey, as Humbert becomes convinced that they are being pursued by a man in an Aztec red convertible who looks uncannily like his relative, Gustave Trapp. He suspects that his pursuer is a secret lover conspiring with Lolita to torment and elude him, but Quilty proves to be an elusive enemy, becoming a series of "identical detectives in prismatically changing cars," who Humbert assumes are "figments of my persecution mania."[93] Reality and fantasy blur as Humbert descends into paranoid breakdown. No longer in control of fate, he believes he is its hapless victim, subject to "cycle[s] of persecution,"[94] longing to "break some pattern of fate in which I obscurely felt myself being enmeshed."[95] Late in the novel, Humbert reveals a gun that he has withheld from the reader. While the gun suggests the intensification of violence that accompanies his paranoia, it becomes another opportunity to caricature Freudian symbolism: "We must remember that a pistol is the Freudian symbol of the Ur-father's central forelimb."[96]

Humbert withholds the identity of his adversary until the end of the novel, although he offers hints along the way: "I had been keeping Clare Quilty's face masked in my dark dungeon."[97] Quilty is at once a detective, a lover, a secret agent, a prankster, an imposter, and a distinctly Humbertian rival. As Humbert pursues his adversary in his third journey across the United States, Quilty leaves him with a trail of "derisive hints" of his and Lolita's whereabouts, planting "insulting pseudonyms," obscure literary references, sexual innuendos, anagrams, puns, and locutions that only Humbert could decode, revealing that he is every bit the intellectual equal of Humbert ("No detective could discover the clues Trapp had tuned to my mind and manner").[98] A verbal trickster like Humbert, Quilty deposits a maze of false names to disorient his pursuer and enmeshes Humbert in elaborate games of wordplay and "logomancy," laying traps that reveal how meticulously patterned the novel's self-references are (one of Quilty's pseudonyms is "Harold Haze, Tombstone, Arizona"). Humbert observes, "I noticed that whenever he felt his enigmas were becoming too recondite, even for such a solver as I, he would lure me back with an easy one."[99] The truth shimmers beneath these cryptic locutions, and Humbert becomes the desperate over-reader that he satirizes.

The Freudian frenzy for verbal decoding is not unlike the "cryptogrammic paper chase"[100] Humbert pursues to discover Quilty's identity. Humbert is described as "groping in a border-land mist with verbal phantoms";[101] but psychoanalysis is associated with the same game of verbal decryption. Psychoanalytic riddles become hoaxes writ large, elaborate contrivances that offer tantalizing answers to complex truths; and yet there is no way to separate Humbert's own cryptic verbal constructions and his intensifying interpretive paranoia from the "hermeneutics of suspicion" that he disdains. In the final section of *Lolita*, every detail becomes a clue, one that could either point to hidden meaning or throw Humbert off the trail. Humbert becomes a ruthless detective or paranoid madman revisiting the scenes of his crimes against Lolita for clues to Quilty's identity. In this he is not unlike Freud, who portrayed himself as a detective methodically untangling clues, reading dreams, wordplay, and slips of the tongue as messages to be decoded.

Even as the novel burlesques psychoanalysis and its habits of reading for occulted meanings, its formal patterning invites a readerly distrust, not only of Humbert but of Nabokov, who plays an elaborate verbal game with the reader. *Lolita* is filled with clues and patterns that await deciphering; the more we read the more we discover. Nabokov's fictions capitalize on this interpretive paranoia, while they burlesque the obsessive reading of signs. When Van Veen is on the verge of his long-awaited sexual tryst with his sister after the deaths of his family members remove all obstacles to their taboo romance, he sees "a dead and dry hummingbird moth . . . on the window ledge of the lavatory." Van quickly moves to disarm the symbolization that the moth invites: "Thank goodness, symbols did not exist either in dreams or in the life between."[102] In his short story "Symbols and Signs," which first appeared in the *New Yorker* in 1948, an older couple from Minsk have a mentally ill and suicidal son who is afflicted with "referential mania."[103] The condition consists of an elaborate system of delusions in which everything that happens around the son forms a veiled reference to his own fate. The son's "referential mania" has been studied by a psychiatrist in a scientific paper and is described as follows:

> Everything is a cipher and of everything he is the theme. All around him, there are spies. Some of them are detached observers, like glass surfaces and still pools; others, such as coats in store windows, are prejudiced witnesses, lynchers at heart; others, again (running water, storms), are hysterical to the point of insanity, have a distorted opinion of him, and grotesquely misinterpret his actions. He must be always on his guard and devote every minute and module of life to the decoding of the undulation of things.

The son is convinced that he is at the center of a conspiracy and that he is surrounded by spies, witnesses, lynchers, and grotesque misreaders, so he must be ever wary and alert. Everything is a clue that leads back to himself, revealing "the ultimate truth of his being."[104] As the story progresses, the reader is invited to decode several unexplained events: an underground train that loses its current between train cars, a bird "helplessly twitching in a puddle," a series of misdialed telephone calls by a girl anxiously asking for "Charlie." The story closes on a telephone ringing with a caller who is never identified, which leads us to wonder whether this is another wrong number or the asylum calling about the son's suicide. Nabokov invites us to puzzle over these enigmatic signs, which could be random occurrences, coded messages, omens, or empty signifiers. As a story that is also about the practice of interpretation, it asks whether attending closely to symbols and signs is a "referential mania," a form of insanity or solipsism. On the one hand, the story parodies the critical sensibility that looks for latent meanings in every sign; on the other hand, it relies upon this critical sensibility to fill out the shadowy and elliptical gaps in the tale. As in *Lolita*, although on a much smaller scale, Nabokov plants clues (like the plaintive phone call and the twitching bird) that bait the reader into entering the referential mania that afflicts his characters; but they also make us wonder if the critical impulse is just madness.

The Hermeneutics of Suspicion, or Referential Mania

This raises a question: Is the "hermeneutics of suspicion," as an interpretive methodology, a form of referential mania? While Nabokov preempts discussions of the "hermeneutics of suspicion" and "paranoid" reading by several decades, we can see him thinking through these hermeneutical questions. "The hermeneutics of suspicion" is a phrase famously coined by Paul Ricoeur in *Freud and Philosophy* to capture a style of textual interpretation that envisions a gap between a text's surface and its hidden meanings. Ricoeur called Marx, Nietzsche, and Freud the "masters of suspicion" for their shared conviction that one had to look "behind" or "beneath" appearances to locate the motivations of conscious phenomena.[105] In Rita Felski's words, "The 'hermeneutics of suspicion' is the name usually bestowed on [a] technique of reading texts against the grain and between the lines, of cataloging their omissions and laying bare their contradictions, of rubbing in what they fail to know and cannot represent."[106] Felski suggests elsewhere that a hermeneutics of suspicion has come to be "synonymous with intellectual rigor, theoretical sophistication, and intransigent opposition to the status quo."[107] Wanting to grant more authority to everyday readers, Felski, Anker, and others have introduced the idea of the "postcritical" as a set of dispositions that are not just suspicious, but are characterized by other affective relations to texts, including engagement, identification, appreciation, and pleasure. Critique, they suggest, does not have to be our exclusive orientation to texts, but it could be just one orientation among many.

The eclipse of orthodox psychoanalytic approaches in contemporary literary studies—especially in its psycho-biographical and applied psychoanalytic forms—and the increasing skepticism of the "hermeneutics of suspicion" that it helped inspire, has occasioned its own set of post-Freudian modes and practices, which propose alternatives to reading "deeply," "suspiciously," or "symptomatically." The attempt to orient literary studies away from a "hermeneutics of suspicion" has been no easy task, as suspicion, according to Felski and others, has become almost synonymous with the discipline's habits of reading. Recent scholars have attempted to offer alternative methods to suspicion, what Paul Saint-Amour calls "lower-pitched alternatives to certain 'strong' theoretical habits of thought,"[108] the seeds of which are found within literary studies, affect studies, queer theory, and in non-humanities fields such as sociology, with its methods of observation, description, and object-oriented analysis. As Saint-Amour points out, surface reading, distant reading, thick description, the sociological turn, and new formalism all constitute attempts to circumvent "strong" critical modes in favor of "weak" theories that reflect a "new modesty" in critical approaches.[109] Eve Sedgwick's groundbreaking essay on "paranoid" and "reparative" reading in *Touching Feeling* (2003) argued that our literary critical habits have been dominated by "paranoid" procedures for decades, that our disposition in literary studies has aligned so exclusively with a "hermeneutics of suspicion" that it has foreclosed other interpretive possibilities. As Sedgwick's essay argues, "to apply a hermeneutics of suspicion is,

I believe, widely understood as a mandatory injunction rather than a possibility among other possibilities."[110] Sedgwick is interested in whether or not the knowledge we unearth from paranoid reading is true, and what kind of work paranoid reading performs—"the pursuit of it, the having and exposing of it."[111] She claims that Freud left in his wake a mandate to decode: "in the hands of thinkers after Freud, paranoia has by now candidly become less a diagnosis than a prescription."[112] Her conclusion is that paranoia is contagious, requiring imitation to be understood: One must imitate or embody paranoia to know paranoia, and one can never be paranoid enough. And yet, to practice forms of knowing that are not paranoid, or to have an unmystified view of reality, does not mean that one is suffering from denial or false consciousness. There are other ways of accessing knowledge that are not paranoid; "paranoia knows some things well and others poorly."[113]

In their well-known 2009 essay "Surface Reading: An Introduction," Stephen Best and Sharon Marcus attempt to broaden the scope of textual analysis by offering alternatives to symptomatic style.[114] Rather than view texts as resistive surfaces that disclose deeper and truer meanings to the expert interpreter, they focus on the ways in which texts disclose their own interpretive operations to the reader. They are particularly invested in modes of reading that attend to surfaces of texts rather than "plumb the depths" in search of meaning taken to be "hidden, repressed, deep, and in need of detection and disclosure by an interpreter."[115] As they point out, symptomatic reading gives tremendous power to the act of interpretation, a power that may be difficult for scholars to surrender given as that act is so firmly wedded to ethical and political imperatives to expose ideology and unmask injustice in its various guises. While not synonymous with modernist arguments about aesthetic autonomy, their emphasis on an immersive experience of the text that is forged without suspicion resembles the arguments of late modernist critics such as Adorno and Sontag. As Best and Marcus declare: "We want to reclaim from this tradition the accent on immersion in texts (without paranoia or suspicion about their merit or value), for we understand that attentiveness to the artwork as itself a kind of freedom."[116] Surface reading, as Felski understands it, teaches us to "respect rather than reject what is in plain view," focusing on the observable and describable, rather than the submerged or symptomatic.

We might argue that modernism did much to cultivate this wariness in readers, as its literary objects frequently solicited a distrustful engagement and a zealousness to decipher the text's unreliable speakers, disjointed chronology, and arcane references. Nabokov's novels both solicit and diffuse this impulse toward suspicion. Toward the end of *Ada*, when Van Veen is asked how he explains his mother's deathbed delusion that he and Ada are actually brother and sister and romantically linked, Van responds: "I try not to 'explain' anything, I merely describe."[117] We might read Van's anti-hermeneutical posture here as a clever dodge and a refusal to acknowledge the ethical consequences of his behavior.

Lolita makes us aware of the ethical and epistemological costs of reading without suspicion. Part of what propels the narrative forward is the increasing friction between Humbert's discourse and the reader's interpretation of events. For example, Humbert would have us believe he is composing a hasty confession over the course of fifty-six days, rather than a meticulously patterned text with an elaborate network of cross-references. As a canny manipulator of language, Humbert offers a discourse littered with arcane allusions, puns, double-entendre, untranslated phrases, inventive malapropisms, obsolete words, and references to other parts of the text; he wields his "fancy prose style" to orient his readers away from his darker deeds. If some of Humbert's references are accessible, others are not and can lead the reader on long referential detours. Humbert's shifting self-presentation likewise solicits our mistrust: He portrays himself by turns as an old-world gentleman, an exotic émigré, a "quiet scholar," a child therapist, a "poet *à mes heures*," a "sad eyed degenerate cur," and a "brute." While he frames his narrative as the memoirs of a convicted pedophile and murderer, he asks us to imagine him as a movie-star hunk with a "clean-cut jaw, muscular hand, deep sonorous voice, broad shoulder."[118] Humbert manipulates our romantic fantasies and our sympathies so skillfully that he seems to disarm our critique at the very moments we should be most critical.

At his most outrageous, Humbert asks the reader to sympathize with him at the very moments he recounts his abuse of Lolita, presenting himself as a morally conflicted and "tenderhearted" soul overtaken by his rapture for the ideal nymphet. He even makes us an accessory, inviting us to imagine abusing Lolita ourselves. Pressing his case, Humbert insists: "We do not rape as good soldiers do. We are unhappy, mild dog-eyed gentlemen, sufficiently well integrated to control our urges in the presence of adults, but ready to give years and years of life for one chance to touch a nymphet. Emphatically, no killers are we. Poets never kill."[119]

With signature eloquence, Humbert pleads for our sympathy and tolerance, describing himself as part of a class of "innocuous, inadequate, passive, timid strangers." Yet the plea emerges while he considers drowning Charlotte in Hourglass Lake so that he can have his way with her daughter. The statement is thick with irony as the poet turns out to be every bit the rapist and killer he maligns.

Ultimately, the confinement to Humbert's perspective is the closest approximation the reader has to Dolores's captivity. If the lyrical prose of the early chapters lulls us into a sympathetic identification with Humbert, we eventually find ourselves trapped inside his discursive manipulation and intensifying cruelty. And yet, in spite of our dependence on Humbert's perspective, the narrative *still* affords us a critical interpretation of Humbert himself: We learn to be skeptical of Humbert's self-interest and solipsism, and to read his discourse against his own intentions. To do this demands a "hermeneutics of suspicion," as suspicion remains the only ethical orientation to *Lolita*. To see past the mists and mirages that Humbert places before us requires more than a "surface" approach; it requires a critical approach. Part of our ethical work as readers of *Lolita* is to surface what we can of Lolita's experience given the distortions, obfuscations, and obliquities of Humbert's account.

Nabokov oscillated between claims that *Lolita* was a "highly moral affair" and that it floated above common morality. In "On a Book Entitled *Lolita*," he writes, "I am neither a reader nor a writer of didactic fiction, and, despite John Ray's assertion, *Lolita* has no moral in tow. For me, a work of fiction exists only insofar as if affords me what I shall bluntly call aesthetic bliss. . . ."[120] If we take Nabokov at his word, *Lolita* is a book without social intent, no more answerable to ordinary morality than it is to psychoanalysis. Yet, Nabokov goes to great lengths to distance himself from his morally compromised narrator and to encourage his readers to read against the grain of Humbert's discourse. Just as the novel satirizes the complacency of those characters in the text who "wrestle with dark doubts" and look the other way, it also satirizes the reader who accepts without scrutiny the polished and poetic surfaces of Humbert's tale. As Nabokov invites a suspicious reading of Humbert's story, reading with suspicion becomes a mode of reading *with* the grain, not against it. Hence, failing to read Humbert's discourse with a critical eye is not only a form of naïveté but of ethical complicity. Suspicious reading remains another Freudian form to which *Lolita* is attached.

Which returns us to a modernist tradition of secret sharing. As I said in the book's introduction, Nabokov declared his works invulnerable to psychoanalysis, yet he engaged obsessively with Freud's ideas—in parody, in comical misreadings, in the fictional reinvention of Freudian forms. The blanket dismissals of Freud in his literary forewords and afterwords obscure a long-standing engagement with psychoanalytic ideas, which shape his fictions in indelible ways. Nabokov's fictions may not be answerable or reducible to psychoanalysis, but in their parodic acts of imitation they acknowledge their debt to, and affinity with, the century's most ubiquitous discourse. We cannot seem to be done with psychoanalysis, or at least Nabokov cannot.

Conclusion
Modernist Afterlives and the Legacies of Suspicion

> It unlocks phenomena, but falls short of the phenomenon of art.
> —THEODOR ADORNO ON PSYCHOANALYSIS, *AESTHETIC THEORY*

My book has endeavored to trace a genealogy of secret sharing between literary modernism and psychoanalysis, focusing on the productive entanglements and intense competitive rivalries that helped shape Anglo-American modernism as a field. Although I often refer to them as proximate discourses with shared preoccupations, I want to conclude by thinking through some of the animating tensions between these adjacent fields, and how such tensions return to haunt literary studies in the present. Anglo-American modernism achieved a measure of its cultural and intellectual identity as a field through its intimate agon with psychoanalysis, which played out in explicit criticism, inventive misreadings, and revisions of Freudian forms—from Lawrence's redescriptions of the unconscious to Nabokov's parody of the Freudian case study. The intimate rivalries between fields also centered critical conversations about the meaning and motivation of art, and about the nature of the artistic process—concerns that preoccupied modernists and psychoanalysts alike. At stake was whether literature could be used as psychoanalytic evidence, and whether psychoanalytic interpretations enhanced or distorted aesthetic meaning. These debates and disagreements between modernism and psychoanalysis about the nature of art and the role of interpretation pivoted around a familiar set of tensions: abstraction and intuition, amateurism and expertise, surface and depth. These same binaries have resurfaced in our own historical moment, as scholars debate how best to orient themselves to cultural objects. In what follows, I hope to limn some of the connections between early and late modernist responses to psychoanalysis and more contemporary re-evaluations of suspicions and symptomatic reading—to suggest the longue durée of these critical conversations.

As I have suggested throughout, modernist writers were especially resistant to psychoanalysis's habit of turning literary texts into allegories for its own speculations. Even the authors most closely associated with psychoanalysis—Conrad, Lawrence, Mann, and Woolf—challenged the reduction of their fictions to psychoanalytic evidence and articulated strong distinctions between literary and psychoanalytic discourse. Toward the end of his life, Conrad offered an intriguing response to the hermeneutics of depth that had been relentlessly applied to his fictions. When H. R. Lenormand, the French playwright and Freud enthusiast, attempted to interest Conrad in psychoanalysis, the latter responded: "I have no wish to probe the depths. I like to regard reality as a rough and rugged thing over which I can run my fingers—nothing more."[1] By framing reality as a rough and rugged thing and his literary practice as a feeling of surfaces, Conrad emphasizes exteriority and texture over depth, defining his practice against a psychoanalytic depth hermeneutic. Conceding, perhaps, that reality has a depth that he does not wish to probe, Conrad privileges a mode of representation that does not recuperate deep content at the expense of surface. His response to psychoanalysis expresses ambivalence about the activity of interpretation as, respectively, an imposition of theory or a recovery of repressed meaning. Yet, the formal difficulty of Conrad's work and the complexity he affords his characters seem to solicit the very interpretive practice that he disavows.

Which returns us to Conrad's trope of the "secret sharer" that animates this study. Many of the familiar works of modernism seem thematically compatible with psychoanalysis (for example, *Sons and Lovers* and *To the Lighthouse*, which read as if they were fortified in the soil of psychoanalysis, with their intricate portraits of inner life and their Oedipalized accounts of family dynamics). Other works seem methodologically compatible, soliciting the suspicious, probing style and intensive decipherment equated with psychoanalytic interpretation. There is a reason why modernist artifacts have been so hospitable to psychoanalytic readings: Both revel in the pleasures of the puzzle; in the delights of decoding; in the slippery play of meanings. Suspicion seems baked into the very medium of modernism, into its cryptic formulations and daunting opacities. Rita Felski writes that modernist writers "are drawn to formal devices that systematically block readers from taking words at face value."[2] With their "unreliable narrators, conflicting viewpoints, fragmented narratives, and metafictional devices that alert us to the ways in which words conceal rather than reveal" modernist experiments invite the suspicious modes of interpretation that contemporary theoretical orientations extend and revise.[3] For Felski, the suspicious style of reading so pervasive in our current moment "riffs off, revises, and extends the classic themes of literary and artistic modernism."[4]

The ubiquitous figure of the unreliable narrator seems like the offspring of these two fields. Will Norman suggests that Freud "helped to birth the modernist unreliable narrator in his accounts of deceitful, manipulative, and treacherous patients."[5] Freud argued that the analysand's discourse is unreliable, and that the work of the analyst is to "fill in the gaps in memory" and "overcome resistances due to repression."[6] Just as the analyst learns to bridge the gaps of the patient's fragmented testimony, the reader struggles to make sense of the modernist text's difficulty and disjointedness. But does it follow that the skillful complexities and dizzying puzzles of modernism lend themselves best to psychoanalytic scrutiny? Or do modernist texts rely on forms of indeterminacy and opacity that psychoanalytic criticism would seek to resolve?[7]

Modernists often expressed ambivalence about the probing, symptomatic style of interpretation that psychoanalysis helped introduce and that was increasingly applied to literary texts. Writers responded to this emergent psychoanalytic literary criticism with a redoubling of arguments for aesthetic autonomy, formal self-consciousness, and amateurism. Lawrence disputed psychoanalytic claims to expertise and insisted that we adopt an amateurish style of literary interpretation rooted in our own intuition: "I am an amateur of amateurs . . . I am not a scholar of any sort . . . I proceed by intuition."[8] Woolf disparaged what she saw as the new genre of "Freudian fiction," and disputed the idea that psychoanalysis could offer a hermeneutic "key" to literature. Woolf was also a defender of amateurism, as Melanie Micir and Aarthi Vadde have shown. Recognizing the gendered entailments of expertise, she championed a female amateurism in pointed contrast to the expertise concentrated in "credentialed (predominantly) male bodies."[9] W. H. Auden, for his part, readily adapted the styles of encryption made available to him through psychoanalysis in his early poetic experiments. But by the mid-1930s he had begun to question the diagnostic priorities of psychoanalysis and psychiatry, especially in their objectifying relationship to subjects deemed sexually deviant. Not only did Auden's poetry become more accessible in the mid-1930s, more directed to the reader than the critic, but it made the case for amateurism over expertise—a "homeopathic" poetry that was less reliant on the interventions of critical experts.

Modernists as diverse in aesthetic and political sensibility as Roger Fry, Gertrude Stein, Clive Bell, Virginia Woolf, Wyndham Lewis, James Joyce, D. H. Lawrence, Ezra Pound, and T. S. Eliot were skeptical of psychoanalysis's territorial overreach and problematic accounts of art. Freudian psychoanalysis endeavored to discover art's secret, to lay bare its concealed truths, truths of which the author was presumed to be unaware. Such truths amounted to a set of psychoanalytic formulas only slightly adjusted to the nuances of literary works. As Thomas Mann's metaphor of the X-ray suggests, authors felt exposed and reduced under the X-ray beam of analysis, especially as they were analyzed through their works. Modernists objected to the predictable plots of psychoanalysis as well as its psychosexual reductions, totalizing ideas, and presumed authority as a hermeneutic key to culture. Modernists argued that psychoanalytic criticism was invasive, oblivious to the aesthetic, and in the words of Virginia Woolf: "a key to fit all locks." Jean-Michel Rabaté captures some of these concerns in a more contemporary register, "canonical psychoanalytic readings only confirm the truth of psychoanalysis about the Oedipus complex, archaic fantasies, the primal scene, castration, childhood memories, and so on. This does not mean that the results are false. Simply, and more damagingly, they are entirely predictable."[10]

Susan Sontag and Modern Interpretation

While my intention is not to posit any easy or direct line of transmission, I want to observe the connections between early twentieth-century disagreements into midcentury and more recent critical conversations. As psychoanalysis became even more entrenched within literary critical discourses at midcentury, writers and intellectuals from Vladimir Nabokov to Susan Sontag to Theodor Adorno warned of the impoverishing effects of this new critical paradigm on works of art. In her eponymous essay, "Against Interpretation" (1966), Sontag defends modernist artworks from a "modern style of interpretation," which in her words "excavates, and as it excavates, destroys; it digs 'behind' the text, to find a sub-text which is the true one. The most celebrated and influential modern doctrines, those of Marx and Freud, actually amount to elaborate systems of hermeneutics, aggressive and impious theories of interpretation."[11]

Sontag impugns the modern hermeneutics of depth, inspired by the doctrines of Marx and Freud, for its "aggressive" excavations of subtext at the expense of the larger work. She goes on to explain that such interpretations merely bracket "all observable phenomena" as "manifest content," which then must be "probed and pushed aside to find the true meaning—the *latent content*— beneath."[12] She reserves special hostility for the psychoanalytic "ravishing" of modern artworks by Kafka, Proust, Rilke, Lawrence, and Beckett, which are reduced to psychoanalytic allegories, and she warns that such methods result in an abstract engagement with art that precludes any apprehension of its sensual and phenomenal qualities. Such statements evoke Nabokov's oblique command to literary critic: "Ignore allegories. . . . Rely on the sudden erection of your small dorsal hairs. Do not drag in Freud at this point."[13]

Describing modern interpretation as "the revenge of the intellect upon art,"[14] Sontag calls for a historicist reevaluation of interpretation itself, as something other than an absolute and unchanging value: interpretation can be liberating and revolutionary as a means of "escaping the dead past," but it can also be reactionary and stifling. Her most trenchant critique of this modern hermeneutic is its privileging of content over form: "It is the habit of approaching works of art in order to interpret them that sustains the fancy that there really is such a thing as the content of a work of art."[15] Claiming that modern interpretation "violates art" by reducing it to content alone, she suggests that a resistance to interpretation emerges as a force within certain artworks; avant-garde art in particular—including the poetry of Ezra Pound—emerges from of an impulse to reinstate "the magic of the word" over the hegemony of the intellect. Modern abstract painting with its lack of content, and pop art with its "blatant" content, are twin responses to the reductive sense-making activities of interpretation. Like Adorno, Sontag is interested in the artwork's alterity, its built-in capacity to resist the interpretations imposed upon it. Literary critics claim to be making art intelligible by disclosing deeper and truer meanings, but in doing so they suppress the artwork's ability to speak for itself.

Sontag's argument conjures its modernist antecedents in its rejection of the excessively knowing, self-conscious style of interpretation that presumes to look beyond appearances to occulted depths. The essay celebrates the "untranslatable, sensuous immediacy" of aesthetic experience in the face of the "hypertrophy of the intellect."[16] Similar arguments could be found in the writings of Pound, Eliot, and Lawrence, who were less interested in the artwork's latent meanings than in the qualities of the artwork that transcended cognitive knowing. While it is sometimes difficult to distinguish the aesthetic positions of these male modernists from the misogynistic and quasi-fascist dimensions of their thought, their investment in producing an aesthetic that could bypass abstract, rational knowledge became an influential current in early-twentieth-century thought. Like D. H. Lawrence, Sontag sees the supremacy of the intellect as destructive and champions the "untranslatable, sensuous immediacy" of the artwork. Several modernists were fascinated by the notion of depthlessness: Conrad played with opacities, Stein cultivated a grammar of repetition, Lewis used angular geometric forms in his visual art and attempted to translate this aesthetic to his writing. Modernism's fascination with surfaces, exteriors, and opacities suggests an oblique relationship to the idea of psychological depth, and indeed many recent studies of modernist aesthetics have emphasized domains of impersonality, a-humanism, and non-psychological modernism over the subjectivist or psychological models that have been so influential.[17] By emphasizing the artwork's own authority and its capacity to be understood on its own terms, and refusing a hermeneutics of depth, Sontag re-ignites modernist arguments on behalf of aesthetic autonomy while anticipating more recent calls for "reparative reading," "surface reading," and "postcritique."

The Old Is New Again

Arguably, literary and cultural critics from formalist, psychoanalytic, Marxist, feminist, post-structuralist, cultural studies, and New Historicist orientations have honed their skills as interpreters by reading against the grain, reading for silences, gaps, inconsistencies, and ambiguities—symptomatic sites where the text's apparent unity breaks down. In the "symptomatic" readings of Althusser, Macherey, and Jameson—all heirs of Marx and Freud—the literary critic works to expose the "unconscious" of the text, whether that unconscious reflects the conflicting impulses of the text or the conflicting forces of history. As the critic, Fredric Jameson, writes in *The Political Unconscious*, "interpretation proper . . . always presupposes, if not a conception of the unconscious itself, then at least some mechanism of mystification or repression in terms of which it would make sense to seek a latent meaning behind a manifest one, or to rewrite the surface categories of a text in the stronger language of a more fundamental interpretive code. . . ."[18] For Jameson, the critic "restores to the surface the deep history that the text represses."[19] Jameson's reliance on tropes of the unconscious and repression, and on spatial metaphors of latent and manifest, depth and surface, render all too clearly his debt to psychoanalytic theory.

In the last few decades, however, the dissatisfaction with such "suspicious" and "symptomatic" methods has inspired a reevaluation of the ways literary studies scholars approach literary objects. Everything from the mood, to the method, to the disposition of the critic has come under scrutiny, as literary studies inventories its zeal for suspicious reading, one dedicated to decoding resistant surfaces and demystifying ideological structures. In her monumental work *Touching Feeling* (2003), Eve Kosofsky Sedgwick argues that psychoanalysis as a "strong theory," with its "reach and reductiveness," can only ever misrepresent literary meaning.[20] Her argument became the foundation for a reevaluation of "paranoid" reading practices that psychoanalysis and Marxism helped inspire. There have since been a number of initiatives to expand our critical practices beyond the epistemologies and methods of suspicion, demystification, and decryption.[21] Sedgwick's "reparative" reading, Sharon Marcus and Stephen Best's "surface" reading, Heather Love's sociological description,

Rita Felski and Elizabeth Anker's "postcritical" reading, Lee Clark Mitchell's "Mere Reading," to Heather Love's sociological description and Paul Saint-Amour's "weak theory"[22] are among the most visible efforts to move away from the strong stance of suspicion. Some scholars have turned to the anti-Oedipal theories of Deleuze and Guatarri, to the affect studies of Sylvan Tompkins, Eve Sedgwick, and Lauren Berlant, to the Actor-Network-Theory of Bruno Latour, and to the work of British object relations theorists, Melanie Klein and Donald Winnicott. Many of these initiatives have explicit connections to queer theory and feminism, to sociology, and to non-orthodox strands of psychoanalysis. But rather than identify this postcritical turn as a decisive shift away from long-standing critical practices, I want to suggest that such dispositions have their antecedents in the milieu of early twentieth-century modernism and in the epistemologies and reading practices that modernism helped inspire.

Recent reevaluations of "suspicious" and "symptomatic" reading hark back to early twentieth-century writers concerned about the authority of literature in an era defined by the emergence of the professional literary critic. The debates that emerged during the first half of the century over the value of psychoanalytic criticism seem uncannily predictive of more recent discussions of literary form, the hermeneutics of suspicion, and the authority over literary meaning—whether that authority should lie with the text, the critic, the general reader, or some combination of those stakeholders. Contemporary literary studies has inherited a long-standing debate over the relationship between psychoanalysis and literary discourse, an inheritance that is especially pronounced in current conversations about "postcritical" reading, which often turn on an ambivalence to the "strong" metalanguages of Marxism and psychoanalysis. Stephen Best and Sharon Marcus's "surface" reading endorses a return to the text's "own" voice over that of the literary critic. Rita Felski's "postcritique" encourages us to recognize the authority of everyday readers over critical experts, and to supplement paranoid and disinterested critical postures with pleasure, attachment, and identification.[23]

But what does it mean that psychoanalysis continues to play an antagonist in some of these debates, despite its diminishing authority in literary studies and other fields? We might argue that contemporary scholars have placed too much emphasis on psychoanalysis for diminishing the authority of literary texts and everyday readers. We might also argue that the suspicious style of reading is hardly the detached, aloof, or bloodless sport that some have declared it to be, and does in fact contain much of the affect, passion, wonder, identification, and self-reflexivity that other methodologies have claimed. It is hard to think of psychoanalytic literary critics like Adam Phillips or Leo Bersani as bereft of these affective orientations. Peter Brooks, who has referred to orthodox modes of psychoanalytic criticism as embarrassing, has transformed Freud's concepts of the pleasure principle and the death drive into a neo-formalism attentive to the dynamics of narrative desire and the erotics of reading.[24] Recent psychoanalytic criticism is certainly capable of grasping the *eros* of cultural production without necessarily grafting allegorical Oedipal plots or rigid developmental schemas onto culture.

What I have shown throughout this book are the lineaments of a professional tussle: Early twentieth-century psychoanalysts made efforts to control literary meaning; modernists wanted to wrest it back. Modernists frequently blamed psychoanalytic criticism for a loss of authority and struggled to recuperate literature's authority in this critique. But what does it mean that critics are still doing this now, struggling to recuperate literary authority from psychoanalysis? Is the study of literature still haunted by this proximity to psychoanalysis? Everyone seems to agree that our current moment is marked by a diminishment in the authority of literature, and the humanities more broadly, although we disagree on how much "postcritical" debates are or are not a symptom of that diminishment.

I would like to suggest that our own contemporary moment furnishes yet another crisis of legitimacy for literature in which scholars struggle to make the case for the continuing value and relevance of literary studies. Literary studies scholars (not unlike their modernist precursors) are anxious about their conceptual authority being superseded by a range of actors and factors: by cognitivist approaches, by the social sciences, by statistical and quantitative methods (including the digital humanities), by social media, by amateurism, and by movements adjacent to textual literary studies, such as object-oriented ontology.[25] Anna Kornbluh views the "latest trends in the academic humanities—big data, thin description, positivist historicism, and the critique of critique" as the current front in "the humanities' permanent war for legitimacy."[26]

What has been dubbed the "method wars" in contemporary literary studies speaks to tensions between surface reading and depth hermeneutics, critique and postcritique, New Historicism and formalism, political orientations and aesthetic ones. But such rivalries are never merely two camps opposed to one another: There is a broader crisis of legitimacy at play, and we should recognize the generative connections that are easy to miss in highly polarized moments. Although framed in the militaristic terms of warfare, both sides of each debate share much in common, including the effort to legitimize literary studies while offering a foundation from which to move forward. Such methods do not necessarily exclude one another: Most literary critics offer some combination of these methodological positions rather than an exclusive adherence to one or the other.

I am less interested in taking a position on these debates than in underscoring that such contentious dynamics reappear in periods in which literature perceives itself as embattled. While humanistic study garnered prestige and cultural capital after World War II and offered the promise of class mobility in a society that increasingly valued higher education, contemporary literary studies confronts its survival in a corporatist and neoliberal environment that threatens the humanities more broadly. The erosion of state funding for higher education, the targeting of humanities disciplines by college administrations for austerity measures, the attacks on the humanities by the right (and the especially virulent critique of critical race theory and identity politics), the accumulation of financial debt for undergraduates, and the ongoing precarity for humanities scholars have all contributed to the sense of threat and fears of extinction experienced by the field. The "method wars" are not just symptomatic of this sense of threat, they bear historical precedent: We might do better to think of these debates about surface and depth, amateurism and expertise, explanation and description—as longstanding dialectical tensions within the field that become especially pronounced in moments of disciplinary crisis.

The reality of the crisis makes the tenor of these debates understandably intense. But is it the case that psychoanalysis, as a literary critical discourse, is as strong or totalizing as some of its critics have claimed? We might argue that though psychoanalysis has become decidedly weaker as a field since the 1970s and 1980s, it continues to cast a long shadow over literary and cultural studies, over its conceptual vocabulary and habits of reading (even as Freud's theories about the artistic process and authorial neurosis have been mostly discredited). Peter Brooks suggests that an enduring blind spot of psychoanalytic literary criticism has been its presumption that it could analyze or explain literature, that it had the upper hand in investigations of the deepest levels of literary meaning.[27] But a promising development in recent literary critical discussions of psychoanalysis can be found in the work of Maud Ellmann, who limns the "frictional interplay" between these discourses, rather than "seiz[ing] the psychoanalytic truth disguised within the literary work."[28] My book has suggested something similar about the dynamics of literature and psychoanalysis: that these fields have stood in a complex relation of engagement and debate since the early part of the century, reading the other, misrepresenting the other, or refusing to read the other altogether, offering insights about the other, popularizing the other, while placing the other's cross-disciplinary ambitions in check. And as I suggest early on, modernists were not only participants in, but producers of, the many forms of psychoanalytic knowledge that circulated at the time. Even Lawrence and Nabokov reflect the charismatic allure of Freudian ideas in their ongoing efforts to disarm them. All four of the authors in this study use psychoanalysis productively to catalyze their creative and intellectual projects.

Psychoanalysis still seems to have something to offer literary studies: as an archive of cultural artifacts with their own literary and rhetorical properties; as a mode of cultural criticism; as a hermeneutic that can work in limited, yet necessary, ways to complicate surface meanings and reveal the over-determination of meaning; as a neo-formalism that can interpret the textual dynamics of delay, postponement, repetition, and suspense.[29] Concepts such as mourning and melancholia, fantasy and fetish, transference and the uncanny remain crucial to our understandings of symbolic phenomena, and are not likely to disappear anytime soon. For all its evident shortfalls and insufficiently historicized and outdated theories, Freudian psychoanalysis furnishes some stubbornly relevant concepts: for example, the destructive and aggressive forces behind human behavior; the crucial impact of childhood experience on psychic development and attachment; the human capacity for denial, disavowal, and compulsive repetition. As Beth Blum points out, so many of the key concepts of psychoanalysis, such as self-destructive behavior, childhood trauma, and wishful thinking, remain central to the industry of modern self-help.[30]

Although psychoanalysis is a predominantly white, eurocentric body of literature, certain psychoanalytic ideas have remained remarkably useful for critical readings of race, and for parsing the experiences of minority subjectivity and racial melancholia, articulated so well by Anne Anlin Cheng, Cathy Park Hong, David Eng, and Shinhee Han. These critics make salient links between the psychic process of excessive mourning that Freud describes in "Mourning and Melancholia" and the psychic and social experiences of minoritized subjectivity, immigration, displacement, diasporic consciousness, and assimilation. Given its association with an enduring loss that becomes part of one's identity, melancholia has become a provocative metaphor for racial trauma in America, where the narratives of freedom and progress conflict so markedly with experiences of exclusion, othering, violence, and micro-aggression for members of ethnic, racial, and sexual minorities. Freud's belief that the melancholic subject incorporates the lost object into the self has been repurposed as a model for how racial trauma is digested, internalized, and repurposed, and how the media packages racial trauma as spectacle designed for consumption.

Though many of Freud's conclusions were wrong and absurd, psychoanalytic methods remain durable in thinking through the dynamics of loss, desire, attachment, and identification; as well as the affective, rhetorical, and temporal dynamics of literary texts. Psychoanalytic criticism combines affect, eroticism and unspoken desires with an acute sensitivity to the surfaces of language. Moreover, a number of contemporary authors—including Alison Bechdel, Lidia Yuknavitch, and Carmen Maria Machado—are reinventing psychoanalysis in their turn. These writers have processed classic psychoanalytic texts through the lenses of fiction and memoir, taking what they need from psychoanalysis and discarding the rest, while revealing the "frictional interplay" of these discourses. As these contemporary writers and critics suggest, literature continues to engage in a dynamic of sharing—sometimes in secret—with this intimate other.

Acknowledgments

It is no secret how much sharing it took to bring this book into the world. This project, which began over ten years ago, has become a book because of the endless generosity, intellectual and emotional support, and good will of colleagues, mentors, friends, students, and family members.

Patrick Deer, my adviser and friend, has shepherded me through this project for years, with wisdom, enthusiasm, patience, and grace. Everyone should be so lucky to have Patrick Deer, Heather Love, Martin Harries, and Elaine Freedgood as readers, mentors, and interlocutors. They offered continuous feedback on chapter drafts and countless opportunities to process my ideas with them. I am grateful to Peter Nichols who was also a brilliant reader for this project. I would like to thank Laura, Shirley, Lenora, Christian, Brendan, and my beloved NYU cohort.

I am especially indebted to colleagues and friends who read sections of the book and offered generous and incisive feedback, including Shirley Wong, Tyler Bradway, Caroline Levine, Chris Holmes, Masha Raskolnikov, Laura Fisher, Martha Schulman, Lily Sheehan, Kate Kallal, Bob Volpicelli, Patty Zimmerman, Emily Sharpe, and Elisha Cohen.

The love of my job comes largely from my colleagues and friends at Ithaca College, including Chris Holmes, Claire Gleitman, Shaianne Osterreich, Jen Tennant, Alexis Becker, Eleanor Henderson, Dyani Johns Taff, Hugh Egan, Jon Peeters, Dan Breen, Derek Adams, Kasia Bartoszynska, Elizabeth Bleicher, Lenora Warren, Carla Golden, Kevin Murphy, Eleanor Henderson, Peter Martin, Joslyn Brenton, Katharine Kittredge, Mat Fournier, Sarah Sutton, Rachel Balzano, Patty Zimmerman, Christine Kitano, Emilie Weisner, Aaron Weinberg, Sherry Deckman, Chris Matusiak, Jonathan Ablard, Kenesha

Chatman, Carlos Figueroa, Te-Wen Lo, Sherry Deckman, Ellie Fulmer, Mike Twomey, Jim Swafford, Paul Hansom, Luca Maurer, and others. I am also indebted to Wade Pickren, Colette Matisco, and the Center for Faculty Excellence for offering course release time as well as editorial feedback from the wonderful Sheri Englund and support from the Provost's Office and Brad Hougham in particular.

I have the best students at Ithaca College: They have challenged me and sharpened my ideas and asked enthusiastic questions about my work. I am especially grateful to three incredible students: Sawyer Hitchcock, who helped me with research; Kathleen Pongrace, who assisted with editing, citations, and bibliography; and Margaret McKinnis, who was an intellectual, emotional, and moral buoy during these trying years of the pandemic.

I owe an immense debt to Richard Morrison at Fordham University Press for his graciousness and communication throughout this process, and to the external readers who offered probing, insightful, and generous suggestions to move this project forward. I am also grateful to Michelle Scott and Westchester Publishing Services for their terrific copyedits.

To my friends who are my joy and my life lines: Megan, Shirley, Laura, Kara, Caroline, Tyler, Chris, Hailey, Jen, Shaianne, Claire, Alexis, Masha, Momo, Paul, Kate, Katie H., Nell, Joselin, Miri, Xak, Carolyn, Kate K., Andy, Rachel, Jen, Hope, Kate, Jess, Amalia, Sandy, Lily, Domenick, Lauren, John, Betsy, Eleanor, Philipa, Amit and Dasi, Beth, Rachel, Sylvia, Suki, Jonah, Cassie, Naomi, Aaron, Elyssa, Eyal, Veronica, Amanda, Emily, Gabi, Morgan, Rachel, Arthur, Lauren, Darcy, Dave, Rebecca, and Ivan. I am also grateful for friends and interlocutors who have helped me improve this and other projects, including Timothy Wientzen, Andrew Van der Vlies, Patrick Flanery, Gayle Rogers, Aarthi Vadde, Stephanie Hawkins, Lori Cole, Corey McEleney, and Urmila Seshagiri. I am impossibly grateful to my "Ithaca School," my sister life-lifes, and my cohorts from Wesleyan, NYU, Ithaca College, Cornell English, Cornell SCT, and Early Career Lady Modernists. I am infinitely grateful to Lezlie Namaste and my Covid bereavement network, who have helped me through two trying years of the pandemic.

I am eternally indebted to my mom and dad who nurtured a love of literature and poetry: my father, who read me Sir Walter Raleigh and Robert Frost growing up and typed my childhood stories for me; and my mother, who modeled a voracious love of reading and helped edit my literature essays from middle school to college. My parents did not look askance when I applied to graduate school in literature, and for this I am grateful. I adore and look up to my sister Laura, and am so grateful for Todd, Slader, and Shay. I am grateful to my family-in-law, Jim and Eileen, who have supported me in every way possible and understood when I had to miss the holidays for work. I am grateful to my extended family, including Lisa, Elaine, Michelle, Paul, Nell, Hamish, Gabe, Nate, Paul, Sarah Lewis, Willy, Lawren, and Alec.

None of this would be possible without the love, support, patience, wit, intelligence, calm energy, and humor of my husband, Jacob White, and the joy, charm, and sweetness of my son, Auden, who keeps asking for a copy of the book. You two make this all worthwhile.

An earlier version of Chapter 1 appeared as "On Not Reading Freud: Amateurism, Expertise, and the 'Pristine Unconscious' in D. H. Lawrence," *Modernism/Modernity* 21, no. 1 (January 2014). An earlier version of Chapter 3 appeared as "The Heterodox Psychology and Queer Poetics of Auden in the 30s," *Journal of Modern Literature* 42, no. 3 (Spring 2019). I am grateful to these publications for the permission to reprint.

Notes

Introduction: Intimate Others

1. Joseph Conrad, "The Secret Sharer," in *The Portable Conrad* (New York: Penguin Classics, 2007), 7–46.
2. The narrator of Conrad's tale alternates between analysand and analyst, sharing his tale with the reader while serving as analyst to another character whose account of events solicits reworking and revision.
3. I borrow this last phrase from Barbara Johnson and Marjorie Garber, "Secret Sharing: Reading Conrad Psychoanalytically," *College English* 49 no. 6 (October 1987): 630.
4. Conrad, "The Secret Sharer," 14.
5. Johnson and Garber, "Secret Sharing," 628–29.
6. Johnson and Garber, "Secret Sharing," 628.
7. David Trotter, *Paranoid Modernism: Literary Experiment, Psychosis, and the Professionalization of English Society* (Oxford: Oxford University Press, 2001). Trotter highlights the anti-mimetic "will to abstraction" and "striving toward structure" that characterize the paranoid modernism of Lawrence, Lewis, and Hulme. He connects such paranoid structures to the rise of a professional class in turn-of-the-century England, and specifically to the professional identity of the author under pressure within a rapidly developing literary marketplace.
8. D. H. Lawrence, *Psychoanalysis and the Unconscious; and, Fantasia of the Unconscious*, ed. Bruce Steele (Cambridge: Cambridge University Press, 2004), 5.
9. Renato Poggioli, *The Theory of the Avant-Garde*, trans. Gerald Fitzgerald (Cambridge, MA: Harvard University Press, 1968), 201.
10. See especially Lawrence Rainey, introduction to *Institutions of Modernism: Literary Elites and Public Culture* (New Haven, CT: Yale University Press, 1999), 1–9.

11. Sigmund Freud, "A Short Account of Psychoanalysis," in *The Standard Edition of the Complete Psychological Works of Sigmund Freud*, 24 vols., trans. from the German under the general editorship of James Strachey, in collaboration with Anna Freud (London: Hogarth Press, 1953–74; repr., New York: Vintage, 1999), 19:208. Going forward, I will use *SE* to refer to the *Standard Edition*. Also quoted in Andrea Freud Loewenstein, *Loathsome Jews and Engulfing Women: Metaphors of Projection in Wyndham Lewis, Charles Williams, and Graham Green* (New York: New York University Press, 1993).

12. T. S. Eliot, "Tradition and the Individual Talent," in *Selected Prose of T S. Eliot*, ed. Frank Kermode (New York: Harcourt, 1975), 41.

13. Malcolm Bradbury and James McFarlane, "The Name and Nature of Modernism," in *Modernism, 1890–1930* (Harmondsworth, UK: Penguin Books, 1978), 47.

14. In Michael North's words, "certain modern writers helped to create the category of 'the psychological." *Reading 1922: A Return to the Scene of the Modern* (New York: Oxford University Press, 1999), 80.

15. For the reception history of psychoanalysis in Britain see Henri F. Ellenberger, *The Discovery of the Unconscious: The History and Evolution of Dynamic Psychiatry* (New York: Basic Books, 1970); Philip Rieff, *Freud: The Mind of the Moralist* (University of Chicago Press, 1979); Janet Malcolm, *In the Freud Archives* (New York: Knopf, 1984); Paul Roazen, *Freud and His Followers* (New York: New American Library, 1976); Lisa Appignanesi and John Forrester, *Freud's Women* (New York: Basic Books, 1993); and Mikkel Borch-Jacobsen and Sonu Shamdasani, *The Freud Files: An Inquiry into the History of Psychoanalysis* (Cambridge: Cambridge University Press, 2012). For discussions of the popularization and dissemination of Freud in Britain, see Dean Rapp, "The Reception of Freud by the British Press: General Interest and Literary Magazines, 1920–1925," *Journal of the History of the Behavioral Sciences* 24, no. 2 (April 1988): 191–201; and Graham Richards, "Britain on the Couch: The Popularization of Psychoanalysis in Britain, 1918–1940," *Science in Context* 13, no. 2 (2000): 183–230.

16. Michael Levenson, *Modernism* (New Haven, CT: Yale University Press, 2001), 5.

17. Quoted in Patricia Moran, "The Sudden 'Mushroom Growth' of Cheap Psychoanalysis: Mansfield and Woolf Respond to Psychoanalysis," *Virginia Woolf Miscellany* 86 (Fall 2014/Winter 2015): 11–13.

18. T. S. Eliot, "The Contemporary Novel," *Times Literary Supplement*, 1927, reprinted August 14, 2015, 14–15.

19. Maud Ellmann, *The Nets of Modernism* (Cambridge: Cambridge University Press, 2010).

20. Lyndsey Stonebridge, *The Destructive Element: British Psychoanalysis and Modernism* (New York: Routledge, 1998).

21. Laura Marcus, *Dreams of Modernity: Psychoanalysis, Literature, Cinema* (Cambridge: Cambridge University Press, 2014).

22. According to Luke Thurston, it was at this talk that Beckett heard Jung say that the unconscious "consists of an indefinite, because unknown, number of

complexes or fragmentary personalities." "Outselves: Beckett, Bion and Beyond," *Journal of Modern Literature* 32, no. 3 (Spring 2009): 121–43, 126.

23. Sigmund Freud, "The Moses of Michelangelo" (1914), in SE, 13:221.

24. Trotter, *Paranoid Modernism*.

25. See Sigmund Freud, *The Interpretation of Dreams*, in SE, 4:102.

26. Lionel Trilling, "Freud and Literature," in *Freud: A Collection of Critical Essays*, ed. Perry Meisel (Englewood Cliffs, NJ: Prentice-Hall, 1981), 52.

27. For additional analysis, see Laura Marcus, *Dreams of Modernity*, 184.

28. See Hanns Sachs, *The Creative Unconscious: Studies in the Psychoanalysis of Art* (Cambridge, MA: Sci-Arts Publishers, 1942).

29. See North, *Reading 1922*, 67–68.

30. As Elizabeth Abel points out, the characterization of psychoanalysis as a literary rather than a scientific *discourse* was a leitmotiv in England. Reviewers and correspondents made derogatory reference to the lack of scientific validity of psychoanalysis—to the absence of controlled tests or verifiable data—and therefore to its greater relationship to imaginative literature. See Abel, *Virginia Woolf and the Fictions of Psychoanalysis* (Chicago: University of Chicago Press, 1989), 15.

31. For a fuller analysis of Bloomsbury's attraction to psychoanalysis see James Strachey and Alix Strachey, *Bloomsbury/Freud: The Letters of James and Alix Strachey, 1924–1925*, ed. Perry Meisel and Walter M. Kendrick (New York: Basic Books, 1985); and Abel, *Virginia Woolf and the Fictions of Psychoanalysis*. For accounts of early British psychoanalysis, see Edward Glover, "Psychoanalysis in England," in *Psychoanalytic Pioneers* (New York: Basic Books, 1966); and Ernest Jones's autobiography, *Free Associations: Memories of a Psycho-analyst* (New Brunswick, NJ: Transaction, 1990).

32. Leonard Woolf's remarks were published in *The New English Weekly* in 1914. Quoted in Perry Meisel, *The Literary Freud* (New York: Routledge, 2007), 5. Freud's work began appearing in English with A. A. Brill's first translations and the publication of Freud's Clark lectures in the *American Journal of Psychology*.

33. The Hogarth Press's publication of Freud's *Collected Papers* in four volumes between 1924 and 1925 would be followed by the comprehensive publication of the twenty-four volumes of the *Standard Edition*, translated by James Strachey, between 1953 and 1966.

34. Elizabeth Abel notes that the Stephens were both in analytic training at the time Melanie Klein gave the lecture at their house at 50 Gordon Square. The event had captured the attention of the British psychoanalytic movement. It also "dramatized the intellectual home psychoanalysis had found in Bloomsbury." *Virginia Woolf and the Fictions of Psychoanalysis*, 13.

35. Freud famously offered an Oedipal reading of *Hamlet* in *The Interpretation of Dreams* (1900), translated into English by A. A. Brill in 1900. Ernest Jones extended Freud's insights in *Hamlet and Oedipus* (1910).

36. Quoted in Potter, *Modernist Literature* (Edinburgh: Edinburgh University Press, 2012), 138. Graham Richards deploys the term "Freudish" to refer to the

popular concepts and terminology that the public identified as being psychoanalytic (185).

37. Quoted in Susan Stanford Friedman, *Psyche Reborn: The Emergence of H.D.* (Bloomington: Indiana University Press, 1981), 18 (ellipses in Friedman). Bryher would correspond with Freud during the 1930s while being analyzed by Hanns Sachs.

38. See Nathan Hale, *The Rise and Crisis of Psychoanalysis* (New York: Oxford University Press, 1995), Chapter 4; and Dorothy Ross, "Freud and the Vicissitudes of Modernism in the United States, 1940–1950," in *After Freud Left: A Century of Psychoanalysis in America* (Chicago: University of Chicago Press, 2012), 167.

39. See Laura Marcus, *Dreams of Modernity*, 152.

40. For an extensive discussion of Freud's impact on American culture, see Nathan G. Hale Jr., *Freud and the Americans: The Beginnings of Psychoanalysis in the United States, 1876–1917* (New York: Oxford University Press, 1971).

41. Freud famously said of America: "America is a mistake, a giant mistake."

42. Henry Abelove, "Freud, Male Homosexuality, and the Americans," in *The Lesbian and Gay Studies Reader*, ed. Henry Abelove, Michèle Aina Barale, and David M. Halperin (New York: Routledge, 1993), 381.

43. Richard Ellman, *James Joyce* (Oxford: Oxford University Press, 1959), 538.

44. Lawrence, *Psychoanalysis and the Unconscious*, 3–4.

45. Pfister also describes the glamorization of psychological depth in U.S. culture in the 1910s and 1920s, and the way the introspective qualities of modern art rendered it a marketable commodity for middle- and upper-class consumers. See "Glamorizing the Psychological: The Politics of the Performances of Modern Psychological Identities," in *Inventing the Psychological: Toward a Cultural History of Emotional Life in America*, ed. Joel Pfister and Nancy Schnog (New Haven, CT: Yale University Press, 1997), 167–216.

46. Lawrence, *Psychoanalysis and the Unconscious*, 4.

47. Lawrence, *Women in Love* (London: Heinemann, 1954), 51.

48. Richards, "Britain on the Couch," 200.

49. Laura Marcus, *Dreams of Modernity*, 153.

50. Joel Pfister puts it this way: "The psychiatric treatment of soldiers who suffered shell shock in World War I gave cultural legitimation and value to the notion of therapy as a process of psychic repair." "Glamorizing the Psychological," 169.

51. See Katherine Ebury, "Diagnosing Shell Shock in Literary Representations of the Military Death Penalty after World War I," in "Modernism and Diagnosis," *Modernism/Modernity* 5, cycle 2 (June 23, 2021).

52. Richards, "Britain on the Couch," 202.

53. In the words of John Brenkman, Freud's thought "stylizes in the sense that it scans the conflicts within society and transposes them to family life, whose conflicts are in turn transposed from the politics of the family to the individual's intrapsychic representations of the family." "Freud the Modernist," in *The Mind of Modernism: Medicine, Psychology, and the Cultural Arts in Europe and America, 1880–1940*, ed. Mark S. Micale (Stanford, CA: Stanford University Press, 2003), 173.

54. As Paul Saint-Amour has argued, "in the immediate wake of the First World War, the dread of another massive conflict saturated the Anglo-European imagination, amounting to a proleptic mass traumatization, a pre-traumatic stress syndrome. . . ." *Tense Future: Modernism, Total War, Encyclopedic Form* (Oxford: Oxford University Press, 2015), 7–8.

55. Rebecca West, *The Return of the Soldier* (New York: Penguin Books, [1918] 1998), 79.

56. Freud also makes the point that anxiety, as a preparation for future trauma, can insulate the subject from a traumatic response—an argument that Paul Saint-Amour complicates by examining sites of pre-traumatic stress in interwar modernist writing.

57. Anne-Claire Mulder, *Divine Flesh, Embodied Word* (Amsterdam: Amsterdam University Press, 2006), 28–29.

58. Jean-Michel Rabaté, *The Cambridge Introduction to Literature and Psychoanalysis* (Cambridge: Cambridge University Press, 2014), 2.

59. Meisel, *The Literary Freud*, 1.

60. Meisel, *The Literary Freud*, xiii.

61. Stephen Marcus, "Freud and Dora: Story, History, Case History," in *In Dora's Case: Freud—Hysteria—Feminism*, ed. Charles Bernheimer and Claire Kahane (New York: Columbia University Press, 1985), 64.

62. Stephen Marcus, "Freud and Dora," 66.

63. Sigmund Freud, *Studies on Hysteria* (1895), in SE, 2:160.

64. Astradur Eysteinsson, *The Concept of Modernism* (Ithaca, NY: Cornell University Press, 1990), 27.

65. Eysteinsson, *The Concept of Modernism*, 28.

66. George Lukács, "The Ideology of Modernism," in *Meaning of Contemporary Realism*, trans. John Mander and Necke Mander (London: Merlin Press, 1963), 20–21.

67. We might also include Wallace Stevens and, at times, Woolf in this impersonal, anti-psychological strand of modernism.

68. See Martin Jay, "Modernism and the Specter of Psychologism," *Modernism/Modernity* 3, no. 2 (1996): 93–111.

69. Quoted in Humphrey Carpenter, *A Serious Character: The Life of Ezra Pound* (London: Faber and Faber, 2010), 395.

70. Eliot, "Tradition and the Individual Talent," 37–44.

71. Douglas Mao, *Solid Objects: Modernism and the Test of Production* (Princeton, NJ: Princeton University Press, 1998), 8.

72. Wyndham Lewis, *Tarr* (London: Oxford World's Classics, [1918] 2010), 265.

73. Martin Jay, Peter Nicholls, Rachel Potter, and Jesse Matz have all offered compelling accounts of the suspicion of inwardness that dominated this strand of Anglo-American modernism, and Anglo-American poetry, in particular. Jay locates a transitional phase in modernism in which several modernists turn away from an earlier allegiance to subjectivism, and begin to define themselves against contemporary psychology, in "Modernism and the Specter of Psychologism." Along similar lines, Matz demonstrates how T. E. Hulme's rejection of Henri

Bergson's vitalist psychology helped set the stage for the ways in which antipsychologism would come to define high modernism. Hulme, who had been pivotal in translating and disseminating Bergson's ideas, eventually committed himself to overturning the intuition and fluidity that Bergson inspired, equating these qualities with a feminized mass cultural aesthetic. Rejecting sentiment and mysticism, Hulme turned to a "hard dry classicism" that would offer a foundation for Pound, Eliot, and Lewis's aesthetic positions. See Matz, "T. E. Hulme, Henri Bergson, and the Cultural Politics of Psychologism," in Micale, *The Mind of Modernism*, 339–51.

74. For a discussion of Pound's adversarial stance vis-à-vis impressionism and "mimetic" art, see Peter Nicholls, *Modernisms: A Literary Guide* (New York: Palgrave Macmillan, 2009), 165–74.

75. Pound's "Prolegomena" first appeared in the *Poetry Review* in 1912.

76. Article in *The New English Weekly*, May 2, 1935. Thank you to Peter Nicholls for pointing me to this quotation. Given its timing, Pound's outburst may have been provoked by H.D.'s decision to pursue analysis with Freud.

77. For further discussion of the relationship between H.D. and Pound, and the impact of her embrace of Freud on their relationship, see Norman Holmes Pearson's foreword to her memoir, *Tribute to Freud* (New York: New Directions, 1974); and Susan Stanford Freidman's study of H.D., *Psyche Reborn: The Emergence of H.D.* (Bloomington: Indiana University Press, 1981).

78. For a discussion of antisemitism and modernism, see Lara Trubowitz, "Concealing Leonard's Nose: Virginia Woolf, Modernist Antisemitism, and 'The Duchess and the Jeweller,'" *Twentieth-Century Literature* 54, no. 3 (Fall 2008): 273–306.

79. In an influential essay, published in the *New Left Review* in 1968, "Components of the National Culture," Perry Anderson argued that the resistance to psychoanalysis in England was a reflection of the "most conservative [society] in Europe." The quotation from Pound is from Carpenter, *A Serious Character: The Life of Ezra Pound*, 395.

80. For more on this entanglement of Pound's politics and aesthetics, see David Barnes, "Fascist Aesthetics: Ezra Pound's Cultural Negotiations in 1930s Italy," *Journal of Modern Literature* 34, no. 1 (Fall 2010): 19–35.

81. Robert Casillo, "Nature, History, and Anti-Nature in Ezra Pound's Fascism," *Papers on Language and Literature: A Journal for Scholars and Critics of Language and Literature* 22, no. 3 (Summer 1986): 287.

82. Quoted in Casillo, "Nature, History, and Anti-Nature in Ezra Pound's Fascism," 287. Sander Gilman points out that even within turn-of-the-century psychiatry it was widely believed that Jews bore innate propensities to hysteria and nervousness.

83. As Casillo demonstrates, the antisemitic slurs and stereotypes that proliferated in Pound's writing and radio broadcasts of the thirties, forties, and fifties coalesced around liquid metaphors, in which Jews were associated with "swamps," "bogs," "morass," and "slime"—with a contaminating confusion that threatened to

dissolve cultural boundaries. Elsewhere, Pound deploys the Oedipus complex, Freud's signature invention, as evidence of the Jewish inclination toward tribalism and incest.

84. In a stunning set of contradictions, Pound associates Jews with an atavist, primordial formlessness and with an introspective excess born of exacerbated consciousness. It is difficult not to read Pound's early statements on fluidity and solidity in art in light of his later antisemitic depictions of Jews, who are associated with images of swamps, bogs, and floods. Pound embraced fascism as a force of order that could combat human instincts toward softness, fluidity, and femininity—qualities that he consistently associated with Jews. As Casillo argues, to understand Pound's antisemitism is to understand its metaphorical link with misogyny.

85. Indeed, such anxieties were in the ether: for example, the influential Austrian philosopher, Otto Weininger argued in his pseudo-scientific treatise *Geschlecht und Charakter* or *Sex and Character* (1903), that to achieve autonomous identity and spiritual transcendence as a man it was necessary that one repudiate both the feminine and Jewish aspects of oneself.

86. Lyndsey Stonebridge summarizes Lewis's rejection of psychoanalysis in the following terms: "Psychoanalysis reaffirms interiority and, as such, supports a narcissistic, effeminate and decadent culture based on a regressive and degenerate notion of the self." *The Destructive Element*, 9.

87. See Bradley Buchanan Bradley, *Oedipus Against Freud: Myth and the End(s) of Humanism in Twentieth-Century British Literature* (Toronto: University of Toronto Press, 2010), 49.

88. Wyndham Lewis, *Paleface; the Philosophy of the "Melting-Pot"* (New York: Haskell House Publishers, 1969), 179, 183–84.

89. In *Paleface* Lewis burlesques Lawrence for being "beneath the spell of this evolutionist, emotional, non-human, 'mindless' philosophy" (176).

90. Andreas Huyssen, *After the Great Divide: Modernism, Mass Culture, Postmodernism* (Bloomington: Indiana University Press, 1986), 47, 52.

91. See Friedman, *Psyche Reborn*; and Laura Marcus, *Dreams of Modernity*, 161–75.

92. H.D., *Tribute to Freud* (New York: New Directions, 1974).

93. H.D., *Tribute to Freud*, 14.

94. H.D., *Tribute to Freud*, 45.

95. W. H. Auden, *Another Time* (New York: Random House, 1940).

96. The elegy appeared as "For Sigmund Freud," *The Kenyon Review*, Winter 1940.

97. Quoted in Thomas Szasz, *"My Madness Saved Me": The Madness and Marriage of Virginia Woolf* (New Brunswick, NJ: Transaction, 2006), 71.

98. The accidental invention of X-ray photography by Wilhelm Conrad Röntgen in 1895 occurred one year before Freud coined the term "psychoanalysis."

99. Jean-Michel Rabaté, *1913: The Cradle of Modernism* (Malden, MA: Wiley Blackwell, 2007), 141.

100. Such anxieties on the part of early twentieth-century artists were intensified by the fact that they were some of the first figures to come into contact with psychoanalysis. Rainer Maria Rilke was introduced to Freud's theories via his lover, the trained analyst, Lou Andreas-Salomé. He was curious about its potential benefits for writer's block, but ultimately refused treatment out of fear that it would inhibit his ability to create art in the future. For more information see Matthew von Unwerth, *Freud's Requiem: Mourning, Memory, and the Invisible History of a Summer Walk* (New York: Riverhead Books, 2005); and Kamna Kirti, "The Woman Who Was a Muse to Nietzsche, Rilke, and Freud," *Medium*, January 14, 2021.

101. "Why Nabokov Detests Freud," interview by Robert Hughes, *New York Times*, January 3, 1966.

102. Virginia Woolf, "Freudian Fiction," *Times Literary Supplement*, 1920. Found in Woolf, *Collected Essays*, 1st American ed. (New York: Harcourt, Brace & World, 1967), 3:197.

103. Woolf imagined female authorship in material, spatial, and psychic terms as "a room with a lock on the door." Woolf, *A Room of One's Own and Three Guineas*, Oxford World's Classics (Oxford: Oxford University Press, 1992), 137. Adorno uses a similar metaphor when he states that psychoanalysis "unlocks phenomena, but falls short of the phenomenon of art." *Aesthetic Theory* (Minneapolis: University of Minnesota Press, 1997), 11.

104. In the words of Jean-Michel Rabaté, "the author cannot control or even know anything of the dark forces that made the work happen." *Cambridge Introduction to Literature and Psychoanalysis*, 5.

105. Unsigned review, "The Dream Books," *The Athenaeum* 4460, April 19, 1913, p. 424. Quoted in Helen Groth and Natalya Lusty, *Dreams and Modernity: A Cultural History* (London: Routledge, 2013), 100.

106. Jones's speech to the Newcastle Literary and Philosophical Society was given on November 28, 1927, and printed in the journal *Psyche* 8 (1928): 73–88. I refer to the reprinted version, Ernest Jones, "Psycho-analysis and the Artist," *Psicoart* 1, no. 1 (2010).

107. Jones, "Psycho-analysis and the Artist," 7.

108. Jones, "Psycho-analysis and the Artist," 7.

109. Jones, "Psycho-analysis and the Artist," 8.

110. Ezra Pound, "Hugh Selwyn Mauberley," in *Selected Poems of Ezra Pound* (New York: New Directions, 1956), pt. v.

111. Sigmund Freud, *Civilization and Its Discontents*, trans. and ed. James Strachey (New York: W. W. Norton, 1961), 23.

112. Freud, *Civilization and Its Discontents*, 24.

113. Sigmund Freud, "Creative Writers and Day-dreaming" (1908), in *SE*, 9:143–53.

114. Sigmund Freud, *Introductory Lectures on Psycho-analysis* (New York: W. W. Norton, 1989), 314.

115. Freud, *Introductory Lectures*, 314.

116. Freud, *Introductory Lectures*, 314.
117. Freud, *Introductory Lectures*, 314.
118. Trilling, "Freud and Literature," 104.
119. Adorno, *Aesthetic Theory*, 15.
120. Adorno recognized in his later works the validity of Freud's conception of group identity in *Group Psychology and the Analysis of the Ego*. Freud argues that civilization requires individuals to repress instinctual impulses in order to function in groups.
121. Adorno, *Aesthetic Theory*, 9.
122. Rita Felski, "The Hermeneutics of Suspicion," https://stateofthediscipline.acla.org/entry/hermeneutics-suspicion.
123. Susan Sontag, "Against Interpretation," in *A Susan Sontag Reader* (New York: Vintage Books, 1966), 3–14.

1. On Not Reading Freud: Amateurism, Expertise, and the "Pristine Unconscious" in D. H. Lawrence

1. D. H. Lawrence, *Psychoanalysis and the Unconscious; and, Fantasia of the Unconscious*, ed. Bruce Steele (Cambridge: Cambridge University Press, 2004), 5. Going forward, I will use *PU* and *FU* to refer to Lawrence's essays.
2. Lawrence, *PU*, 24.
3. Lawrence defines idealism elsewhere as "the motivizing of the great affective sources by means of ideas mentally derived" (*PU*, 14).
4. Lawrence, *PU*, 3.
5. *The Letters of D. H. Lawrence*, ed. James T. Boulton, vol. 2, *June 13–October 1916* (Cambridge: Cambridge University Press, 1979), 80.
6. Fiona Beckett, "Lawrence and Psychoanalysis," in *The Cambridge Companion to D. H. Lawrence*, ed. Anne Fernihough (Cambridge: Cambridge University Press, 2001), 217.
7. Letter to Mabel Dodge Luhan, December 4, 1921, in *The Letters of D. H. Lawrence*, ed. James T. Boulton, vol. 4, 1921–1924 (Cambridge: Cambridge University Press, 2002), 142.
8. Quoted in Frederick J. Hoffman, *Freudianism and the Literary Mind* (Baton Rouge: Louisiana State University Press, 1957), 154.
9. Bruce Steele points out that Lawrence mostly ignored psychoanalysis both as a system of investigation and as therapeutic procedure. Introduction to Lawrence, *PU and FU*, 220.
10. Beckett, "Lawrence and Psychoanalysis," 219–20.
11. Lawrence, *FU*, 62.
12. Hoffman, *Freudianism and the Literary Mind*, 153.
13. Lawrence, *PU*, 18.
14. Lawrence, *PU*, 17.
15. Lawrence, *PU*, 14.

16. Sigmund Freud, "The Future Prospects of Psycho-Analytic Therapy," in *The Standard Edition of the Complete Psychological Works of Sigmund Freud*, 24 vols., trans. from the German under the general editorship of James Strachey, in collaboration with Anna Freud (London: Hogarth Press, 1953–74; repr., New York: Vintage, 1999), 11:145. Also quoted in Reuben Fine, *A History of Psychoanalysis* (New York: Columbia University Press, 1979), 32.

17. Fine, *A History of Psychoanalysis*, 32.

18. Lawrence's introduction to Freud was facilitated by Frieda Weekley, the German wife of his professor, whom Lawrence had an affair with and eventually married.

19. Letter of Freud to Fliess, October 15, 1897, in *The Complete Letters of Sigmund Freud to Wilhelm Fliess, 1887–1904*, ed. J. M. Masson (Cambridge, MA: Harvard University Press, 1985).

20. Moreover, despite Freud's sometimes more progressive theories of homosexuality, Freud suggested that an incomplete resolution of the Oedipus complex could lead to homosexuality, caused by the child's identification with their opposite-sex parent instead of their same-sex one. Thus, homosexuality becomes linked to a deviation in "normal" sexual development, a sexuality ultimately shaped by traumatic childhood experience.

21. D. H. Lawrence, *Sons and Lovers*, Cambridge Edition of the Works of D. H. Lawrence (Cambridge: Cambridge University Press, 1992), xlv.

22. For an excellent discussion of Lawrence's Vitalist ideas, within the context of the politics of reflex, see Timothy Wientzen's *Automatic: Literary Modernism and the Politics of Reflex* (Baltimore: Johns Hopkins University Press, 2021). According to Wientzen, Lawrence challenges the "automaticity engendered by modern institutions" (64), seeing institutions as promoting ready-made ideas and collective forms of reflex behavior.

23. D. H. Lawrence, *Sons and Lovers* (New York: Penguin Books, 1976), 279.

24. Alfred Kuttner, "Sons and Lovers: A Freudian Appreciation," *Psychoanalytic Review* 3, no. 3 (July 1916): 295–317.

25. Kuttner, "Sons and Lovers: A Freudian Appreciation," 295.

26. Kuttner, "Sons and Lovers: A Freudian Appreciation," 316.

27. Lawrence, *PU and FU*, xxviii.

28. Fredric Jameson, *The Political Unconscious: Narrative as a Socially Symbolic Act* (Ithaca, NY: Cornell University Press, 1981), 60.

29. Jameson, *The Political Unconscious*, 60.

30. We might view Lawrence's refusal of Kuttner's reading practice not only along the lines of disciplinary rivalry, but as a resistive stance which prefigures the contemporary backlash against forms of symptomatic reading, as articulated by Stephen Best and Sharon Marcus in their manifesto "Surface Reading: An Introduction," *Representations* 108, no. 1 (Fall 2009): 1–21.

31. D. H. Lawrence, "The Spirit of Place," in *Studies in Classic American Literature* (New York: Viking, 1961), 2.

32. Gordon's interpretation of Lawrence's remarks is found in *D. H. Lawrence: Modern Critical Views*, ed. Harold Bloom (New York: Chelsea House Publishers, 1986), 20.

33. Reflecting on the appropriations of psychoanalytic themes and methods by literary theory over the last several decades, Françoise Meltzer asks pointedly: "Literary theory has, after all, been able to find itself in psychoanalytic theory, so why shouldn't psychoanalysis be allowed to find its unconscious inside literature?" Françoise Meltzer, "Unconscious," in *Critical Terms for Literary Study*, ed. Frank Lentricchia and Thomas McLaughlin (Chicago: University of Chicago Press, 1990), 155.

34. Hoffman, *Freudianism and the Literary Mind*, 71.

35. R. A. Gekoski, "Freud and English Literature, 1900–30," in *The Context of English Literature, 1900–1930*, ed. Michael Bell (New York: Holmes & Meier, 1980), 206.

36. See Mathew Thompson, *Psychological Subjects: Identity, Culture and Health in Twentieth-Century Britain* (Oxford: Oxford University Press, 2006).

37. Lawrence, *PU*, 3.

38. Lawrence, *FU*, 62.

39. Quoted in David J. Gordon, "Lawrence as Literary Critic," in Bloom, *D. H. Lawrence: Modern Critical Views*, 24.

40. From Eliot, *After Strange Gods*. Quoted in Gordon, "Lawrence as Literary Critic," 24, 27.

41. May 25, 1921, 5. Quoted in Steele's introduction to Lawrence, *PU and FU*, xlviii.

42. Philip Rieff, "The Therapeutic as Mythmaker," in Bloom, *D. H. Lawrence: Modern Critical Views*, 31.

43. Eugene Goodheart makes a similar point in *D. H. Lawrence: The Utopian Vision* (Chicago: University of Chicago Press, 2006), 207.

44. Lawrence, *FU*, 55.

45. Michel Foucault, *The History of Sexuality*, trans. Robert Hurley (New York: Random House, 1990), 1:26.

46. Lawrence's "centres" generally describe the loci of the embodied unconscious, which Lawrence will discuss at great length in *Fantasia*. The most important centres for Lawrence were the solar plexus and the lumbar ganglion.

47. Lawrence, *FU*, 60.

48. In *Three Essays on the Theory of Sexuality* (New York: Basic Books, [1905] 1963). Freud allows for a wide range of sexual objects and behaviors; however, he still views consummated sex with a person of the opposite gender as the most complete and fulfilling sex act.

49. Lawrence, *PU*, 85.

50. Lawrence, *PU*, 11.

51. Freud would go on to constitute the unconscious in a topographical sense, as a system comprised of contents that are refused access to the conscious mind due to the machinations of repression.

52. Lawrence, *PU*, 13.
53. Beckett, "Lawrence and Psychoanalysis," 221.
54. Lawrence, *PU*, 3–4.
55. Steele, introduction to *PU and FU*, xxi.
56. Steele, introduction to *PU and FU*, xxi.
57. Rieff, "The Therapeutic as Mythmaker," 41.
58. Lawrence, "The Spirit of Place," 85.
59. Lawrence, "The Spirit of Place," 85.
60. D. H. Lawrence, "Benjamin Franklin," in *Studies in Classic American Literature*, 26.
61. Lawrence, "Benjamin Franklin," 26.
62. Thanks to Timothy Wientzen for pointing me to this passage in *Studies*.
63. Quoted in Eli Zaretsky, *Secrets of the Soul: A Social and Cultural History of Psychoanalysis* (New York: Alfred A. Knopf, 2004), 159.
64. D. H. Lawrence, *Study of Thomas Hardy and Other Essays*, ed. Bruce Steele (Cambridge: Cambridge University Press, 1985), 175.
65. The term "resistance" as I apply it in this opening section might also be used as cognate for "adversarial" or "bad," two terms applied retroactively to modernism. In their introduction to *Bad Modernisms*, Douglas Mao and Rebecca Walkowitz foreground the conventional reading of modernism as "bad": "no kind of art . . . has been more dependent upon a refractory relationship between itself and dominant aesthetic values, between itself and its audience, between itself and the bourgeoisie, between itself and capitalism, between itself and mass culture, between itself and society in general." Douglas Mao and Rebecca L. Walkowitz, *Bad Modernisms* (Durham, NC: Duke University Press, 2006), 3.
66. Jean LaPlanche and Jean Bertrand Pontalis, "Resistance," in *The Language of Psycho-Analysis* (New York: Norton, 1973), 394–96.
67. "We know, in fact, from the technique of interpreting dreams, that of all the random notions which may occur, those against which such doubts are raised are invariably the ones to yield the material which leads to the uncovering of the unconscious." Sigmund Freud, *Introductory Lectures on Psycho-Analysis*, "Part III: A General Theory of the Neuroses," in *SE*, 16: 249.
68. Sigmund Freud, *General Introduction to Psychoanalysis* (New York: Boni & Liveright, 1920), 252.
69. Sigmund Freud, "On Beginning the Treatment," in *SE*, 12:134–35: "You will notice that as you relate things various thoughts will occur to you which you would like to put aside on the grounds of certain criticisms or objections. You will be tempted to say to yourself that this or that is irrelevant here, or is quite unimportant, or nonsensical, so that there is no need to say it. You must never give in to these criticisms, *but must say it precisely because you feel an aversion to doing so*. . . . Finally, never forget that you have promised to be absolutely honest, and never leave anything out because, for some reason or other, it is unpleasant to tell it." Freud also says in "Notes Upon a Case of Obsessional Neurosis" (1909): "I made him pledge

himself to submit to the one and only condition of the treatment—namely, to say everything that came into his head, even if it was unpleasant to him, or seemed unimportant or irrelevant or senseless" (in *SE* [New York: Boni & Liveright Publishers, 1920], 10:6).

70. Sigmund Freud, *The Interpretation of Dreams*, in *SE*, 5:101.

71. Critics have highlighted the self-authorizing maneuvers of psychoanalysis, its branding of all forms of intellectual resistance, from both inside and outside the analytic session, as pathological symptoms of repression. As Groth and Lusty point out, "A resistance to Freud's theory thus becomes a resistance to the unconscious wish." See Laura Marcus, *Dreams and Modernity: Psychoanalysis, Literature, Cinema* (Cambridge: Cambridge University Press, 2014), 94.

72. Lawrence Rainey describes this dynamic as the "adversarial model of culture, the belief that only cultural activity inimical to or in opposition to dominant social values can be genuine true culture." Rainey, *Institutions of Modernism: Literary Elites and Public Culture* (New Haven, CT: Yale University Press, 1999), 8. Lionel Trilling also famously called modernism an "adversary culture." Trilling, preface to *Beyond Culture* (1965), in *The Moral Obligation to Be Intelligent: Selected Essays*, ed. Leon Wieseltier (New York: Farrar, Straus and Giroux, 2000), 549–66.

73. D. H. Lawrence, *Women in Love* (London: Penguin Classics, 1995), 39.

74. Lawrence, *Women in Love*, 86.

75. Lawrence, *Women in Love*, 106.

76. Lawrence, *Women in Love*, 108.

77. Lawrence, *Women in Love*, 279.

78. Sigmund Freud, *Civilization and Its Discontents*, trans. and ed. James Strachey (New York: W. W. Norton, 1961), 38.

79. For a fuller discussion of Freud's primitivism and its connection to colonialist anthropology, see Amy Allen, *Critique on the Couch: Why Critical Theory Needs Psychoanalysis* (New York: Columbia University Press, 2021), particularly Chapter 3, "Beyond Developmentalism."

80. Lawrence, *Women in Love*, 73.

81. Lawrence, *Women in Love*, 78.

82. Marianna Torgovnick, *Gone Primitive: Savage Intellects, Modern Lives* (Chicago: University of Chicago Press, 1990), 159.

83. Torgovnick, *Gone Primitive*, 7.

84. Lawrence, *PU*, 12.

85. Lawrence, *PU*, 13.

86. Lawrence, *PU*, 15.

87. Perry Meisel, *The Myth of the Modern* (New Haven, CT: Yale University Press, 1987).

88. Allison Pease, *Modernism, Mass Culture, and the Aesthetics of Obscenity* (Cambridge: Cambridge University Press, 2000), 137.

89. Lawrence, *PU*, 16.

90. Lawrence, *FU*, 162.

91. Taylor Stoehr, "'Mentalized Sex' in D. H. Lawrence," *Novel: A Forum on Fiction* 8, no. 2 (Winter 1975): 101–22.

92. Lawrence, *PU*, 18.

93. Elisabeth Ladenson, *Dirt for Art's Sake: Books on Trial from "Madame Bovary" to "Lolita"* (Ithaca, NY: Cornell University Press, 2007), 145.

2. The Soul under Psychoanalysis: Virginia Woolf and the Ethics of Intimacy

1. The home-based Hogarth imprint was to publish all of Woolf's novels, giving her a felt approximation of the kind of creative independence that she had theorized in *A Room of One's Own*. As she wrote in September 1929, "I'm the only woman in England free to write what I like." Virginia Woolf, *The Diary of Virginia Woolf* (New York: Harcourt Brace Jovanovich, 1977), 3:42.

2. Elizabeth Abel reads this language of "handling" to illustrate Woolf's phobic response to Freud. Elizabeth Abel, *Virginia Woolf and the Fictions of Psychoanalysis* (Chicago: University of Chicago Press, 1993), 14.

3. Virginia Woolf, *The Letters of Virginia Woolf* (New York: Harcourt Brace Jovanovich, 1975), 4:387.

4. The Hogarth Press survived many of its competitors, largely because of the profits of the International Psycho-analytical Library, which published Freud's *Collected Papers* and the work of Ernest Jones, Melanie Klein, Helene Deutsch, and Karl Abraham. After the war the alliance between the Hogarth Press and the Psycho-analytical Library produced the twenty-four volumes of the *Standard Edition* of Freud, which has come down in English as the official textual corpus.

5. Woolf, *Letters*, 5:36.

6. Abel, *Virginia Woolf and the Fictions of Psychoanalysis*, 15.

7. In her autobiographical essay "A Sketch of the Past," Woolf asks: "why it is so difficult to give any account of the person to whom things happen." In *Moments of Being*, 2nd ed., ed. Jeanne Schulkind (New York: Harcourt Brace Jovanovich, 1985), 69.

8. Woolf, "A Sketch of the Past," 70.

9. Woolf, *Diary*, 3:62.

10. A 1921 article entitled "Psycho-analysis à La Mode" reported that the new science has "a double string in its bow. It professes to dissect the soul and wallows in sex." "Psycho-analysis à La Mode," *The Saturday Review*, December 2, 1921, 129–30, 129.

11. Woolf also described her "tunneling process" as "telling the past by installments." Woolf, *Diary*, 2:272, 263.

12. Virginia Woolf, "Modern Fiction," in *Collected Essays*, 1st American ed. (New York: Harcourt, Brace & World, 1967), 2:156.

13. Raymond Williams, *Marxism and Literature* (Oxford: Oxford University Press, 1977), 134.

14. Woolf rejected Victorian fiction's attachment to comedy, suspense, and romance, and argued that fiction should present a more nuanced account of the indeterminate nature of everyday reality.

15. Woolf, "Modern Fiction," 2:160.

16. She later criticized Richardson for her failure to grant psychological access to the "hidden depths" of her characters. Quoted in Judith Ryan, *The Vanishing Subject* (Chicago: University of Chicago Press, 1991), 191. The original review of Richardson's *Revolving Lights*, the seventh chapter of *Pilgrimage*, appeared in the *Times Literary Supplement* on May 19, 1923.

17. Woolf, "Modern Fiction," 2:33.

18. Sigmund Freud, *Beyond the Pleasure Principle* (London: International Psycho-analytic Press, 1920).

19. Woolf and Freud's understanding of the ordinary as constituted by trauma is most fully realized in the figure of Septimus Smith. Smith seems to be so receptive to the stimuli of the outside world that he no longer possesses that protective shield that might mitigate the intensity of sensations: "Scientifically speaking, the flesh was melted off the world. His body was macerated until only the nerve fibres were left. It was spread like a veil upon a rock." Virginia Woolf, *Mrs. Dalloway* (New York: Modern Library, 1928), 68. Conveyed in Woolf's elastic style, with the poetic syntax that indexes Septimus's perspective, the narration tells us that "Red flowers grew through his flesh," *Mrs. Dalloway*, 68.

20. Freud, *Beyond the Pleasure Principle*, 10.

21. Freud, *Beyond the Pleasure Principle*, 30.

22. Virginia Woolf, "Freudian Fiction," in *The Essays of Virginia Woolf*, vol. 3, 1919–1924, ed. Andrew McNeille (London: Hogarth Press, 1988), 197.

23. Woolf, "Freudian Fiction," 3:196. Freud's founding narrative for psychoanalysis, derived from his self-analysis, was what he described to Wilhelm Fliess as "the love of the mother and jealousy of the father . . . a general phenomenon of early childhood." Sigmund Freud, *The Origins of Psychoanalysis: The Letters of Freud and Fliess (1887–1902)* (London: Imago Press, 1954), 213.

24. That Woolf can exploit the clichéd nature of the Oedipus complex is evidence of its popularization as a concept by 1920.

25. Woolf, "Freudian Fiction," 3:195.

26. Woolf, "Freudian Fiction," 3:196.

27. Thomas Mann articulated similar sentiments, suggesting that the author "is a man essentially not bent upon science, upon knowing, distinguishing, and analyzing . . . he stands for simple creation"; which is to say, that the epistemological activities of science are distinct from the creative work of authorship. The quotation is from Mann's homage to Freud, which Mann delivered at Freud's eightieth birthday. "Freud and the Future," in *Death in Venice, Tonio Kröger, and Other Writings*, ed. Frederick A. Lubich (New York: Continuum, 1999), 279.

28. Woolf, "Freudian Fiction," 3:197.

29. Cited in Peter Nicholls, *Modernisms: A Literary Guide* (Berkeley: University of California Press, 1995), 8.

30. Graham Richards, "Britain on the Couth: The Popularization of Psychoanalysis in Britain, 1918–1940," *Science in Context* 13, no. 2 (2000): 185.

31. Perry Meisel, *Literary Freud* (New York: Routledge, 2007), 115.

32. Hermione Lee, *Virginia Woolf* (New York: Vintage Books, 1999), 172.

33. Lee, *Virginia Woolf*, 172.

34. For a more extensive discussion of Woolf's treatment by various doctors and specialists see Lee, *Virginia Woolf*; Stephen Trombley, *All That Summer She Was Mad: Virginia Woolf and Her Doctors* (New York: Continuum, 1981); and Jane Marcus, "On Dr. George Savage," *Virginia Woolf Miscellany*, no. 17 (1981): 3–4.

35. For more on this subject, see Lee's biography, particularly Chapter 10: "Madness."

36. Woolf, *Letters*, 3:180.

37. Elaine Showalter, *The Female Malady: Women, Madness, and English Culture, 1830–1980* (London: Time Warner Books, 1985), 154.

38. See Phyllis Chesler, *Women and Madness* (Garden City, NY: Doubleday, 1972); Sandra M. Gilbert and Susan Gubar, *The Madwoman in the Attic: The Woman Writer and the Nineteenth-Century Literary Imagination* (New Haven, CT: Yale University Press, 1979); and Showalter, *The Female Malady*.

39. Showalter, *The Female Malady*, 150.

40. Lee, *Virginia Woolf*, 174.

41. See Abel, *Virginia Woolf and the Fictions of Psychoanalysis*.

42. For more information on Woolf's interest in Klein, see Abel, *Virginia Woolf and the Fictions of Psychoanalysis*.

43. See Amy Allen, "Kleinian Realism," Chapter 1 in *Critique on the Couch: Why Critical Theory Needs Psychoanalysis* (New York: Columbia University Press, 2021).

44. Sigmund Freud, "The Psychical Consequences of the Anatomic Differences between the Sexes" (1925), in *Three Essays on the Theory of Sexuality* (New York: Basic Books, 1963).

45. Freud, "The Psychical Consequences."

46. Sigmund Freud, "Femininity," *Introductory Lectures on Psycho-Analysis*, in *The Standard Edition of the Complete Psychological Works of Sigmund Freud*, 24 vols., trans. from the German under the general editorship of James Strachey, in collaboration with Anna Freud (London: Hogarth Press, 1953–74; repr., New York: Vintage, 1999), 22:125. Going forward, I will use *SE* to refer to the *Standard Edition*.

47. Sigmund Freud, "Femininity," *SE*, 22:135.

48. Woolf, *Diary*, 3:254.

49. Leonard Woolf, *Beginning Again: An Autobiography of the Years 1911 to 1918* (New York: Harcourt Brace Jovanovich, 1975), 80.

50. Quoted in Douglas Orr, *Psychoanalysis and the Bloomsbury Group* (Clemson, SC: Clemson University Press, 2004), 31.

51. Woolf, *Diary*, 2:242.

52. Virginia Woolf, *On Being Ill* (London: Hogarth Press, 1930), 14.

53. See Victoria Rosner, *Modernism and the Architecture of Private Life* (New York: Columbia University Press, 2008).

54. Virginia Woolf, *A Room of One's Own* (London: Hogarth Press, 1929).

55. Catherine A. MacKinnon, "Feminism, Marxism, Method, and the State: Toward Feminist Jurisprudence," *Signs* 8, no. 4 (Summer 1983): 656–57.
56. Woolf, *Letters*, 4:180.
57. Woolf, *Diary*, 2:248.
58. Woolf, *Mrs. Dalloway*, 5.
59. Woolf, *Mrs. Dalloway*, 15.
60. Franco Moretti, *Graphs, Maps, Trees: Abstract Models for Literary History* (London: Verso, 2005), 82; D. A. Miller, *Jane Austen, or the Secret of Style* (Princeton, NJ: Princeton University Press, 2003).
61. Herman Rapaport, *The Literary Theory Toolkit: A Compendium of Concepts and Methods* (Hoboken, NJ: Blackwell, 2011), 78.
62. Woolf, *Mrs. Dalloway*, 14.
63. Woolf, *Mrs. Dalloway*, 14.
64. Woolf, *Mrs. Dalloway*, 67.
65. Woolf, *Mrs. Dalloway*, 101.
66. Rebecca Walkowitz, "Virginia Woolf's Evasion: Critical Cosmopolitanism and British Modernism," in *Bad Modernisms*, ed. Douglas Mao and Rebecca Walkowitz (Durham, NC: Duke University Press, 2006), 129.
67. Ulysses D'Aquila, *Bloomsbury and Modernism* (New York: Peter Lang, 1989), 158–59.
68. According to Hermione Lee, Craig viewed mental illness as "anti-social or non-conformist behavior" while Hyslop associated insanity with the "morbid manifestations" of modern art like symbolism. George Savage believed in the "degenerative symptoms of hereditary insanity" and treated his "hysterical" female patients with rest cures and excessive feeding. Lee, *Virginia Woolf*, 179.
69. Lee, *Virginia Woolf*, 178.
70. Woolf, *Mrs. Dalloway*, 101.
71. Woolf, *Mrs. Dalloway*, 91.
72. Woolf, *Mrs. Dalloway*, 91, 92.
73. A similar scenario occurs in *The Voyage Out* (1915). When Hughling Elliot falls ill, a Dr. Rodriguez is called in for an assessment. Like Holmes, Rodriguez exudes confidence in his abilities while dismissing the severity of the patient's condition: "Rodriguez appeared to think that they were treating the illness with undue anxiety." And like Holmes, Rodriguez is described as "looking furtively around the room . . . more interested in the furniture . . . than in anything else." Woolf, *The Voyage Out* (New York: George H. Doran Company, 1920), 333. As the first appearance of a doctor in any of Woolf's fictions, Rodriguez anticipates the medical charlatans to come, those who defraud their patients while exerting a domineering will over them. Doctors in Woolf's fictions betray excessive confidence in their abilities but are incompetent in treatment and diagnosis; they exhibit a callous disregard for the suffering of patients and family members, and a keen interest in economic profit.
74. Woolf, *Mrs. Dalloway*, 94.

75. Woolf, *Mrs. Dalloway*, 96.
76. Walkowitz, "Virginia Woolf's Evasion," 129, 137.
77. Michel Foucault, *Madness and Civilization: A History of Insanity in the Age of Reason* (New York: Vintage Books, 1973), 253.
78. Woolf, *Mrs. Dalloway*, 99.
79. Molly Hite, "The Public Woman and the Modernist Turn: Virginia Woolf's *The Voyage Out* and Elizabeth Robins's *My Little Sister*," *Modernism/Modernity* 17, no. 3 (Sept. 2010): 523–48.
80. Walkowitz, "Virginia Woolf's Evasion," 137.
81. Woolf, *Mrs. Dalloway*, 102.
82. Walkowitz, "Virginia Woolf's Evasion," 129.
83. Woolf, *Mrs. Dalloway*, 130.
84. Woolf, *Mrs. Dalloway*, 100.
85. An important distinction between psychoanalysis and traditional psychiatry, however, is that psychoanalysis takes stories and testimony seriously and was established through the spoken narratives of hysterical patients.
86. Foucault, *Madness and Civilization*, 187.
87. For a fuller exploration of the connections between Woolf and Foucault, see Michèle Barrett, "Virginia Woolf Meets Michel Foucault," in *Imagination in Theory* (New York: New York University Press, 1999).
88. Woolf, *Mrs. Dalloway*, 101.
89. Woolf, *Mrs. Dalloway*, 101.
90. Woolf, *Mrs. Dalloway*, 140.
91. Woolf, *Mrs. Dalloway*, 184.
92. Woolf, *Mrs. Dalloway*, 39.
93. Megan Quigley has argued convincingly about Woolf's commitment to vagueness and to her understanding of the slipperiness of language. See *Modernist Fiction and Vagueness: Philosophy, Form, and Language* (Cambridge: Cambridge University Press, 2015).
94. Woolf, *Mrs. Dalloway*, 184–85.
95. Woolf, *Mrs. Dalloway*, 186.
96. Woolf, *Mrs. Dalloway*, 184.
97. D. H. Lawrence, *Psychoanalysis and the Unconscious and, Fantasia of the Unconscious*, ed. Bruce Steele and D. H. (David Herbert) Lawrence (Cambridge: Cambridge University Press, 2004), 16.
98. Virginia Woolf, "The Russian Point of View," in *Collected Essays*, 4:181–89.
99. Michel Foucault, *Discipline and Punish: The Birth of the Prison* (New York: Vintage Books, 1979), 30.
100. Foucault, *Discipline and Punish*, 29.
101. Michel Foucault, *The History of Sexuality*, 1st American ed. (New York: Pantheon Books, 1978), 59.
102. Foucault, *History of Sexuality*, 59.

103. Sigmund Freud, *The Uncanny* (New York: Penguin Classics, 2003), 141.

104. J. Hillis Miller, *Fiction and Repetition* (Cambridge, MA: Harvard University Press, 1982), 178.

105. Anna Snaith, *Virginia Woolf: Public and Private Negotiations* (Houndmills, UK: Palgrave Macmillan, 2000), 64.

106. Miller, *Fiction and Repetition*, 178. Along similar lines, Paul Saint-Amour classifies *Mrs. Dalloway*'s unsettling narrator "as mobile, surveillant, penetrating, sometimes totalizing, and possessed of an archivist's retentive and cross-referencing powers." *Tense Future: Modernism, Total War, Encyclopedic Form* (Oxford: Oxford University Press, 2015), 119.

107. Woolf, *Mrs. Dalloway*, 14.

108. Sigmund Freud, "Papers on Technique," in *SE*, 12:118.

109. Mann, "Freud and the Future," 281.

110. As Kily Valentine points out, Freud had little to do with Hogarth's publication of the International Psycho-analytical Library with the exception of occasional disagreements over book titles, but he expressed gratitude to the Woolfs for their efforts on his behalf. *Psychoanalysis, Psychiatry, and Modernist Literature* (New York: Palgrave Macmillan, 2003), 1.

111. Woolf's diary gives the following synopsis of the encounter: "Dr. Freud gave me a narcissus. Was sitting in a great library with little statues at a large scrupulously tidy shiny table. We like patients on chairs. A screwed up shrunk very old man: with a monkeys light eyes, paralyzed spasmodic movements, inarticulate: but alert. On Hitler, Generation before the poison will be worked out. About his books. Fame? I was infamous rather than famous. Didn't make £50 by his first book. Difficult talk. An interview" (*Diary*, 5:202).

112. Woolf, *Diary*, 4:24.

113. Woolf, *Diary*, 5:249.

114. Woolf, *Diary*, 6:250.

115. Woolf, *Moments of Being*, 116.

116. Sanja Bahun, "Woolf and Psychoanalytic Theory," Chapter 8 in *Virginia Woolf in Context*, ed. Bryony Randall and Jane Goldman (Cambridge: Cambridge University Press, 2012).

117. Virginia Woolf, *To the Lighthouse* (San Diego: Harcourt Brace Jovanovich, 1989), 83.

118. Virginia Woolf, *Three Guineas* (London: Hogarth Press, 1938), 120.

119. Virginia Woolf, "A Sketch of the Past," in *Moments of Being*, 81.

120. Julia Briggs, "Virginia Woolf Meets Sigmund Freud," https://www.charleston.org.uk/virginia-woolf-meets-sigmund-freud/. From an edited version of a talk given by Briggs at the Charleston Festival in 2006.

121. Sigmund Freud, "Totem and Taboo," in *SE*, 13:146.

122. Woolf, *To the Lighthouse*, 12.

123. Maud Ellmann, *The Nets of Modernism: Henry James, Virginia Woolf, James Joyce, and Sigmund Freud* (Cambridge: Cambridge University Press, 2010), 85.

3. The Heterodox Psychology and Queer Poetics of Auden in the 1930s

1. See Eve Kosofsky Sedgwick, *Epistemology of the Closet* (Berkeley: University of California Press, 2008); and Michel Foucault, *The History of Sexuality*, vol. 1, trans. Robert Hurley (New York: Vintage Books, 1990).

2. Auden configured his early poetics as a psychoanalytically informed diagnostic tool for interpreting personal and social neurosis. He first encountered the work of Freud through his father, who had begun incorporating psychoanalysis into his medical practices in 1920 when Auden was only thirteen. George Auden, a member of the Royal-Medico Psychological Association and an honorary psychologist of a children's hospital in Birmingham, as well as a medical advisor for an institution of the mentally handicapped, spent years classifying a range of mental disorders, including "feeblemindedness," juvenile delinquency, and dyslexia. Auden had privileged access to George Auden's psychological texts and eventually acquired his own copies of the works of Freud, Jung, and Rivers. Richard Davenport-Hines has described how the adolescent Auden brandished his burgeoning knowledge of psychoanalysis as a tool of intellectual mastery, diagnosing his friends' behaviors, analyzing their motives, and dissecting their words for hidden meanings.

3. For more information on Auden's interest in psychology, see Edward Mendelson, *Early Auden* (New York: Viking, 1981); Randall Jarrell, *Randall Jarrell on W. H. Auden*, ed. Stephanie Burt and Hannah Brooks-Motl (New York: Columbia University Press, 2005); Richard Davenport-Hines, *Auden* (London: Heinemann, 1995); and Richard Bozorth, *Auden's Games of Knowledge* (New York: Columbia University Press, 2001).

4. The largely unpublished manuscript of the 1929 Berlin journal is held at the Berg Collection of the New York Public Library. Quoted in John Fuller, *A Reader's Guide to W. H. Auden* (New York: Farrar, Straus and Giroux, 1970), 294.

5. Peter Firchow, *W. H. Auden: Contexts for Poetry* (Newark: University of Delaware Press, 2002), 9.

6. Peter Porter, "Auden's English: Language and Style," in *The Cambridge Companion to W. H. Auden*, ed. Stan Smith (Cambridge: Cambridge University Press, 2004), 125.

7. Foucault, *The History of Sexuality*, 101.

8. Valentine Cunningham, *British Writers of the Thirties* (Oxford: Oxford University Press, 1988), 125.

9. Jarrell, *Randall Jarrell on W. H. Auden*, 33.

10. See Michael Warner, Chapter 1 in *The Trouble with Normal* (Cambridge, MA: Harvard University Press, 1999).

11. See Sedgwick's argument in *Epistemology of the Closet* about the overlap of "universalizing" and "minoritizing" definitions of queer experience (54).

12. Penny Farfan, *Performing Queer Modernism* (New York: Oxford University Press, 2017), 2. Farfan's use of the phrase "odd or at odds" is from Anne Herrmann, *Queering the Moderns* (New York: Palgrave, 2000), 6.

13. As Richard Bozorth points out, "Auden is surely one of the earliest poets to engage extensively with recognizably modern conceptualizations of sexual identity," *Auden's Games of Knowledge*, 56.

14. Over the last twenty-five years, queer theory has evolved into a range of political, critical, and academic commitments. It was initially inspired by poststructuralist efforts to highlight the constructed and relational nature of identity, and has retained the impulse to transcend essentializing categories of gender and sexuality by focusing on non-normative models of gender and sexual behavior and performance. In their introduction to the 2015 special issue of *differences*, "Queer Theory Without Antinormativity," Robyn Wiegman and Elizabeth A. Wilson argue that queer theory's governing rationale has been a commitment to anti-normativity. Coalescing around this commitment, some strands of queer theory have emphasized the specific sex practices socially constituted as non-normative, while other strands have embraced a more capacious politics based on the resistance to all norms. My own reading focuses on the way Auden's early poetry foregrounds sexual dissidence in relation to models of heteronormativity, but it is also energized by queer critiques that recuperate negative affects and think about queer experience in the shadow of pathology and stigma. Love's *Feeling Backward* and Sedgwick's *Epistemology of the Closet* are especially helpful in this regard. The works of Foucault, Sedgwick, Love, Gayle Rubin, and Michael Warner are helpful in contextualizing Auden's poetry against the backdrop of sexological, psychological, and medical disciplines and other heteronormative models of sex and identity.

15. Quoted in Davenport-Hines, *Auden*, 106.

16. I borrow this phrase from the title of Bozorth's book, *Auden's Games of Knowledge*.

17. Sedgwick, *Epistemology*, 71.

18. Sedgwick, *Epistemology*, 5.

19. Heather Love, "Introduction: Modernism and Night," *PMLA* 124, no. 3 (May 2009): 745.

20. Piotr Gwiazda, *James Merrill and W. H. Auden: Homosexuality and Poetic Influence* (New York: Palgrave Macmillan, 2007), 13.

21. W. H. Auden, *The English Auden: Poems, Essays and Dramatic Writing, 1927–1939* (London: Faber, 1973), 31.

22. Auden, *English Auden*, 60.

23. Auden, *English Auden*, 31.

24. Auden, *English Auden*, 25.

25. Mendelson, *Early Auden*, 36.

26. Sedgwick, *Epistemology*, 70.

27. Sedgwick, *Epistemology*, 20.

28. Fuller, *A Reader's Guide to W. H. Auden*, 34. Fuller points out that the verses of the Old English poem are almost the same as Auden's: "They can easily part that which was never joined together."

29. For more on the 1928 private printing of *Poems* by Spender, and on the sexual politics of Auden's coterie poetry, see Bozorth, *Auden's Games of Knowledge*.

30. Gregory Woods, *Homintern: How Gay Culture Liberated the Modern World* (New Haven, CT: Yale University Press, 2016), 178.

31. W. H. Auden, *The Collected Poems of W. H. Auden*, ed. Edward Mendelson (New York: Vintage Books, 1976), 619.

32. Bozorth, *Auden's Games of Knowledge*, 25.

33. Edmund White, *The Burning Library* (New York: Random House, 1994), 159.

34. Bozorth, *Auden's Games of Knowledge*, 54.

35. Didier Eribon argues against Foucault's emphasis on the performative powers of psychiatry and for a fuller recognition of the "autoproduction" of gay identity through popular, philosophical, and literary culture. Didier Eribon, *Insult and the Making of the Gay Self* (Durham, NC: Duke University Press, 2004), xiv.

36. Heather Love, *Feeling Backward* (Cambridge, MA: Harvard University Press, 2007), 7.

37. Auden, *English Auden*, 30.

38. W. H. Auden, quoted in Humphrey Carpenter, *W. H. Auden: A Biography* (Boston: Houghton Mifflin, 1981), 49.

39. Sigmund Freud, quoted in Henry Abelove, "Freud, Male Homosexuality, and the Americans," in *Lesbian and Gay Studies Reader*, ed. Henry Abelove, Michele Aina Barale, and David M. Halperin (New York: Routledge, 1993), 385.

40. Sigmund Freud, quoted in Abelove, "Freud, Male Homosexuality, and the Americans," 381.

41. Sigmund Freud, *Three Essays on the Theory of Sexuality* (New York: Basic Books, 2000), 145.

42. Tim Dean and Christopher Lane, "Homosexuality and Psychoanalysis: An Introduction," in *Homosexuality and Psychoanalysis* (Chicago: University of Chicago Press, 2001), 4.

43. Sedgwick, *Epistemology*, 84.

44. To reiterate, Freud would not have endorsed the use of psychoanalysis to treat or cure homosexuality, as he did not view it as an illness.

45. Quoted in Davenport-Hines, *Auden*, 70.

46. Auden, *English Auden*, 36.

47. Auden, quoted in Carpenter, *W. H. Auden*, 84.

48. Mendelson, *Early Auden*, 55.

49. Auden, quoted in Carpenter, *W. H. Auden*, 90.

50. Norman Page, *Auden and Isherwood: The Berlin Years* (Houndmills, UK: Palgrave Macmillan, 1998), 94, 102.

51. Auden, *English Auden*, 37.

52. Patrick Deer, "Two Cities: Berlin and New York," in *W. H. Auden in Context*, ed. Tony Sharpe (Cambridge: Cambridge University Press, 2013), 26.

53. Critics also interpret this verse as alluding to Auden's reunion with Isherwood in March 1929. See Fuller, *A Reader's Guide to W. H. Auden*, 41.

54. Page, *Auden and Isherwood*, 15.

55. Auden, *English Auden*, 39.
56. W. H. Auden, *Selected Poems*, ed. Edward Mendelson (New York: Vintage, 2007), 12.
57. Auden, *Selected Poems*, 12.
58. Auden composed the first two parts of "1929" in Berlin, and the latter two parts while back home in England.
59. Auden, *English Auden*, 195.
60. The renunciation of "Art" for life and love may also suggest a waning interest in the impersonal and elliptical style of modernist poetry he associated with Eliot.
61. For additional discussion of Layard's influence on Auden, see Davenport-Hines, *Auden*, 90–100; and Carpenter, *W. H. Auden*, 103–35.
62. For more information about the Commonwealth School and its philosophy, see E. T. Bazeley, *Homer Lane and the Little Commonwealth* (London: New Education Book Club, 1948).
63. Homer Lane, *Talks to Parents and Teachers* (New York: Schocken Books, 1969), 111.
64. Carpenter, *W. H. Auden*, 87.
65. André Gide, quoted in Carpenter, *W. H. Auden*, 87.
66. According to Groddeck's theory of the "It," "man is animated by the Unknown," a "wondrous force which directs both what he himself does, and what happens to him" (11). See Georg Groddeck, *The Book of the It* (New York: Vintage Books, 1961).
67. In *The Ego and the Id* Freud gives credit to Groddeck for giving a name to the largely unconscious forces that motivate us. Sigmund Freud, "The Ego and the Id," *SE*, 19:23.
68. Sigmund Freud, *Introductory Lectures on Psycho-Analysis* (New York: W. W. Norton, 1989), 27.
69. Sigmund Freud, *Civilization and Its Discontents* (New York: W. W. Norton, 1989), 25.
70. W. H. Auden, "1929 Journal" (Berg Collection). Passage is printed in Auden, *English Auden*, 299, with some variants.
71. Davenport-Hines, *Auden*, 17.
72. Homer Lane, quoted in Carpenter, *W. H. Auden*, 91.
73. Lane, *Talks*, 130.
74. Mendelson, *Early Auden*, 56.
75. W. H. Auden, quoted in Carpenter, *W. H. Auden*, 89.
76. Auden, "1929 Journal" (Berg Collection). Passage is printed in Auden, *English Auden*, 48.
77. Sedgwick, *Epistemology*, 22–23.
78. Carpenter, *W. H. Auden*, 47.
79. Davenport-Hines, *Auden*, 88.
80. Cunningham, *British Writers*, 55.
81. Cunningham, *British Writers*, 55.
82. Auden, "1929 Journal" (Berg Collection).

83. Auden, *English Auden*, 72.
84. Didier Eribon points to the significance of this theme in homophobic discourse in his reading of André Gide's *Corydon*, *Insult*. See Didier Eribon, *Insult and the Making of the Gay Self* (Durham, NC: Duke University Press, 2004), 218.
85. Auden, *English Auden*, 62.
86. It is hard not to think about Auden's own Berlin diary of somewhat incomprehensible jottings.
87. Auden, *English Auden*, 62.
88. Auden, *English Auden*, 62.
89. Mao, *Bad Modernisms*, ed. Douglas Mao and Rebecca Walkowitz (Durham, NC: Duke University Press, 2006), 226.
90. Auden, *English Auden*, 64.
91. Sedgwick, *Epistemology*, 223.
92. Sedgwick, *Epistemology*, 223.
93. David M. Halperin, *Saint Foucault: Towards a Gay Hagiography* (New York: Oxford University Press, 1995).
94. Auden, *English Auden*, 90.
95. Auden, *English Auden*, 86.
96. J. W. Layard, "Malekula: Flying Tricksters, Ghosts, Gods, and Epileptics," *The Journal of the Royal Anthropological Institute of Great Britain and Ireland* 60 (July–Dec. 1930): 501–524.
97. Auden, *English Auden*, 82.
98. Auden, *English Auden*, 76.
99. Auden, *English Auden*, 85.
100. Auden, *English Auden*, 72.
101. Auden, *English Auden*, 151.
102. Auden, *English Auden*, 196.
103. Auden, *English Auden*, 193.
104. Auden, *English Auden*, 193.
105. Auden, *English Auden*, 195.
106. Bozorth, *Auden's Games of Knowledge*, 3.
107. Auden cut this more affirmative first verse when he revised the poem for *Collected Poems* in 1945.
108. Auden, *English Auden*, 180.
109. Auden, *English Auden*, 190.
110. Auden, *English Auden*, 183.
111. Auden, *English Auden*, 182.

4. Nabokov and the Lure of Freudian Forms

1. Quoted in Jenefer Shute, "Nabokov and Freud: The Play of Power," *Modern Fiction Studies* 30, no. 4 (Winter 1984): 641.
2. Vladimir Nabokov, foreword to *Bend Sinister* (New York: McGraw Hill, 1974), xii.

3. Nabokov's polemic against Freud has been the subject of studies by Jenefer Shute, Leland del la Durantaye, Teckyoung Kwon, and Geoffrey Green, among others. See Shute, "Nabokov and Freud," 637–50; Leland de la Durantaye, *Style Is Matter: The Moral Art of Vladimir Nabokov* (Ithaca, NY: Cornell University Press, 2007), especially chapter 8; Teckyoung Kwon, *Nabokov's Mimicry of Freud; Art as Science* (Lanham, MD: Lexington Books, 2017); Geoffrey Green, *Freud and Nabokov* (Lincoln: University of Nebraska Press, 1981); and Stephen H. Blackwell, "Nabokov's Wiener-schnitzel Dreams: *Despair* and Anti-Freudian Poetics," *Nabokov Studies* 7 (2002/2003): 129–50.

4. Green, *Freud and Nabokov*, 1.

5. Quoted in Jeffrey Berman, *The Talking Cure: Literary Representations of Psychoanalysis* (New York: New York University Press, 1985), 211. See Michal Oklot and Matthew Walker, "Psychoanalysis," in *Nabokov in Context*, ed. David Bethea and Siggy Frank (Cambridge: Cambridge University Press, 2018), 211–18.

6. Joanna Trzeciak, "Viennese Waltz: Freud in Nabokov's *Despair*," *Comparative Literature* 61, no. 1 (2009): 54–68.

7. Nabokov despised the writing of D. H. Lawrence, as well as that of Pound. He said in a 1967 interview, later published in *Strong Opinions*: "I must fight a suspicion of conspiracy against my brain when I see blandly accepted as 'great literature' by critics and fellow authors Lady Chatterley's copulations or the pretentious nonsense of Mr. Pound, that total fake." *Strong Opinions* (New York: Vintage, 1990), 102.

8. Vladimir Nabokov, "Good Readers and Good Writers," in *Lectures on Literature*, ed. Fredson Bowers (San Diego: Harcourt Brace Jovanovich, 1980), 1–6, 1.

9. John Burnham points out that Freud's contempt for the culture and character of America only intensified over time. *After Freud Left* (Chicago: University of Chicago Press, 2012), 15–16.

10. Nathan Hale, *The Rise and Crisis of Psychoanalysis in America* (Oxford: Oxford University Press, 1994).

11. Burnham, *After Freud Left*, 3.

12. Burnham, *After Freud Left*, 3.

13. Vladimir Nabokov, *Lolita: A Screenplay* (New York: McGraw-Hill, 1974), 728.

14. Alvin Toffler, Interview with Nabokov, *Playboy*, January 1964, http://reprints.longform.org/playboy-interview-vladimir-nabokov.

15. "Why Nabokov Detests Freud," *New York Times*, January 3, 1966, http://movies2.nytimes.com/books/97/03/02/lifetimes/nab-v-freud.html.

16. Vladimir Nabokov, *Speak, Memory: An Autobiography Revisited* (London: Everyman's Library, 1967), 10.

17. Nabokov, *Speak, Memory*, 10.

18. Andrew Field, *Nabokov: His Life in Art* (Boston: Little, Brown, 1967), 262–63. Also quoted in Shute, "Nabokov and Freud," 638.

19. Shute, "Nabokov and Freud," 642.

20. Quoted in Kenneth Warren, *What Was African American Literature?* (Cambridge, MA: Harvard University Press, 2011), 49.

21. Du Bois, *Dusk of Dawn*, 86.

22. Mary Esteve, "When Psychoanalysis Was in Vogue," in *American Literature in Transition, 1950–1960* (Cambridge: Cambridge University Press, 2018), 46.

23. Esteve, "When Psychoanalysis Was in Vogue," 46.

24. Vladimir Nabokov, *The Annotated Lolita*, revised and updated, ed. Alfred Appel (New York: Vintage, 1991), 36.

25. Nabokov, *The Annotated Lolita*, 37.

26. Nabokov, *Strong Opinions*, 66.

27. Will Norman, "Freudian Time: Lolita, Psychoanalysis and the Holocaust," in *Nabokov, History and the Texture of Time* (New York: Routledge, 2012), 107.

28. See Kwon, *Nabokov's Mimicry of Freud*, 149.

29. Lionel Trilling, "Freud and Literature," in *The Liberal Imagination* (New York: Viking, 1951), 34.

30. Peter Brooks, "The Idea of a Psychoanalytic Literary Criticism," *Critical Inquiry* 13, no. 2 (Winter 1987): 336.

31. Nabokov, *Strong Opinions*, 115–16.

32. De la Durantaye, *Style Is Matter*, 120.

33. Nabokov, *Speak, Memory*, 230.

34. Kwon, *Nabokov's Mimicry of Freud*, 27.

35. Anne Guérin, "Entretien: Vladimir Nabokov," *L'Express*, January 26, 1961.

36. Vladimir Nabokov, *Ada, or Ardor: A Family Chronicle* (New York: Vintage, 1970), 577.

37. Nabokov, *The Annotated Lolita*, 34.

38. Nabokov, *The Annotated Lolita*, 34.

39. Nabokov, *The Annotated Lolita*, 13.

40. Sigmund Freud, *The Interpretation of Dreams* (1900), in *The Standard Edition of the Complete Psychological Works of Sigmund Freud*, 24 vols., trans. from the German under the general editorship of James Strachey, in collaboration with Anna Freud (London: Hogarth Press, 1953–74; repr., New York: Vintage, 1999), 4:183. Going forward, I will use *SE* to refer to the *Standard Edition*.

41. Sigmund Freud, "An Outline of Psychoanalysis," in *SE*, 23:141–307, 187.

42. See Esteve, "When Psychoanalysis Was in Vogue," 48.

43. Sigmund Freud, *Three Essays on the Theory of Sexuality* (New York: Basic Books, 1963), 37.

44. See, for example, Sigmund Freud, *Dora: An Analysis of a Case of Hysteria*, introduction by Philip Rieff (New York: Simon and Schuster, 1963), 43.

45. Sigmund Freud, "Remembering, Repeating and Working-Through" (1914), in *Further Recommendations on the Technique of Psycho-Analysis*, in *SE*, 12:151.

46. Nabokov, *The Annotated Lolita*, 333.

47. Nabokov, *The Annotated Lolita*, 124.

48. Nabokov, *Strong Opinions*, 116.
49. Nabokov, *The Annotated Lolita*, 10.
50. Nabokov, *The Annotated Lolita*, 10.
51. Nabokov, *The Annotated Lolita*, 10–11.
52. Nabokov, *The Annotated Lolita*, 167.
53. See Joel Pfister's discussion of psychological reading as an exercise of cultural power, in "Glamorizing the Psychological: The Politics of the Performances of Modern Psychological Identities," in *Inventing the Psychological: Toward a Cultural History of Emotional Life in America*, ed. Joel Pfister and Nancy Schnog (New Haven, CT: Yale University Press, 1997), 167–216, 170.
54. Shute, "Nabokov and Freud," 641.
55. L. Hutcheon and M. Woodland, "Parody," in *The Princeton Encyclopedia of Poetry and Poetics*, 4th ed., ed. Roland Greene (Princeton, NJ: Princeton University Press, 2017).
56. Nabokov, *The Annotated Lolita*, 5.
57. Nabokov, *The Annotated Lolita*, 4.
58. Nabokov, *The Annotated Lolita*, 17.
59. Freud, *Dora*, 2.
60. Freud, *Dora*, 3.
61. Freud, *Dora*, 3.
62. Freud, *Dora*, 5.
63. Nabokov, *The Annotated Lolita*, 6.
64. Freud, *Dora*, 13.
65. Pamela Thurschwell, *Sigmund Freud* (London: Routledge, 2000), 71.
66. Stephen Marcus, "Freud and Dora: Story, History, Case History," in *Dora's Case: Freud—Hysteria—Feminism*, ed. Charles Bernheimer and Claire Kahane (New York: Columbia University Press, 1985), 206.
67. Freud, *Dora*, 4.
68. Nabokov, *The Annotated Lolita*, 72.
69. Sigmund Freud, *Studies on Hysteria*, in *SE*, 2:160.
70. For example, Freud reads Dora's dream about the box, which he views as symbolic of the female genitals, as evidence that Dora desires Herr K. sexually: "there lay concealed behind the first situation in the dream a phantasy of defloration." *Dora*, 91.
71. Nabokov, *The Annotated Lolita*, 120.
72. Nabokov, *The Annotated Lolita*, 119, 124.
73. Nabokov, *The Annotated Lolita*, 133.
74. Nabokov, *The Annotated Lolita*, 124–25.
75. Nabokov, *The Annotated Lolita*, 139.
76. Rieff, introduction to Freud, *Dora*, x.
77. Felski, "Suspicious Minds," *Poetics Today* 32, no. 2 (Summer 2011): 221.
78. See also David Stewart, "The Hermeneutics of Suspicion," *Literature and Theology* 3, no. 3 (1989): 296–307.

79. Sigmund Freud, "The Moses of Michelangelo" (1914), in *SE*, 13:22.
80. Nabokov, *The Annotated Lolita*, 285.
81. Nabokov, *The Annotated Lolita*, 314.
82. Nabokov, *The Annotated Lolita*, 250.
83. Nabokov, *The Annotated Lolita*, 54.
84. Nabokov, *The Annotated Lolita*, 54.
85. Sigmund Freud, *Dora*, 9.
86. Nabokov, *Ada*, 362. Although Nabokov hated the standard interpretations of Freud, he was fascinated by dreams and kept a dream diary himself, which was posthumously assembled into *Insomniac Dreams* (2018). Like Van Veen, Nabokov was obsessed with locating patterns in dreams and classifying them into categories: erotic, professional, nostalgic, etc.
87. Melanie Weiss reappears again at the end of the novel when Quilty offers to show Humbert his collection of erotica, including more than 800 photos of male organs taken by Weiss.
88. Humbert's idealizations of the nymphet give way to the frustrations that Lolita is a "disgustingly conventional little girl" with properly American tastes in musicals, magazines, and tourist traps. Nabokov, *The Annotated Lolita*, 148.
89. Nabokov, *The Annotated Lolita*, 60.
90. Nabokov, *The Annotated Lolita*, 62.
91. Nabokov, *The Annotated Lolita*, 211.
92. Nabokov, *The Annotated Lolita*, 211.
93. Nabokov, *The Annotated Lolita*, 238.
94. Nabokov, *The Annotated Lolita*, 227.
95. Nabokov, *The Annotated Lolita*, 215.
96. Nabokov, *The Annotated Lolita*, 216.
97. Nabokov, *The Annotated Lolita*, 290.
98. Nabokov, *The Annotated Lolita*, 248, 249.
99. Nabokov, *The Annotated Lolita*, 250.
100. Nabokov, *The Annotated Lolita*, 250.
101. Nabokov, *The Annotated Lolita*, 251.
102. Nabokov, *Ada*, 510.
103. Nabokov, "Symbols and Signs," *The New Yorker*, May 15, 1948, https://www.newyorker.com/magazine/1948/05/15/symbols-and-signs.
104. The son's condition is not wholly unlike that of Humbert, whose interpretive paranoia and solipsism intensify after the abduction of Lolita.
105. Related to Christian theories of interpretation, hermeneutics presupposes that the textual surface, made up of material and fleshy words, were merely signs to be transcended in the pursuit of a more meaningful spiritual reality. See Paul Ricoeur, *Freud and Philosophy: An Essay on Interpretation*, trans. Denis Savage (New Haven, CT: Yale University Press, 1979).
106. Rita Felski, "Context Stinks!," *New Literary History* 42, no. 4 (Autumn 2011): 573–91.

107. Rita Felski, "Critique and the Hermeneutics of Suspicion," *M/C Journal* 15, no. 1 (March 2012), https://journal.media-culture.org.au/index.php/mcjournal/article/view/431.
108. Paul Saint-Amour, "Weak Theory, Weak Modernism," *Modernism/Modernity* 25, no. 3 (September 2018): 437–59.
109. Saint-Amour, "Weak Theory," 438–39.
110. Eve Kosofsky Sedgwick, "Paranoid Reading and Reparative Reading, or, You're So Paranoid, You Probably Think This Essay Is About You," in *Touching Feeling: Affect, Pedagogy, Performativity* (Durham, NC: Duke University Press, 2003), 123–52, 125.
111. Sedgwick, "Paranoid Reading and Reparative Reading," 124.
112. Sedgwick, "Paranoid Reading and Reparative Reading," 125
113. Sedgwick, "Paranoid Reading and Reparative Reading," 130.
114. Stephen Best and Sharon Marcus, "Surface Reading: An Introduction," *Representations* 108, no. 1 (Fall 2009): 1–21.
115. Best and Marcus, "Surface Reading," 1.
116. Best and Marcus, "Surface Reading," 16.
117. Nabokov, *Ada*, 519.
118. Nabokov, *The Annotated Lolita*, 43.
119. Nabokov, *The Annotated Lolita*, 89.
120. Nabokov, afterword, in *The Annotated Lolita*, 314.

Conclusion: Modernist Afterlives and the Legacies of Suspicion

1. Bernard Meyer, *Joseph Conrad: A Psychoanalytic Biography* (Princeton, NJ: Princeton University Press), 1967.
2. Rita Felski, *The Limits of Critique* (Chicago: University of Chicago Press, 2015), 42.
3. Felski, *The Limits of Critique*, 42.
4. Felski, *The Limits of Critique*, 42.
5. Will Norman, "Freudian Time: Lolita, Psychoanalysis and the Holocaust," in *Nabokov, History and the Texture of Time* (New York: Routledge, 2012), 108.
6. Sigmund Freud, "Remembering, Repeating and Working-Through," in *Further Recommendations on the Technique of Psycho-Analysis*, in *The Standard Edition of the Complete Psychological Works of Sigmund Freud*, 24 vols., trans. from the German under the general editorship of James Strachey, in collaboration with Anna Freud (London: Hogarth Press, 1953–74; repr., New York: Vintage, 1999), 12:148. Going forward, I will use *SE* to refer to the *Standard Edition*.
7. Vicki Mahaffey discerns the similarities between modernist literature and the detective genre, by focusing on the "interpretive authority" of both the detective and the reader, and by linking, by way of example, the Sherlock Holmes stories with the stories of *Dubliners*, which both rely on difficulty and analyze backwards from what is observed. Quoted in Laura Marcus, *Dreams of Modernity* (New York: Cambridge University Press, 2014), 6.

8. D. H. Lawrence, "Fantasia of the Unconscious," in *Psychoanalysis and the Unconscious; and, Fantasia of the Unconscious*, ed. Bruce Steele (Cambridge: Cambridge University Press, 2004), 62.

9. Melanie Micir and Aarthi Vadde, "Obliterature: Toward an Amateur Criticism," *Modernism/Modernity* 25, no. 3 (September 2018): 518.

10. Jean-Michel Rabaté, *The Cambridge Introduction to Literature and Psychoanalysis* (Cambridge: Cambridge University Press, 2014), 5.

11. Susan Sontag, "Against Interpretation," in *A Susan Sontag Reader* (New York: Vintage Books, 1966), 98.

12. Sontag, "Against Interpretation," 98.

13. Vladimir Nabokov, *Strong Opinions* (New York: Vintage, 1990), 66.

14. Sontag, "Against Interpretation," 98.

15. Sontag, "Against Interpretation," 97.

16. Sontag, "Against Interpretation," 98.

17. For example, the "Cold Modernism" of Jessica Burnstein "engages a world without selves or psychology . . . not antihumanism but ahumanism." *Cold Modernism: Literature, Fashion, Art* (University Park: Pennsylvania State University Press, 2012), 2. This reading deemphasizes the individualist, psychological, libidinal sensibility so long emphasized in modernist studies.

18. Fredric Jameson, *The Political Unconscious* (Ithaca, NY: Cornell University Press, 1982), 60.

19. Jameson, *The Political Unconscious*, 3.

20. Eve Kosofsky Sedgwick, "Paranoid Reading and Reparative Reading, or, You're So Paranoid, You Probably Think This Essay Is About You," in *Touching Feeling: Affect, Pedagogy, Performativity* (Durham, NC: Duke University Press, 2003), 134.

21. Sedgwick, "Paranoid Reading and Reparative Reading."

22. As Saint-Amour points out, such alternatives have the benefit of dispensing with "all-or-nothing arguments," offering "lower-pitched alternatives to certain 'strong' theoretical habits of thought in literary studies." "Weak Theory, Weak Modernism," *Modernism/Modernity* 25, no. 3 (September 2018): 437–59, 438–39.

23. For Rita Felski, suspicion has been the dominant "mood" of literary studies for decades, so much so that it has become equivalent to a demystified view of the text, while a lack of critical suspicion indexes a kind of false consciousness or resignation to the status quo.

24. See, for example, Brooks's *Reading for the Plot* (Cambridge, MA: Harvard University Press, 1984) and *Psychoanalysis and Storytelling* (Cambridge, MA: Blackwell, 1994).

25. As Heather Love points out, critics have been turning to more distant fields such as the natural sciences, economics, quantitative and digital methods, and cognitive psychology to approach reading anew. Love, "Close Reading and Thin Description," *Public Culture* 25, no. 71 (Fall 2013): 401–34.

26. Anna Kornbluh, "We Have Never Been Critical: Toward the Novel as Critique," *Novel: A Forum on Fiction* 50, no. 3 (2017): 397–408, 387.

27. Peter Brooks, "The Idea of a Psychoanalytic Literary Criticism," *Critical Inquiry* 13, no. 2 (Winter 1987): 334–48, 335–36.

28. Maud Ellmann, *The Nets of Modernism* (Cambridge: Cambridge University Press, 2010), 11.

29. For the latter, see especially Peter Brooks and his psychoanalytic understandings of the erotics of form and intratextual temporal relations in "The Idea of a Psychoanalytic Literary Criticism."

30. Beth Blum, *The Self-Help Compulsion* (New York: Columbia University Press, 2020), 19.

Index

Aaron's Rod (Lawrence), 42
Abel, Elizabeth, 7, 60, 161n30
Abelove, Henry, 12
Abraham, Karl, 172n4; Hogarth Press and, 59
abstraction, 8, 143; Lawrence and, 33, 45, 57, 58, 159n7
Actor-Network-Theory, 149
Ada, Or Ardor: A Family Chronicle (Nabokov), 122–23, 126, 134; impulse toward suspicion and, 139–41
"Address for a Prize-Day" (Auden), 108–10
Adorno, Theodor, 27, 30, 139, 147, 166n103, 167n120
adversary culture, 171n72
aesthetic: Woolf and psychoanalysis and extension of rationalism into, 62; Woolf and soul of, 82
aesthetic autonomy: Lawrence and, 4; Sontag and, 147–48; Woolf and, 66
aesthetic creation, psychoanalysis seen as threat to, 4–5
aesthetic experience, Sontag and immediacy of, 147
aesthetic meaning, psychoanalytic interpretations and, 143. *See also* psychoanalytic literary criticism
aesthetic theory, 24
Aesthetic Theory (Adorno), 27, 30
"Against Interpretation" (Sontag), 146
alterity, 147
Althusser, Louis, 133, 148

amateurism: Auden and, 145; expertise *vs.*, 143; Lawrence and, 28, 33, 34, 114; Woolf and, 145
ambivalence, Woolf and, 84–85
Andreas-Salomé, Lou, 166n100
Anker, Elizabeth, 138, 149
"Annabel Lee" (Poe), 125
anti-Semitism: belief Jews had propensity to hysteria and nervousness, 164n82; directed at Freud from modernists, 8, 20; Pound and, 8, 20, 164–65n83, 165n84
anti-subjective modernism, 18, 19–20
anxiety, Freud on, 163n56
Appel, Alfred, 125
"Arlesienne" (Van Gogh), 120
art: modernism and psychoanalysis and nature of, 143; modernist anxiety over demystification of by psychoanalysis, 24–27; modernist suspicion of psychoanalysis's accounts of, 145–46; psychoanalytic theories of, 25–27
artist, psychoanalysis and conflation of art and, 23–27
Auden, George, 178n2
Auden, W. H.: amateurism and, 145; ambivalence about psychoanalysis, 29–30; attempt to "cure" his homosexuality, 97–98; backwardness trope and, 92, 96, 112; circumventing censorship, 91–95; diagnosis and, 30, 88, 89, 91, 97–98, 114; discourse of gay self-affirmation and, 90–91, 103, 112–13; Eliot and, 181n60; engagement

Auden, W. H. (*continued*)
    with psychoanalysis, 3, 8, 178n2; Freud and, 8, 22–23, 96–97, 105; Groddeck and, 103; "In Memory of Sigmund Freud," 22–23; intuition and, 114; Lane and, 98, 103–4, 105–6, 107; Lawrence and, 89, 90, 103; Layard and, 103, 104; mentors and, 102–6; poetic taxonomies, 109–10; psychoanalysis, rival psychologies, and, 88–91; Pure-in-heart and, 111–14; queer poetic criticism and, 7; theorizing same-sex desire, 29, 90–91, 92, 95, 96–102, 110, 113; in Weimar Berlin, 89, 96, 98, 99–102, 107–8; wrestling with legacy of psychoanalysis, 87. *See also individual works*
Auden group, fascination with World War I, 107
authoritarianism, 8. *See also* medical authoritarianism
authority, modernists efforts to retain literary, 66, 118, 150
authorship, gay identity and, 114

"backward love," Auden and, 96
backwardness, Auden and, 92, 96, 112
Bacon, Francis, 118
Bad Modernisms (Mao & Walkowitz), 170n65
Barker, Pat, 16
Barthes, Roland, 133
Baudelaire, Charles, 66
Bauer, Ida (Freud's Dora), 129–30
Bechdel, Alison, 153
Beckett, Fiona, 34
Beckett, Samuel, 8, 146, 160–61n22
Beginning Again (Leonard Woolf), 68–69
Bell, Clive: psychoanalysis on art and, 6, 145; rejection of psychoanalysis, 7–8, 13, 29, 60
Bellow, Saul, 119
Bend Sinister (Nabokov), 115, 116
Beresford, John, 64
Bergson, Henri, 163–64n73
Berlant, Lauren, 149
Berlin. *See* Weimar Berlin
Berman, Jeffrey, 116
Bersani, Leo, 149
Best, Stephen, 9, 139, 148, 149
Beyond the Pleasure Principle (Freud), 16–17, 63, 64
Bion, Wilfred, 8
blood-consciousness, Lawrence's, 21, 48–49; mind-consciousness vs., 48–49, 52; qualities affiliated with, 55

blood-knowledge, Lawrence defining, 49
Bloomsbury Group, psychoanalysis and, 5–6, 11–12, 60
Blum, Beth, 6, 152
Bodkin, Maud, 120
Bonaparte, Marie, 4
Bozorth, Richard, 88, 95, 110, 113, 179n13
Bradbury, Malcolm, 5
Brenkman, John, 162n53
Briggs, Julia, 86
Brill, A. A., 11
British Psychoanalytical Society, 15, 38
British Psychological Society, 11
Brooks, Peter, 121–22, 149–50, 151
Brooks, Van Wyck, 121
Bryher (Annie Winifred Ellerman), 8, 12
Burke, Kenneth, 121
Burnham, John, 117
Burnstein, Jessica, 188n17
Bwili people, 110–11
Byron (Lord), 113, 114

Campbell, Joseph, 120
Cantos, The (Pound), 20
case study. *See* psychoanalytic case study
Casillo, Robert, 20
censorship: Auden and, 91–95; Nabokov's defense against in *Lolita* foreword, 128
centres, Lawrence's, 44, 169n48
Cheng, Anne Anlin, 152
Chesler, Phyllis, 67
Civilization and Its Discontents (Freud), 25, 54, 85, 105
Clarissa Dalloway, 71, 75, 77, 79–80, 82, 83, 84
"Cold Modernism," 188n17
Collected Papers (Freud), 12, 59, 66, 161n33, 172n4
Collins, Ernest, 47
Conrad, Joseph: hermeneutics of depth and, 144; opacity and, 147; "The Secret Sharer," 1–3
conscious mind, Lawrence and unconscious vs., 47–49
consciousness: Freud on, 63; interwar years and fascination with, 5; multiple centers of, 18; *Women in Love* and limits of, 52–58; Woolf on, 63, 73–74
"Control of the passes" (Auden), 93–94
Craig, Maurice, 73, 175n68
"Creative Writers and Day-dreaming" (Freud), 26

INDEX

Criterion, The (journal), 69
Cunningham, Valentine, 107–8

D'Aquila, Ulysses, 73
Das Ich und Das Es (Freud), 49
Davenport-Hines, Richard, 88, 105, 107, 178n2
Dean, Tim, 97
Deer, Patrick, 100
defiance, in *Mrs. Dalloway*, 79–80
degeneration, Auden and theme of, 101
Degeneration (Nordau), 101
Deleuze, Gilles, 70, 149
depth: Conrad and, 144; Lane and, 106; Nabokov and, 115, 120; surface vs., 143, 144; Woolf, Freud, and metaphors of, 64
depth hermeneutics: Sontag on, 146–48; surface reading vs., 150–51
depthlessness, modernists and, 147–48
desire, "1929" and temporality of, 101–2
Destructive Element, The (Stonebridge), 6
detective story, *Lolita* as, 132–33, 135–36
determinism, Nabokov's offense at, 122
Deutsch, Helene, 59, 172n4
diagnosis, 8, 18, 88; Auden and, 30, 88, 89, 91, 97–98, 114; self-diagnosis, 95–99, 121; social, 107–11
distant reading, 138
Dr. Holmes, 74, 78–80. See also *Mrs. Dalloway* (Woolf)
doctor-patient dynamics in *Mrs. Dalloway*, 74–80
Don Juan (Byron), 113
"Dora: An Analysis of a Case of Hysteria" (Freud), parallels between *Lolita* and, 17–18, 128–32, 185n70
dream formation, 10
dream interpretation: Freud and, 10, 134, 170n67; Nabokov and, 118, 186n86
Dreams of Modernity (Marcus), 6
Du Bois, W. E. B., 119–20
Durantaye, Leland de la, 122
Dusk of Dawn (Du Bois), 119–20

Easter, Auden's use of allegory of, 100–1
ego, 11, 49, 85
Ego and the Id, The (Freud), 85
Eliot, T. S., 69; criticism of Lawrence's style, 42; impersonal style of, 5, 19, 181n60; on novel and psychoanalysis, 6; response to psychoanalysis, 7–8, 13, 145
Ellison, Ralph, 23, 119
Ellmann, Maud, 6, 7, 87, 151

embodied response, psychoanalysis and, 7
encoding, Auden and, 91, 93
Eng, David, 152
England: hostility from scientific and medical establishment in, 15–16; psychoanalysis in, 11–12, 14 (*see also* Bloomsbury Group)
English Auden, The (Mendelson), 95
English boarding school, Auden's parody of, 107, 108–10, 111–14
English liberalism, Auden and fascist underside of, 107
Epistemology of the Closet (Sedgwick), 179n14
epistemophilia, Lawrence and, 53–54
Eribon, Didier, 95, 180n35, 182n84
Esteve, Mary, 120
eugenic psychiatry, 78–79
euphemism, Woolf's critique of, 76–77
expertise: amateurism vs., 143; gendered entailments of, 145; Lawrence and, 14–15, 40–41, 145
Eye, The (Nabokov), 115
Eysteinsson, Astradur, 18

Faber, 94
fall, Christian allegory of the, 45–46, 49
Fantasia of the Unconscious (Lawrence): challenging psychoanalysis in, 13, 28, 32; embrace of amateurism in, 34; epistemophilia and, 53–54; inversion of Christian morality in, 104; on psychoanalysis and transformation of sex, 43–45; as sequel to *Psychoanalysis and the Unconscious*, 42–43; on true unconscious, 57
Farfan, Penny, 90
fascism: Auden on education and, 107; blood-consciousness and, 55; misogyny and, 21; modernism and, 20; Pound and, 8, 20, 165n84
Feeling Backward (Love), 96, 179n14
Felski, Rita, 9, 28, 30; on detective and science of suspicion, 132; on hermeneutics of suspicion, 138; postcritical reading and, 149; on surface reading, 139; on suspicious reading, 144–45, 188n23
Female Malady, The (Showalter), 67
feminine, male modernists and repudiation of feminized cultural aesthetic, 20–21
"Femininity" (Freud), 68
Field, Andrew, 118
Finnegans Wake (Joyce), 13
Firchow, Peter, 89, 90, 110

First World War: acknowledgment of invisible wounds and, 64; Auden group and fascination with, 107; pre-traumatic stress syndrome and, 163n54, 163n56; psychoanalysis and treatment of shell shock following, 15–16

Fliess, Wilhelm, 35, 36, 173n23

forewords, Nabokov's, 115, 116, 128

form: Freud on, 26; privileged over content, 147; psychoanalytic literary interpretations and, 26–27

Foucault, Michel: on authority vested in psychologists, 15; discourse reducing objects discussed and, 45; interpreting Woolf and, 78; on madness and truth, 70; on the medicalization of homosexuality, 95–96; on modern psychiatry, 78; on modern soul, 82; on patriarchy, 75; on performative powers of psychiatry, 180n35; on psychological frameworks and homo/heterosexual definition, 88; on relation of sexual taxonomies to power, 109; on reverse discourse, 90

Franklin, Benjamin, 49

free association, 10

free indirect discourse, Woolf and, 7, 62, 64, 72, 83

"Free One, A" (Auden), 93

Freud, Anna, 84

Freud, Sigmund: ahistorical soul and, 82; anti-Semitic attacks against, 8, 20; Auden and, 8, 88, 89, 105; contempt for American culture, 117, 183n9; Dora and, 17–18, 130–31, 185n70; on dream interpretation, 170n67; emphasis on unconscious as origin of artistry, 4–5, 17; expansion of definition of sex, 43–44, 45, 169n48; founding narrative for psychoanalysis, 173n23; H.D. and, 8, 19–20, 21–22; on homosexuality, 96–97; on id and ego, 11, 49; interest in how modern life impinges psychologically on subject, 63; Lane and, 106; Lawrence and, 20, 116; lectures at Clark University, 12; literary qualities of writing, 17–18; on melancholic subject, 152; midcentury American obsession with, 117; modernists engaging with, 3, 10; Nabokov's rejection of, 115, 116–18, 125, 183n3; Oedipus complex and, 36; on overcoming resistances, 50–51; on parallels between detective and analyst, 9, 133; parallels with Nabokov, 117; paranoia and, 139; positioned as fraud in *Lolita*, 125; the primitive and, 54, 55; on psyche's management of pleasure and pain, 16–17; psychoanalytic readings of *Oedipus* and *Hamlet*, 12; as "sharer" with Lawrence, 28–29, 51–52; theory of art, 25–27; unconscious and, 56, 58; on United States and England, 12–13; unreliable narrator and, 145; on value of repression, 105; viewing literary works as case studies, 4; views on women, 68; on visibility of psychic pain, 64; Woolf and, 5–6, 29, 82–85, 177n111. *See also individual works*

"Freud and Literature" (Trilling), 10, 121

Freud and Philosophy (Ricoeur), 138

"Freudian Fiction" (Woolf), 6, 24, 29, 64–66

"Freudian Revolution Analyzed, The" (Kazin), 124

Freudian symbol, Nabokov and, 133–34

Freudianism: entrenched in literary criticism, 119–22; Pound on, 19

Freudianism and the Literary Mind (Hoffman), 41

Friedman, Susan Stanford, 7, 21

Fry, Roger: debate with Jones over meaning and function of art, 24–25; psychoanalysis on art and, 6, 145; reaction to psychoanalysis, 7–8, 13, 29, 60

Frye, Northrop, 120

Fuller, John, 94, 110

Future of an Illusion, The (Freud), 85, 105

Garber, Marjorie, 2–3

gay identity, authorship and, 114

gay sexuality, Auden's discourse of, 90. *See also* homosexuality

Gekoski, R. A., 41

General Introduction to Psychoanalysis (Freud), 50–51

Geschlecht und Charakter (Sex and Character) (Weininger), 165n85

"Get there if you can" (Auden), 104

Gide, André, 103, 104, 182n84

Gilbert, Sandra, 67

Ginsberg, Allen, 119

Glover, Edward, 15

Goethe, Johann Wolfgang von, 17

Gordon, David J., 39

Green, Geoffrey, 116

Groddeck, Georg, 106, 181n66; Auden and, 89–90, 91, 103

INDEX

Gross, Otto, 36
group identity, Freud's conception of, 167n120
Group Psychology and the Analysis of the Ego (Freud), 85, 167n120
Guattari, Félix, 70, 149
Gubar, Susan, 67
Gwiazda, Piotr, 92

Hale, Nathan, 117
Hall, Radcliffe, 94
Halperin, David, 109
Hamlet and Oedipus (Jones), 161n35
Hamlet (Shakespeare), Freud's Oedipal reading of, 12, 161n35
Han, Shinhee, 152
"Hatreds," Auden's, 106, 109
Hawthorne, Nathaniel, 48–49
H.D. (Hilda Doolittle): Freud and, 8, 19–20, 21–22; Pound and, 19–20; technologies of modernity and, 6
Head, Henry, 73
Heine, Heinrich, 17
Hemingway, Ernest, 125
hermeneutics, Nabokov and fictional text's struggle against, 127
hermeneutics of suspicion, 30, 133, 136–41
Hirschfeld, Magnus, 99
historicist reevaluation of interpretation, 147
History of Sexuality, The (Foucault), 82, 90, 95–96
Hite, Molly, 76
Hoffman, Frederick J., 7, 34, 41
Hogarth Press: as Freud's British publisher, 11, 28, 59, 161n33; Freud's relationship with, 177n110; International Psycho-analytical Library and, 11, 12, 28, 29, 59, 172n4; publication of *Standard Edition*, 28; publishing Woolf and, 172n1; survival of, 172n4
homosexuality: Auden's discourse of gay self-affirmation, 90–91, 103, 112–13; Auden's theorization of same-sex desire, 29, 90–91, 92, 95–102, 110, 113; Auden's view as regressive stage of development, 96; criminality of same-sex acts in Britain, 94; medicalization of, 95–96; Oedipus complex and, 168n20; psychological frameworks and, 88, 90–91
Hong, Cathy Park, 152
Horney, Karen, 36
Hulme, T. E., 19, 159n7, 163–64n73

Humbert Humbert: contempt for generic and derivative, 134–35; as detective, 133; dreams and, 134; Freudian symbols and, 127, 133–34; friction between reader and, 140–41; introduction of, 123–24; on Lolita's complicity, 132; narrator functioning as analysand and analyst, 125–26; Quilty and, 135–36; ridiculing psychiatrist as reader of his case study, 126–27; speaking on behalf of young woman, 130–31; as suspicious reader, 135; using backstory as psychohistory, 124–25, 126. *See also Lolita* (Nabokov)
Huxley, Aldous, 13, 42
Huyssen, Andreas, 21
Hyslop, Theo, 73, 175n68

id, 11, 49–50, 85
"Idea of a Psychoanalytic Literary Criticism, The" (Brooks), 121–22
idealism, Lawrence and, 34, 35, 51, 167n3
illness: Auden's etiology of, 106; privacy and, 69–71. *See also* mental illness
Imagism, 19, 20
Imago (journal), 10
Imperfect Mother, The (Beresford), 64
"In Memory of Sigmund Freud" (Auden), 22–23
Insomniac Dreams (Nabokov), 186n86
Institute for Sexual Science, 99
Insult (Gide), 182n84
International Psycho-analytical Library, Hogarth Press and, 11, 12, 28, 29, 59, 172n4
Interpretation of Dreams, The (Freud), 24, 34, 51, 124
intersubjective consciousness, Woolf and, 81
Introductory Lectures (Freud), 26
introspection, psychoanalysis and, 43
intuition, 143; Auden and, 114; Lawrence and, 33, 39, 40–41, 42, 114; self-knowledge and, 28, 33
Invisible Man (Ellison), 23, 119
Isherwood, Christopher, 99, 103, 107
"It," Groddeck's concept of, 104, 181n66
"IT," Lawrence's use of, 49–50

James, William, 81
Jameson, Fredric, 39, 133, 148
Jarrell, Randall, 88, 90
Joad, Marjorie, 59–60
Johnson, Barbara, 2–3

Jones, Ernest, 15, 38, 172n4; debate with Fry over meaning and function of art, 24–25; Gross and, 36; Hogarth Press and, 59; psychoanalytic readings of *Oedipus* and *Hamlet*, 12, 161n35; viewing literary works as case studies, 4
Joyce, James, 8, 13, 145
Joyce, Lucia, 8
Jung, Carl, 8, 12, 89, 120, 160–61n22, 178n2

Kafka, Franz, 146
Kangaroo (Lawrence), 42
Kazin, Alfred, 120, 124
Klein, Melanie, 6, 11, 59, 68, 149, 161n34, 172n4
knowledge, Lawrence on senses and, 34–35. *See also* self-knowledge
Kornbluh, Anna, 150
Kris, Ernest, 121
Kuttner, Alfred, 4, 37–38, 40
Kwon, Teckyoung, 122

Lacan, Jacques, 121
Ladenson, Elisabeth, 58
Lady Chatterley's Lover (Lawrence), 45
Lane, Christopher, 97
Lane, Homer: Auden and, 89–90, 91, 98, 103–4, 105–6, 107; Freud and, 106
Latour, Bruno, 149
Lawrence, D. H., 144; abstraction and, 33; aesthetics of unconsciousness and embodied response and, 7; amateurish style of literary interpretation and, 145; amateurism and, 33, 34, 114; anti-Semitism and, 20; argument against reductionism of psychoanalysis, 33; Auden and, 89, 90, 91, 103; blood-consciousness and, 21, 48–49, 52, 55; concept of the "IT," 49–50; criticism of psychoanalysis, 13–15, 28–29; defense of aesthetic autonomy, 4; dissemination of psychoanalytic ideas to public and, 59; engagement with psychoanalysis, 3; on expertise *vs.* intuition, 40–41; on Freudian unconscious, 46–47; hostility toward Freud and psychoanalysis, 33–35, 116; idealism and, 167n3; intuition and, 33, 39, 40–41, 42, 114; Layard and, 104; Lewis's criticism of, 21; literary criticism and, 39–40; mental- *vs.* blood-consciousness and, 48–49, 52; Nabokov and, 183n7; the primitive and, 54–55; on psychoanalysis and transformation of sex, 43–46; on resistance, 50–51; resistance to reading Freud, 6, 33,
34; resistance to systematic approach in writing, 42–43; on review of *Sons and Lovers*, 38–39, 40; as "sharer" with Freud, 28–29, 51–52; Sontag and, 146; soul and, 57, 81; symptomatic reading and, 39; theory of reader response to modern novel, 50–51; true unconscious and, 56–58; on unconscious and repression, 55–56. *See also other individual works. See also Fantasia of the Unconscious* (Lawrence); *Psychoanalysis and the Unconscious* (Lawrence); *Sons and Lovers* (Lawrence); *Women in Love* (Lawrence)
Layard, John: airman's journal and, 110; Auden and, 89–90, 91, 103, 104; fieldwork with Rivers, 103, 110
Leavis, F. R., 92
Lee, Hermione, 66–67, 68
Leggatt and the captain, in "The Secret Sharer," 2–3
"Letter to a Wound" (Auden), 108
"Letter to Lord Byron" (Auden), 91, 102–3; as satire on coerciveness of English boarding school, 107, 111–14
Levenson, Michael, 5
Lewis, Wyndham, 7–8, 13, 145; depthlessness and, 147; misogyny and anti-psychologism of, 20–21; objectivism and, 19
"Liberal Fascist, The" (Auden), 107
literalism, Woolf's critique of, 77
literary criticism: contemporary reevaluation of, 148–53; exposing "unconscious" of the work in, 148; Freudianism entrenched in, 119–22; Lawrence and, 39–40; modernism and emergence of, 9–10; Nabokov's distrust of, 120–21; psychoanalysis and, 7; Sontag and, 146–48
Literary Freud, The (Meisel), 17
literary studies: continued influence of psychoanalysis on, 28; making case for value and relevance of, 150–51; psychoanalysis and contemporary, 30
literature: as allegories for psychoanalysis, 144; connection to psychoanalysis, 17; psychoanalysts and, 4
Little Commonwealth School, 104
Lolita (Nabokov), 28; as case study, 119, 127–32; contempt for American culture in, 120; dependence on Freudian forms in, 116; detective story and, 132–33; foreword, 128; Freudian symbols in, 133–34; narrator dabbling in psychology, 123; as

parody of psychoanalysis, 30, 123–27; reading without suspicion and, 140–41; understanding of Lolita in, 131–32. *See also* Humbert Humbert
Lost Girl, The (Lawrence), 42
Love, Heather, 188n25; on backwardness and queer life, 96; on dark side of queer representation, 102; on emergence of modernism and categories of sexual identity, 92; sociological description and, 148
Low, Barbara, 38
Luckhurst, Roger, 6
Luhan, Mabel, 50
Lukács, György, 18–19

Machado, Carmen Maria, 153
Macherey, Pierre, 133, 148
MacKinnon, Catherine, 70
Madness and Civilization (Foucault), 15, 75, 78
male individuation, Lewis and, 21
Malekula people, 110–11
Mann, Thomas, 144; homage to Freud, 84, 173n27; X-ray metaphor for Freud's methods, 23–24, 146
Mansfield, Katherine, 6
Mao, Douglas, 19, 109, 110, 170n65
Marcus, Laura, 6, 21
Marcus, Sharon, 9, 139, 148, 149
Marcus, Stephen, 7, 17–18, 130
Marx, Karl, 138, 146, 148
Marxism, literary criticism and, 148, 149
McFarlane, James, 5
media, on psychoanalysis in Britain and the United States, 14
medical authoritarianism, Woolf's battle against, 60–61, 65, 67
medical response to shell shock in *Mrs. Dalloway*, 71–80
medicalization of homosexuality, 95–96
Meisel, Perry, 7, 17, 56–57, 66
melancholia, as metaphor of racial trauma in America, 152
Meltzer, Françoise, 40, 57, 169n33
Mendelson, Edward, 94, 95, 99, 110
mental consciousness, blood consciousness vs., 47–49
mental illness: Craig, Hyslop, and Savage on, 175n68; gendered definitions of, 67; Woolf and, 66–67, 68–71
mental life, modernism and psychoanalysis and representation of, 61–62

Mere Reading, 149
"method wars," 28, 150–51
Meyer, Gerhart, 100
Micir, Melanie, 145
military regime, psychiatry as, 77–78
Miller, D. A., 72, 133
Miller, J. Hillis, 83–84
mind-consciousness, blood-consciousness vs., 48–49, 52
misogyny, anti-psychologism and, 20–21
Mitchell, Lee Clark, 149
"Modern Fiction" (Woolf), 29, 62–63
modern life impinging psychologically on subject, Woolf and Freud and, 63
modernism: anti-subjectivist, 18, 19–20; emergence of and interaction with psychoanalysis, 5–11; emergence of literary criticism and, 9–10; Freud and aesthetic experiments and, 7, 10; obsession with recovery of origins, 56–57; psychological, 18–19; secret-sharer relationship with psychoanalysis, 1–3
modernist primitivism, 54
modernist texts: decoding and, 144; suspicious reading and, 144–45
modernists: aesthetic autonomy and, 4; anxiety over demystification of art by psychoanalysis, 24–27; dissemination of Freud's ideas and, 8–9, 59; engagement with psychoanalysis, 3–4; summary of anxieties about psychoanalysis, 27; suspicious reading style and, 9–10
Moments of Being (Woolf), 85
"Morality and the Novel" (Lawrence), 50
Morelli, Giovanni, 9
Moretti, Franco, 72
Moses, Omri, 6
"Moses of Michelangelo, The" (Freud), 9
mourning, minority experience and psychic process of, 152
"Mourning and Melancholia" (Freud), 152
Mr. Noon (Lawrence), 42
Mrs. Dalloway (Woolf), 68; doctor-patient dynamics in, 74–80; lampoon of Freud in, 6; medical community's response to shell shock and, 71–80; narrator, 83, 177n106; ordinary constituted by trauma in, 173n19; as polemic against medical and psychological authority, 60–61; published on same day as Freud's *Collected Papers*, 12, 66; question of scale and, 16; the soul and, 29, 80–81

Mulder, Anne-Claire, 17
Myth of the Modern, The (Perry), 56–57

Nabokov, Vladimir: aligning totalitarianism with psychoanalysis, 122–23; contempt for American culture, 120; distrust of literary criticism, 120–21; dream diary of, 186n86; engagement with psychoanalysis, 3, 117–18; on Freud and demystification of literature, 24; Freudian forms in fiction of, 115–16, 118–19; hermeneutics of suspicion and, 137–41; Lawrence and, 183n7; mocking Freud, 122, 183n3; modernist parody and, 7; parallels with Freud, 117; parodying psychoanalysis in *Lolita*, 123–27, 128; Pound and, 183n7; on psychoanalytic literary criticism, 146–47; rejection of Freud and parody of Freudian forms, 30, 115, 116–18; suspicious reading and, 132; symbol decoding and, 132–37. *See also* Humbert Humbert; *Lolita* (Nabokov); *other individual works*
narrators: unreliable, 145; Woolf's, 83–84, 117n106. *See also* Humbert Humbert
Nazis: Freud and Nabokov's escape from, 117; Nabokov comparing psychoanalysis and analysts to, 122, 123; "1929" and, 102
Nets of Modernism, The (Ellmann), 6
New Criticism, 23
New England Weekly, The (journal), 19
new formalism, 138
New Statesman, The (journal), 24
New York Times (newspaper), 124
New Yorker (magazine), 136
Newcastle Literary and Philosophical Society, 166n106
"1929" (Auden), 91, 100–2
Nordau, Max, 101
Norman, Will, 121, 145
normativity, Auden's satire of, 112

objectivism, 19
obscenity trials, 94–95
Oedipal issues: "Dora" and, 130; in *To the Lighthouse*, 86–87; Woolf's review of *The Imperfect Mother* and, 64–65
Oedipus complex, 173n24; Ellison and, 119; homosexuality and, 168n20; Pound's anti-Semitism and, 165n83; *Sons and Lovers* and, 35–38; *Sons and Lovers* as fictional case study of, 4
Oedipus Rex (Sophocles), 36; psychoanalytic reading of, 12

Oklot, Michal, 116
Olympia Press, 128
"On a Book Entitled *Lolita*" (Nabokov), 141
"On Beginning Treatment" (Freud), 170–71n69
"On Being Ill" (Woolf), 69–70
Orators: An English Study, The (Auden): "Address for a Prize-Day," 108–10; airman's diary, 110–11; indirection in, 91, 92; Lane's views and, 107; wound theme in, 108

Page, Norman, 100
Paleface (Lewis), 21, 165n89
paranoid modernism, 3, 159n7
Paranoid Modernism (Trotter), 9
paranoid reading, 30, 137, 138–39
parody, 127–28
patriarchy: Foucault on, 75; psychiatry and, 77
Pease, Allison, 57
penis envy, 36, 68
perception, psychological theory of, 5
"Petition" (Auden), 91
Pfister, Joel, 14
Phillips, Adam, 149
Plath, Sylvia, 119
Plato, 2
Playboy (magazine), 117
Plumed Serpent, The (Lawrence), 54–55
Poe, Edgar Allan, 124, 125
Poggioli, Renato, 4
Political Unconscious, The (Jameson), 148
popular culture, psychoanalysis and, 14, 41
Porter, Peter, 89, 90
"postcritical," 138
postcritical reading, 30, 149
Pound, Ezra, 7–8, 13, 145, 147; anti-Semitism of, 8, 20, 164–65n83, 165n84; on art as response to age between two world wars, 25; fascism and, 20; Nabokov and, 183n7; objectivism and, 19
power: relation of sexual taxonomies to, 109; reversibility of, 110
pre-traumatic stress, following World War I, 163n54, 163n56
primitive/primitivism: Ellison and, 119; Freud and, 54, 171n79; Lawrence and, 48, 54–55; modernist, 54
privacy, illness and, 69–71
"Prolegomena" (Pound), 19
proportion, 76–77
Proust, Marcel, 146

psychiatry: eugenic, 78–79; psychoanalysis vs., 176n85
"Psychical Consequences of the Anatomic Distinction Between the Sexes, The" (Freud), 68
"Psycho-analysis à La Mode" (The Saturday Review), 172n10
"Psycho-analysis and the Artist" (Jones), 24
psychoanalysis: on art, 25–27, 145–46; assimilation into American culture, 22–23, 117, 119, 120; assimilation into British literature, 22–23, 65–66, 117, 119, 120; Bloomsbury Group and, 5–6, 11–12, 60; conflation of art with artist, 23–27; connection to literature, 17; contemporary relationship with literary discourse, 28, 148–53; cultural literacy and, 41; effort to control literary meaning/authority, 118, 150; emergence of and interaction with modernism, 5–11; Freud's founding narrative for, 173n23; Freud's fundamental rule of, 51; Lawrence's criticism of, 13–15, 28–29; as literary discourse, 161n30; modernists' engagement with, 3–4; Nabokov on, 117–18, 122–23; post-war World War I, 11–18; secret-sharer relationship with modernism, 1–3; seens as threat to aesthetic creation, 4–5; summary of modernist anxieties about, 27; traditional psychiatry vs., 176n85; Woolf's rapprochement with, 85–87; Woolf's resistance to, 60–61; X-ray metaphor for, 23–24. See also Freud, Sigmund
Psychoanalysis and the Unconscious (Lawrence), 13–15, 28, 42; allegory of the serpent and the fall and, 45–46; anti-Semitism in, 20; epistemophilia and, 53–54; on knowledge of the unconscious, 34–35; Lawrence on Freudian unconscious, 46–47; parody of Freud's narrative of unconscious, 31–32; on tension between mental and physical in, 50
psychoanalytic analysis of literature, 38–39
psychoanalytic case study: literature viewed as fictional, 4; Lolita as, 119, 127–32; Sons and Lovers as, 4, 35–40
psychoanalytic ideas, dissemination to public, 8–9, 14, 59
psychoanalytic interpretations, aesthetic meaning and, 143
psychoanalytic literary criticism, 9–10, 119–22, 145
Psychoanalytic Review (journal), 37

psychological authoritarianism, Woolf's battle against, 60–61
psychological modernism, 18–19
psychological reading, as cultural power, 185n53
Psychopathology of Everyday Life, The (Freud), 11, 34
psychosexual model of development, 97
Pure-in-heart, Auden and, 103, 111–14

queer poetics, 29, 114; indirection and censorship and, 91–92; psychoanalysis and, 7; stigmatizing cultural signifiers in, 112. See also Auden, W. H.
queer suffering, Auden and, 111
queer theory, 90, 138, 149, 179n14
"queer," use in modernist period, 90
Quilty, 135–36

Rabaté, Jean-Michel, 7, 23, 146, 166n104
race, psychoanalytic ideas and critical readings of, 152
racism: blood-consciousness and, 55; Du Bois on, 120; Freud's primitive and, 54
Rainey, Lawrence, 4, 171n72
Rapaport, Herman, 72
Raverat, Gwen, 67
Read, Herbert, 121
reader response to modern novel, Lawrence's theory of, 50–51
reality, Auden on, 112
Recollections of Virginia Woolf (Strachey), 69
referential mania, 137–41
Regeneration (Barker), 16
religion, psychoanalysis and authority of, 14–15
"Remembering, Repeating and Working-Through" (Freud), 125
reparative reading, 28, 148
representation, Freud's focus on language and, 17–18
repression: effects of, 105–6; unconscious and, 55–56
resistance: case of Dora and, 131; defined, 170n65; Lawrence, Freud, and, 50–51
Return of the Soldier, The (West), 16
Revolving Lights (Richardson), 173n16
Richards, Graham, 12, 15, 16, 66
Richardson, Dorothy, 6, 12, 63, 173n16
Ricoeur, Paul, 133, 138
Rieff, Philip, 43, 48, 55, 132
Rilke, Rainer Maria, 146, 166n100

Rivers, W. H. R., 15–16, 103, 110, 178n2
Röntgen, Wilhelm Conrad, 165n98
Room of One's Own, A (Woolf), 70
Rosner, Victoria, 69
Roth, Philip, 119
"Russian Point of View, The" (Woolf), 81
Ryan, Judith, 6

Sachs, Hanns, 4, 8, 10, 38
Saint-Amour, Paul, 138, 149, 163n54, 163n56, 177n106, 188n22
Salinger, J. D., 119
Salpêtrière hospital, 67
same-sex desire: Auden on, 29, 90–91, 92, 95, 96–102, 110, 113; sanctions against its expression, 105. *See also* homosexuality
Sassoon, Siegfried, 16, 73
Savage, George, 73, 175n68
Scarlet Letter, The (Hawthorne), 48–49
"Secret Agent, The" (Auden), 93–94, 104–5
secret agent/spy, in Auden's works, 93
"Secret Sharer, The" (Conrad), 1–3
secret sharers: Nabokov and Freud as, 141; relationship between modernism and psychoanalysis as one of, 1–3
Sedgwick, Eve Kosofsky, 9, 30, 149; analysis of gay mutual recognition, 109; on paranoid and reparative reading, 138–39; psychological frameworks and homo/heterosexual definition, 88; on psychosexual model of sexual development, 97; reevaluation of paranoid reading practices and, 148; theories of the closet, 92, 94
self: boundaries with others, 1; Woolf's conception of, 60, 79
self-consciousness, Lawrence and escaping from, 58
self-diagnosis, 95–99, 121
self-division: Lawrence and, 49; "The Secret Sharer" and, 3
self-knowledge: Conrad and, 2; intuition and, 28, 33; Lawrence on, 35; modernism and psychoanalysis and, 1
self-narration, "The Secret Sharer" and, 3
Septimus Smith, 71–80, 83, 84, 173n19. *See also Mrs. Dalloway* (Woolf)
sex: Freud and expansion of definition of, 43–44, 45, 169n48; Lawrence on psychoanalysis and transformation of, 43–46; *Women in Love* and access to sensual body, 52–53. *See also* homosexuality
"sex in the head," 44–45, 46, 58

"Sexual Culture" (White), 95
sexual identity: Auden engaging with own, 96, 97, 100, 179n13; emergence of modernism and categories of, 92
sexual impotence, mentalized sex and, 45
sexual inhibition: Auden on, 106, 109; Groddeck on effect of, 90; Lane on effects of, 106
sexuality, Auden theorizing his, 88–89. *See also* homsexuality
Shakespeare, William, 17, 113, 118
shell shock: *Mrs. Dalloway* as indictment of medical response to, 71; psychiatric treatment of, 162n50; psychoanalysis as treatment for, 15–16
Showalter, Elaine, 67
Shute, Jenefer, 118, 126–27, 127
Sir William Bradshaw, 74–77, 78–80. *See also Mrs. Dalloway* (Woolf)
"Sketch of the Past, A" (Woolf), 60, 85–86, 172n7
Smyth, Ethel, 70
Snaith, Anna, 83
social, Auden and diagnosing the, 111–14
social critique, psychoanalysis as tool for, 27
sociological description, literary criticism and, 148
sociological turn, 138
"Sons and Lovers: A Freudian Appreciation" (Kuttner), 37–38
Sons and Lovers (Lawrence), 45, 144; mental vs. blood consciousness in, 47–48; Oedipal scenario in, 35–38; viewed as fictional case study, 4, 35–40
Sontag, Susan, 121; modern interpretation and, 139, 146–48; on modernism's resistance to demystification, 30
soul: Foucault and, 82; Lawrence and, 57, 81; Woolf and, 60, 61, 80–82
Spa Belgium, 97–98
Speak, Memory (Nabokov), 118, 122
Spender, Stephen, 92, 94
Spitteler, Carl, 10
Standard Edition (Freud), 12, 28, 59, 161n33, 172n4
Stein, Gertrude, 13, 145, 147
Stephen, Adrian and Karin, 11, 161n34
Stevens, Wallace, 19
Stoehr, Taylor, 58
Stonebridge, Lyndsey, 6
Strachey, Alix, 11–12, 69
Strachey, James, 11–12, 49, 59

INDEX

Strachey, Lytton, 11
stream-of-consciousness techniques, 5, 12, 18
Strong Opinions (Nabokov), 122, 125, 183n7
Studies in Classic American Literature (Lawrence), 39, 42, 48–49, 50
Studies on Hysteria (Freud), 18, 131
subjectivism, modernist turn from, 163n73
subjectivity: maternal origins of, 68; Woolf and, 62–63
subterfuge, in Auden's works, 92–94
surface: depth *vs.*, 143, 144; modernism and, 147–48; Woolf, Freud, and metaphors of, 64
surface reading, 28, 138, 148, 149
"Surface Reading: An Introduction" (Best & Marcus), 139
suspicious reading, 28, 30, 188n23; Humbert Humbert and, 135; modernist texts and, 144–45; modernists and, 9–10; Nabokov and, 132–37; reevaluation of, 148–49
Sword, Helen, 6
symbols, Nabokov, psychoanalysis and decoding, 132–37
"Symbols and Signs" (Nabokov), 136–37
symptomatic reading, 39, 139, 149, 168n30
symptomatic style, in criticism, 30

Talks to Parents and Teachers (Lane), 104
Tarr (Lewis), 21
Tavistock Clinic, 8
thick description, 138
"Thought" (Lawrence), 38
Three Essays on the Theory of Sexuality (Freud), 97, 124, 169n48
Three Guineas (Woolf), 85
Thurschwell, Pamela, 6, 130
Times Literary Supplement (periodical), 64
To the Lighthouse (Woolf), 85–87, 144
Tompkins, Sylvan, 149
"Too Dear, Too Vague" (Auden), 96
Torgovnick, Mariannna, 55
totalitarianism, Nabokov's alignment of psychoanalysis with, 122–23
Totem and Taboo (Freud), 119
Touching Feeling (Sedgwick), 138–39, 148
trauma, ordinary constituted by, 173n19
trauma theory, use in *Lolita*, 124
Tribute to Freud (H. D.), 8, 21–22
Trilling, Lionel, 10, 121, 171n72; on psychoanalytic interpretations and neglect of form, 26–27

Trotter, David, 3, 159n7; *Paranoid Modernism*, 9
"Truest Poetry is the Most Feigning, The" (Auden), 95
truth, madness and, 70
Trzeciak, Joanna, 116
tunneling process, 62, 172n11

Ulysses (Joyce), 13
Ulysses trial, 94
unconscious: Lawrence on Freudian, 46–47 (see also *Fantasia of the Unconscious* (Lawrence); *Psychoanalysis and the Unconscious* (Lawrence)); Lawrence's conception of, 47–50; as origin of artistry, 4–5; psychoanalysis and aesthetics of, 7; in topographical sense, 169n51
United States, popularization of psychoanalysis in, 12, 22–23, 117, 119, 120, 162n45

Vadde, Aarthi, 145
vagueness, Woolf's commitment to, 79, 176n93
Van Gogh, Vincent, 120
Voyage Out, The (Woolf), 175n73

Walker, Matthew, 116
Walkowitz, Rebecca, 73, 75, 76–77, 170n65
Warner, Richard, 90
weak theory, 149
Weekley, Frieda, 36, 47, 168n18
Weimar Berlin: Auden group and, 107–8; Auden in, 29, 89, 96, 98, 99–102, 107–8
Weininger, Otto, 165n85
Well of Loneliness (Hall), 94
West, Rebecca, 16, 73
White, Edmund, 95
white supremacy, psychoanalysis and examination of, 119–20
Wientzen, Timothy, 6
Wilde, Oscar, 113
Williams, Raymond, 62
Wilson, Edmund, 121
Wilson, Leigh, 6
Winnicott, Donald, 149
"Woman Who Rode Away, The" (Lawrence), 54–55
women: Freud's views on, 68; illness and privacy for, 69–71
Women in Love (Lawrence), 14, 28, 42, 48; model of unconscious in, 52–58; the primitive and, 54–55; repression and, 55–56

women patient, Woolf and, 66–71
Woods, Gregory, 95
Woolf, Leonard: as Freud's publisher, 6; overseeing wife's medical treatment, 68, 73; review of *The Psychopathology of Everyday Life*, 11; review of *The Interpretation of Dreams*, 34; reviews of Freud's essays, 28; visit to Freud, 84; on wife's creativity and her madness, 68–69
Woolf, Virginia, 3; affinities with Freud, 82–84; amateurism and, 145; on application of psychoanalysis to literature, 64–66, 144; criticism of Freud, 13, 29, 145; dissemination of psychoanalytic ideas to public and, 59; on female authorship, 166n103; free indirect style and, 7, 62, 64, 72, 83; on Freud and demystification of art, 24; on Hogarth Press publishing Psycho-analytical Library, 59–60; medical authoritarianism and, 60–61, 65, 67; meeting Freud, 84, 177n111; mental illness and treatment of, 66–67, 68–71; narrators, 83–84; parallels with life of character Septimus Smith, 73–74; on psychoanalysis's account of art, 146; rapprochement with Freud and psychoanalysis, 84–87; resistance to psychoanalysis, 60–61; resisting reading Freud, 59; Richardson and, 63, 173n16; the soul and, 60, 61, 80–82; technologies of modernity and, 6; tunneling and, 62, 172n11; turn away from humans toward objects, 19. *See also* "Freudian Fiction" (Woolf); *Mrs. Dalloway* (Woolf); *other individual works*
World War I. *See* First World War
"Wulf and Eadwacer" (poem), 94, 179n28

X-ray photography: invention of, 165n98; as metaphor for Freud's methods, 23–24, 146

Yuknavitch, Lidia, 153

JENNIFER SPITZER is Associate Professor in the Department of Literatures in English at Ithaca College. Her work has appeared or is forthcoming in *Modernism/Modernity*, the *Journal of Modern Literature*, *Studies in the Novel*, *Modern Language Quarterly*, the *New York Times*, the *Los Angeles Review of Books*, *Avidly*, and other venues.

Lightning Source UK Ltd.
Milton Keynes UK
UKHW011949090123
415075UK00003B/34

9 781531 502096